The road

MANCHESTER
1824

Manchester University Press

The road

An ethnography of (im)mobility, space, and cross-border infrastructures in the Balkans

DIMITRIS DALAKOGLOU

Manchester University Press

Published by Manchester University Press
Altrincham Street, Manchester M1 7JA, UK
www.manchesteruniversitypress.co.uk

British Library Cataloguing-in-Publication Data
A catalogue record for this book is available from the British Library

Library of Congress Cataloging-in-Publication Data applied for

ISBN 978 1 5261 0933 0 *hardback*
     978 1 5261 0934 7 *paperback*

First published 2017

The publisher has no responsibility for the persistence or accuracy of URLs for external or any third-party internet websites referred to in this book, and does not guarantee that any content on such websites is, or will remain, accurate or appropriate.

Typeset in Sabon by
Koinonia, Manchester
Printed and bound in Great Britain by
CPI Group (UK) Ltd, Croydon CR0 4YY

To Anna, Luca and Toni,
my Gjirokastrit friends,
and
my friends in Mali i Jusit

Contents

List of figures   *page* ix
Preface   xi
Acknowledgements   xiii
Map of Albania   xv

1 From dromocracy toward a new critical dromology   1
2 The road to Albania   15
3 The state(s) of the road   33
4 The city and the road   53
5 Fear of the road and the accident of postsocialism   82
6 The road of/on transition   98
7 Domesticating the road   133
8 Infrastructures, borders, (im)mobility, or the material
   and social construction of new Europe   162

Appendix 1 Notes on language, terminology,
and pseudonyms   172
Appendix 2 Population statistics   175

Bibliography   176
Index   199

Figures

1 A Bektashi priest leaving the Tekke of Haliki (author's
  photograph)   *page* 28
2 A postcard from the 1930s showing the municipality of
  Gjirokastër, then occupied by the Italian forces (public domain)   37
3 An image used in the 1970s in party publications regarding
  the economic development of the regime   42
4 An image from the party's periodical press of the 1970s showing
  women being trained in the use of rifles   43
5 A propaganda collage published in the party's periodical press
  in the 1970s   48
6 A young boy smiles as his father fixes his Mercedes-Benz in an
  abandoned former industrial facility (author's photograph)   51
7 A man walking on a street in the Pazari (author's photograph)   55
8 The plaque celebrating the inclusion of Gjirokastër's old town
  in the UNESCO World Heritage list (author's photograph)   56
9 A shop under construction in Gjirokastër's old town (author's
  photograph)   57
10 A school photo from the early 1980s taken in front of Enver
   Hoxha's statue (private collection)   59
11 The remains of the lower pedestal of Enver Hoxha's statue
   (author's photograph)   60
12 A small corner of Gjirokastër's old town, as seen from the castle
   (author's photograph)   61
13 Remnants of the Gjirokastër metal factory (author's photograph)   63
14 Gjirokastër's main boulevard in the late 1970s (from Riza, 1978)   65
15 Gjirokastër's main boulevard today (author's photograph)   66
16 A bank on Gjirokastër's main boulevard (author's photograph)   67
17 Uncle and nephew: two generations of shop owners in the Pazari
   (author's photograph)   68
18 An informal currency exchanger at the roundabout of the Boulevard
   Shtator, the new center of Gjirokastër (author's photograph)   71
19 Peak afternoon time in the Pazari's narrow cobbled street (author's
   photograph)   73
20 The main street of the Pazari in the 1970s (from Riza, 1978)   76

21 The main street of the Pazari today (author's photograph)   77
22 Construction work on a socialist period building (author's
   photograph)   79
23 The boulevard, as seen from the south side of the street,
   overlooking the new, postsocialist expansion of the city (author's
   photograph)   80
24 A small monument in Gjirokastër commemorating two women
   killed during the 1997 conflict (author's photograph)   84
25 Road signs entering the cross-border highway from a Greek minority
   village (author's photograph)   108
26 The cobbled street of the Pazari meets the asphalt (author's
   photograph)   109
27 One of the largest Greek public works companies constructing
   a road in Gjirokastër (author's photograph)   117
28 Tire and oil technicians at a truck stop on the Gjirokastër–Kakavijë
   highway (author's photograph)   119
29 The main device used for cooking until the early 1990s:
   a petrol-based stove (author's photograph)   128
30 A block of flats in Gjirokastër (author's photograph)   141
31 A house built by migrants in Albania which has been under
   construction for over a decade (author's photograph)   145
32 A doll talisman to protect against the evil eye (author's photograph)   148
33 A door traveling from Greece to Albania on the roof of a car
   (author's photograph)   152
34 Posters calling on owners to register and legalize their buildings
   (author's photograph)   155

Every effort has been made to obtain permission to reproduce copyright material, and the publisher will be pleased to be informed of any errors or omissions for correction in future editions.

Preface

Europe was shocked by the news: a boat full of migrants sinks in the Mediterranean Sea, carrying fifty-seven people to their deaths. The episode occurred when the Italian Navy vessel *Sibilla*, responsible for protecting the common EU borders, collided with the migrants' boat in the course of its duties. There was serious debate as to whether this was an accident or part of a political effort to stop the flow of migrants—and whether the Italian Navy could have done more to save the victims. The year was 1997 and the migrants were Albanians.

This incident is known as the Otranto tragedy. In a historical irony, "Sibilla" refers to the female prophets of the ancient Greek world, who were believed to be capable of foreseeing the future. Almost twenty years later, sinking boats and drowned migrants are common in the Mediterranean. In the past, the "Others" who did not deserve to enter Europe were of different origins than those of today, but the mobility and border regimes we see in 2015–16 were already being rehearsed and shaped in the early 1990s.

This is a book about a cross-border motorway that passes through such an EU/non-EU border, dividing Albania from Greece. In examining this road, we will see not only the flow of people, labor, and things— including cities and houses—but also a road flowing materially in itself. Most importantly, via this road we will see the material and sociopolitical construction that flowed through the whole of Europe after the cold war.

The idea that infrastructures constitute an important element of the anthropological project first appeared many decades ago (see Godelier 1978; Harris 1968). In more recent times, infrastructures have reemerged as a central theme within the discipline (Dalakoglou 2009a; Dalakoglou and Harvey 2012; Harvey and Knox 2015; Humphrey 2005; Larkin 2008, 2013). Roads are one of the best infrastructures through which to study anthropologically. They are the archetypal human-made network; they are physically static, but at the same time they are the infrastructure of mobility per se. Today, when we are surrounded by so many networks—visible or invisible, tangible or intangible—the archetypal properties of these roads—their sense of *roadness*—extend beyond the named category. However, this is not to imply that everything is a road; roads are qualitatively and ontologically unique. This uniqueness refers to the fact that roads, socioculturally, are the most anthropocentric and established of human-made networks.

Ethnographically, the highway examined in this book is part of an explicit cultural–material nexus that includes elements such as houses, urban architecture, building materials, and vehicles. Yet even the most physically rooted of these entities are not static ethnographically, but have fluid and flowing physical materialities, and contain superstructural, infrastructural, or even—as Victor Turner (1995) would put it—antistructural characteristics. Such an infrastructural ethnography provides an approach that allows the anthropological gaze to fall anew on some of the most typical scales of social analysis (e.g. between historical and ethnographic perspectives or between social agent and structure, material and human, static and mobile). Within such a context, complex sociopolitical phenomena such as EU border security, nationalist politics, transnational kinship, social-class divisions, post-cold war capitalism, political transition, and financial crises in Europe—and more precisely in Greece and Albania—can be seen as phenomena paved in and on this cross-border highway.

Moreover, the highway featured in this book helps us to explore anew classical anthropological categories of analysis in direct reference to the infrastructure. Categories such as the house, domestic life, the city, kinship, money, boundaries, nationalism, statecraft, geographic mobility, and distance—to name but a few—seem very different when seen from or on the road. As such, this book is not merely an ethnography *on* the road but an anthropology *of* the road.

Acknowledgements

My warmest thanks go to all my friends in Albania who helped me while I was researching this book. I am deeply grateful to Rigels Halili and his parents Kuitim and Natasa: Rigels for teaching me the Albanian language in London during my pre-fieldwork preparations, and his parents who opened their house to me and became like my parents in Albania. Stephanie Schwandner-Sievers helped me to begin this research. Many others also helped during and after the fieldwork, including: Eliana and Afro Lili, Alqi and Luci Beqo, Mir and Niko Sulani and their family. Thanks should go to Labi Kotra, Christian Gogo Geositch, Thimio and Margarita Petsi, Adil and Sabria Hamko, Katia Saro, Tani Goga and Drago Kovaci.

I would like to thank Anna Christofides for her support and help. Moreover, Michael Herzfeld has been very supportive all these years. I would like to thank Victor Buchli for his careful and intensive mentoring, his patience, great ideas, and some of the most intense discussions I have ever had. I would also like to thank Danny Miller for all of his advice and guidance, for being strict, and, of course, for the endless anthropological chats over tables of alcoholic beverages. I should also thank Caroline Humphrey and Dimitra Gefou-Madianou for their comments on this text.

Warm thanks have to go to my London housemate Liz Abraham who, in addition to offering very affordable accommodation, provided me with a huge amount of moral support and much copy-editing. Special thanks to my parents Konstantinos and Eleni, my brother, Giorgos, and my sister-in-law Maria. Chris Giovanopoulos has also been of great help and a good friend over the last decade. Other people who read or heard my chapters during conferences and seminars and gave me valuable comments include: Martin Holbraad, Chris Tilley, Charles Stewart, and Olivia Harris. Fereniki Vatavali provided very useful information on Gjirokastër and Epirus. I want to thank Chris Simotas for providing the soundtrack to this book and Antonis Vradis for his valuable copy-editing, support and chats. I also have to thank the many people who discussed the various things I write about in this book over the ten years I have been researching highways: Meta Kordis, Sarah Keeler, Kate Michalopoulou, Andrea Undra, Ivana Bajic, Diana Espirito-Santo, Bodil Nielesen, Sophie Thyssen, Giorgos Agelopoulos, Giorgos Tsimouris, Tryfon Bambylis, Gen Fuji (who was a great friend in Albania), Tim Page, Catherine Baker, Evi Chatzipanagiotidou, Clara Jaya Brekke, Penny Harvey, Jon Mitchell, Simon Coleman, Katy Gardner, Jane Cowan, Eugene Michail, Sarah Green, Sam Hardy, and Christos Filippidis. The very final stages of this book were completed while I was a visiting scholar at the Center of Place, Culture, and Politics at the CUNY Graduate Center, and I would like to thank David Harvey for all his help and comments during this time. Setha Low and Michael Blim's help and comments have also been crucial for this book. Of course in NYC everything happened in Tortuga so the crew there should be thanked for everything, especially Elena and Smokey for all the chats and cigarettes.

The Hellenic Republic State Scholarship Foundation (IKY) for the national fellowship in Anthropology (2004–8) too must be thanked. I must also thank the Marie Curie European Doctorate Program in the Social History of Europe and the Mediterranean for the research fellowship they awarded me. Finally, to UCL, which helped me at times of hardship with a hardship fund.

Map of Albania (Ammartivari / Wikimedia Commons / based on UN map in public domain)

1

From dromocracy toward a new critical dromology

As soon as it takes power the Nazi government offers the German proletariat sports and transport. No more riots, no need for much repression;
to empty the streets it's enough to promise everyone the highway. (Virilio
2006 [1977], 49)

Roads and anthropologists

Traditionally, most anthropological work has been devoted to studying
populations that were portrayed as antithetical to the dominant trends in
modern and capitalist society. Roads and automobility were considered
Western and modern elements, far from the ethnographic Other. The
widespread introduction of roads on a global level sparked distinct
reactions within anthropology.

First, many classical disciplinary ancestors underestimated (rather
ineloquently) the impact of highways on their ethnographic "objects."
Most typically, Evans-Pritchard suggested that although the Azande had
changed their pattern of settlement by concentrating around the newly
constructed roads—instead of streams, as they had before—he could
not in fact ascribe to roads "any great change in the life of the Azande"
(1932, 292). Highways, in the eyes of Evans-Pritchard, brought the
imagined exotic a few steps nearer to the nonexotic world. Writing
"a few steps nearer" was, in fact, quite literal, as it seems that his
anthropological objects were constituted mainly of walkers, rather than
drivers and passengers, with a preference for barefoot walkers. Walking
barefoot implied an a priori hierarchical classification of people, as Tim
Ingold (2004) explains in his discussion of cultures characterized by
walking versus those with a culture of vehicle mobility. Thus, Sir Evans-
Pritchard's subjects were indeed walkers—and hence closer to nature.
They were passive receivers of change, unaffected by highways:

I am not concerned here with those changes, which were mostly imposed
on the Azande and are—when I use the present tense the reference is to

the years 1926–30—not regarded by them as part of their way of life but something to be passively accepted or to be circumvented or ignored. To give one example: though the Administration compelled them to maintain wide roads it was noticeable that when a group of Azande walked down them they did so in single file as they were accustomed to do along their bush paths. (Evans-Pritchard 1960, 311)

Given the aforesaid trend toward remote ethnographic subjects, there was, in some respects, an unspoken competition between ethnologists to reach the most isolated and remote places, and as such the most primitive and exotic of peoples. Early anthropological accounts are full of references to isolated subjects accessed by poor-quality (mostly pre-automobile) roads. In 1884, Franz Boas observed that "the natives who had visited Padli in March had reported that the road was very bad; that the land was very nearly clear of snow and that the sledge would have to be carried over high rocks" (1884, 265). Levi-Strauss's early ethnographic explorations in South America were equally explicit: "I occasionally took that step on horseback with some colleagues when we came to the end of one of the few roads available at the time" (Levi-Strauss and Kussell 1971, 45). Moreover, Edmund Leach, in an interview with Adam Kuper (1986, 375), recalled his first type of ethnographic excursion in China, while still a civil engineer: "Chung-king itself was still a mediaeval city, all steps and sedan chairs. No roads or motor vehicles except the odd half-disintegrated bus." Even Paul Rabinow (2007 [1977], 44), the most reflexive anthropologist, stated about his fieldwork that "the road for the first five miles is little more than a path—untarred, pitted, and winding and steep in places." Even anthropologists who later focused their research on networked infrastructures such as Caroline Humphrey (1989, 6) have been explicit about the difficult roads in their place of research: "the road crosses a high mountain pass which is snowy even in midsummer, and plane tickets, unless booked months in advance, are obtainable only on a who-you-know basis."

Nevertheless by the latter half of the twentieth century, ethnologists began to acknowledge that highways had marked the end of the semi-isolated, nonmodern people that comprised the discipline for most of its history. Thus, given the aforesaid enthusiasm for, and informal competition to reach, remote places, to a certain extent the implication is that generally many anthropologists somehow regret the disappearance of remote research subjects. As Levi-Strauss explained, by the 1960s, roads already implied the end of isolated ethnographic subjects: "Likewise, the establishment of the new federal capital of Brazil and the building of roads and aerodromes in remote parts of South America have led to the discovery of small tribes in areas where no native life was thought to exist" (1966, 125). Twenty years later, Michael Herzfeld (1985) was much more clear on the potential sources of anthropological road-phobia: highways "strangulate" the traditional practices of the ethnographic subject.

Finally, as with all things, the arrival of better roads and better access brought more positive assessments of the roads that were reaching the once-isolated ethnographic subject:

> More than anything else, the completion of the jeep road opened up the Fore region, changing it almost overnight from an isolated region to one open to free travel and commerce and, more important, in contact with the outside world ... The power of the road is hard to overestimate. It was a great artery where only restricted capillaries had existed before, and down this artery came a flood of new goods, new ideas, new peoples, and, above all, excitement... . It was to the Fore an opening to a new world. (Sorenson 1972, 366)

Roads and boundary crossing

Within this aforementioned context, Marc Augé's suggestion (1995, 86) that "ethnologists mistrust the journey" is hardly a surprise. At the same time, anthropologists were professional strangers (Agar 1996) and the most typical students of nomadism and semi-nomadism (e.g. see Barth 1964; Campbell 1964; Rao 1987; Vainshtein 1980), and the ones who produced pioneering ethnographic works on migrants and their communities dating from several decades ago (e.g. see Lewis 1964; Watson 1977). Thus, the aforesaid mistrust of roads was not the same as a mistrust of the journey; in fact, it implied an anthropological avoidance of studying the crossing of certain spatial and cultural boundaries rather than the mistrust of the journey per se. This reflected the similar avoidance to cross the respective boundaries of the established epistemological paradigm. These spatial/cultural/epistemological boundaries have to be seen within the culturally relativistic (but simultaneously rationalist) Boasian separation of humanity into semi-sealed culture-areas. Arguably, the issue was what Akhil Gupta and James Ferguson called place-culture isomorphism (1997). Namely that cultures are considered attached to places. Thus, to rephrase Marc Augé, the issue was not the journey or mobility generally, but a dislike for the process of crossing a series of boundaries.

This is more or less to be expected from anthropology; an epistemological offspring of modernity which indeed had as its main focus clear-cut rational classifications and thus the negation of explicitly hybrid formations (Latour 1993) or that which would facilitate such cultural formations, in our case: roads. In the case of British anthropology, the methodological monism of small-scale groups further illustrates this fear of crossing sociospatial boundaries. For instance, while physical mobility, in reference to the Kula Ring of Trobriand islanders, was defining for British social anthropology (Malinowski 1922), the established spatiocultural boundaries of the Trobriand islands were not really crossed as part of the Kula exchange, and thus an ethnography of such mobility that remained within its spatiocultural position was, epistemologically, a safe bet. Perhaps, a potential encounter with the crossing of boundaries would lead to a disruption of the "order of [anthropological] things" (Foucault 2002 [1966]).

Following a Foucauldian line of argument, one could attribute such fear of boundary-crossing to the privileged class and ethnic background of most ancestors of the discipline and their self-determination, in antithetical terms, to the nonmodern and colonized ethnographic subject. This echoes the by now celebrated opposition—but also interdependence—between the nomadic and the settled that Gilles Deleuze and Felix Guattari (1986), among others, discuss, or indeed what in a more anthropological manner James Scott (1998) described as the opposition between state(d) (anthropologists in our case) and stateless/moving people. Or perhaps it even reflects the other famous division between hot and cold societies, if one prefers the more classical Levi-Straussian terminology. Indeed, we should not forget the metaphor encapsulated in this terminology: according to thermodynamics, cold bodies are characterized by slower molecular motility.

Late modernity as dromocracy

Anthropology is no longer able to neglect roads; together with other infrastructures, roads have become a central subject of anthropological inquiry. This should be seen in relation to other concepts, such as mobility (Cresswell and Merriman 2011; Urry 2007), flows (e.g. Appadurai 1990), network society (Castells 2010), or fluidity and liquidity (Bauman 2000), that have entered the standard lexicon of the social sciences in reference to current sociocultural conditions. In addition to allowing for theoretical speculations and heuristic models, the current sociocultural phenomena, described by the aforesaid concepts, refers both to novel forms of sociality and also to some very explicit and tangible materialities (Miller 2005). Thus, from the increased speed and flows to the fact that they are crucial spaces of flow for network society (Castells 2010), it can be argued that highways have become one of the most paradigmatic material infrastructures of the current sociocultural condition. This does not necessarily imply a materialist determinism: highways not only produce other modern materialities and socialities but also comprise the materialization of modernist ways of imagining the—once "utopian"—futures of a previous era.

We describe the modern world in terms of automobility (Featherstone et al. 2005; Miller 2001; Sheller 2004; Urry 2004), yet this generic term, which seems to prioritize the automobile conceptually, can be misleading. Historically, roads for automobility were developed and "produced" on a mass scale well before the mass production and mass use of vehicles (Mom 2005; Vahrenkamp 2002). As such, the priority of modern highways is not only a temporal matter—some of the most insightful students of modernity have been explicit about the "cosmogonical" value of highways for the late modern cosmos. For instance, in *Speed and Politics*, Paul Virilio (2006 [1977]) defined modern society precisely as a "dromocratic society" (from *dromos*, road, and *cratos*, state, power).

Roads of course are not a modern phenomenon; they are the most archetypal human-made networks. For example, James Snead et al. (2010) compiled a collection of archaeological perceptions of different roads and pathways. Moreover, if we consider the paths that animals make, then it becomes clear that humans do not have a monopoly on networks of inland mobility. Thus, a question which emerges at this point is what is meant by modern road-systems? A first, technical answer is that modern roads are roads made with fast, frequent, long-range mobility (of vehicles) in mind. They comprise the combination of two relatively different technologies. First, the hard-surfacing/drainage technology that, in the case of Europe, was initially found in cobbled Roman roads and later in other forms such as macadam, cement, brick, or (much later) asphalt concrete. Second, the technology of rapidly building large-scale, long and wide, hard-surfaced, linear highways with controlled and limited access. Although such infrastructure was sometimes built over older transport networks (even ancient ones), in the twentieth century it was primarily built from scratch. This technology is notoriously linked with the modernist and futurist imagination of the European far-right totalitarian states. After all, the highway built during the 1920s, the early days of Italian fascism, between Milan and the Lakes of the North, is considered to be the first example of a highway as we know it today.

Given that the two largest highway systems (built in Italy and Germany) of the interwar period were surfaced with cement, the two current technologies, asphalt concrete and large-scale, linear highway networks, came together and were standardized after WWII. According to Mom (2005) both highways exclusively for automobility and asphalt surfacing emerge after a long war between the competing technologies. In the first case was a war between mixed and car-only networks, which followed a previous war between automobility and canals, railways etc. In the area of surfacing the fight was equally complicated as it was amongst asphalt, bricks, cement, concrete etc. It can be argued that asphalt concrete dominated the surfacing of highways because the United States won WWII.[1] Famously, Germany lacked the natural resources necessary for asphalt and sought to avoid becoming dependent on a scarce material for what was one of its key propaganda projects. As technology studies have taught us, however, there are complex politics behind the domination of one material over another. Thus, much more instrumental was the existence of a powerful asphalt lobby in the United States (Holley 2003; MacNichol 2005). Indeed, asphalt was far from the perfect material in the early era of the competition. Nevertheless, substantial amounts of capital were injected into the development of asphalt throughout the nineteenth and early twentieth century which led to its victory in that implicitly historical and explicitly economic competition with various other paving technologies. Asphalt triumphed due to the involvement of local and national governments under pressure from, and aided by, corporate agents and interests such as the owner of Trinidad's pit lake, the US petrol industrialists, and the postwar boom in the car industry, to mention but a few (Holley 2003; MacNichol 2005; Mom and Kirsch 2001).

Highways were developed over the same period, marking another victory over alternative transport technologies such as canals and most especially railways (Mom and Kirsch 2001). On a macrohistorical level, colonialism and the exploitation of natural resources in diverse terrains all around the globe contributed to the spread of roads capable of automobility versus the railways and canals which dominated the relatively flat landscapes of Northern and Central Europe. During the twentieth century, newly built networks of unpaved roads were becoming a temporary and inexpensive solution for the opportunistic development of colonial exploitation. Later, during the postcolonial period, roads became the key element in the economic development of "underdeveloped" countries, according to development theorists such as Walt Rostow (1960).

Historically, in the case of Europe, it was WWI that ensured highways triumphed in the competition with other transport infrastructures. The vulnerability of the existing—and thus known—networks played a key role in this. Moreover, outside the flat territories of some Northern European countries, the diversity of landscape in the rest of the continent meant that roads were convenient from a practical perspective, as was the case for the Romans and during the Napoleonic Wars of 1799–1815 (see Mom 2005). The construction of these roads was facilitated by the plentiful supply of gratis labor young conscripts provided between 1914 and 1918. In addition, during this time, the various automobile clubs of Europe saw their upper-class members volunteering, together with their vehicles, to the war effort. Thus, road-building and automobility became an integral part of the technology that corresponded to a modernist perception of how wars were to be fought during the industrial, modern age, after cavalries.

Just a few years after WWI, hard-surfacing technology (cement concrete), together with the introduction of the aforesaid, linear, technical characteristics, elevated large-scale road-building projects into highways as we know them today. Although the first highway technology was a peacetime project and arguably, in the case of Europe, one with primarily aesthetic and leisure purposes, its genealogy would be linked eternally with far-right totalitarian regimes and their modernist and futurist worldview. Rather than an infrastructure with key practical purposes, the first *autostrada* (built just after Mussolini came to power) served the weekend excursions of the wealthy leisure-class of car owners. In Germany, the Third Reich's *autobahnen* of the 1930s were undertaken in order to create employment for the unemployed German proletariat rather than for the purpose of actual mobility. They also connected the nation, providing tangible propaganda for the capabilities of the most modernist regime in Europe by demonstrating its ability to tame nature and make itself visible in every corner of the country. As David Frisby (2001) implied, the straightness of these roads represented very specific perceptions of the social world in comparison to those that winding roads represented. It can be argued that highways were framed within the wider context of the aesthetics of progress, representing unlimited growth, unlimited speed, unlimited length, and a straightforward, unobstructed path to the future of the new world order.

In addition, it is important to highlight the more implicit military purposes of the interwar *autobahn* and *autostrada* systems. For example, the highways in Albania and Libya, built by the Italian fascist regime at the dawn of WWII, were later used by the Italian army to invade these countries, as were the German highways leading to Poland. Despite this, it was not until after WWII, in the United States, that new mass-built highway systems became *explicitly* linked with defense purposes (Patton 1986; Rose 1990; Seely 1987). The famous American expressways were built during the cold war in order to evacuate the cities in the case of a nuclear attack. Ironically, whether by design or by accident,

American cities were eventually evacuated not by an act of war but by suburbanization (Baum-Snow 2007). Moreover, if intercity highways were linked with military purposes after 1945, wide road nexuses within cities were linked with military purposes well before that. The nineteenth-century, postrevolution Parisian boulevards were designed to facilitate the movement of organized military units for counter-insurrectionary purposes, as evidenced by the Paris Commune commentaries on boulevards as a feared new infrastructure (e.g. Blanqui 1972 [1866]). Following the end of WWII, urban road networks would be linked explicitly with intercity nexuses toward the so-called integrated infrastructural ideal that gave birth to the late modern city (Graham and Marvin 2001).

Toward a new critical dromology

Much of the critical thinking addressing the issue of automobile highways considers them one of the most crucial elements in the development of modern capitalism. This is probably embedded within the wider school of thought that considers Nazism and fascism as programmatic of late modern capitalism (Arendt 1951; Bauman 1989; Virilio 1974). For example, Arendt, in her discussion of the banality of evil (1951), suggested that the ontology of the modern capitalist state (dictatorial or democratic) is such that it facilitates the organization and the performance of a potential holocaust, a process that is almost irrelevant to the actual modern agents who were (and are) socialized to treat their activities, even the most evil, heinous actions, in a routinized, professionalized, way. Similarly, in *Holocaust and Modernity*, Bauman (1989) suggests that one reason people are so horrified by the Holocaust is precisely because every modern state apparatus is capable of organizing and implementing a similar mass extermination project. Thus, within that context, some rather romantic but celebrated Marxist authors—based on the capitalist side of the cold war divide—were critical of highways and the centrally organized state apparatuses that build them. Guy Debord (1992 [1967], 174) paved the way for a critique of automobility when he stated that "the dictatorship of the automobile—the pilot product of the first stage of commodity abundance—has left its mark on the landscape with the dominance of freeways, which tear up the old urban centers and promote an ever-wider dispersal." The key critical thinker of modern spaces, Henri Lefebvre, stated categorically that a "motorway brutalizes the country-side and the land, slicing through space like a great knife" (Lefebvre 1991 [1974], 165, 124–5). Paul Virilio (1974) saw the city of Paris as being in a permanent state of siege by the peripheral highway and the flow of cars thereon (2005, 3). As previously mentioned, he is also the person who established an explicit link between highways, fascism, and modernity (Virilio 2006 [1977]). David Harvey (1989) acknowledged the role of highway systems in late capitalism's spatiomaterial relationships—highways, as mega-infrastructures, are embedded within the organic crises of capitalism (2010).

Speed, and so-called time–space compression, is the major point of reference in the aforesaid studies of modern spaces. This phenomenon took place thanks to the increasing use of transportation and communication technologies after 1945, which resulted in what Marx had prophetically termed the "annihilation of space by time" (Marx 1993a, 539). In terms of daily life in the capitalist core of the world-system, time–space compression has become evident by the widespread use of vehicles. In the West, after 1945, highways and cars created the iconic "*autopias*" (Wollen and Kerr 2002) of late capitalism. Highways became the major reference of a gradually speeding and long-distance cultural cosmology (Baudrillard 1988).

Occasionally, however, the critical approach of the modern postwar expansion of highways was ethnocentric. Historically, in noncapitalist or non-Western contexts, the mass construction of roads was not necessarily accompanied by the widespread introduction of automobility or a similar promise. Thus, for the great majority, neither was followed by time–space compression or high speed. On the contrary, in most non-Western and noncapitalist contexts, automobility and high(er) speeds were so exclusive that the asymmetric power divisions were explicitly materialized on roads, where usually the most powerful (e.g. the elite or the colonialist) could enjoy the symbolic and practical benefits of fast(er) and (more) private mobility (see also Ingold 2004). In the *Wretched of the Earth*, Franz Fanon is very specific in his description of the divisional value of the road for the colonial and colonized landscape:

> The zone where the natives live is not complementary to the zone inhabited by the settlers. The two zones are opposed, but not in the service of a higher unity. Obedient to the rules of pure Aristotelian logic, they both follow the principle of reciprocal exclusivity. No conciliation is possible, for of the two terms, one is superfluous. The settlers' town is a strongly built town, all made of stone and steel. It is a brightly lit town; the streets are covered with asphalt, and the garbage cans swallow all the leavings, unseen, unknown and hardly thought about. (Fanon and Sartre 1963, 38–9)

The political value of paved highways is especially evident in places where the people who had no access to automobility were the same ones who were forced to build the roads, as in socialist Albania (Dalakoglou 2009a, 2010b), Portugal (Pina-Cabral 1987), or colonial Africa (Evans-Pritchard 1960; Thomas 2002).

Given this context, a novel critical understanding of highways and automobility, in the case of a noncapitalist Western framework, emerges as a necessary part of the debate. Moreover, what this debate implies is the need for an ethnographically informed perception of roads capable of automobility in order to understand the infrastructural world in which we are dwelling today. Thus, given the unprecedented proliferation of highways today, along with the complex politics incorporated in the macro- and microhistories of modern road construction, and also given the *dromocratic* (Virilio 2006 [1977]) ontology of late modern politics, there has been a renewed interest in automobility and highways within the social sciences (e.g. Edensor 2004; Dalakoglou and Harvey 2012; Featherstone et al. 2005; Harvey and Knox 2015; Merriman 2007; Miller 2001; Urry 2007; Wollen and Kerr 2002). Although roads are arguably less researched by anthropologists in comparison to other universal material forms (e.g. houses, clothing, art), and despite the problematic history of the relationship between roads and the choice of ethnographic sites, roads are no longer just a coincidental brief reference in ethnographies. On the contrary, we can make roads the main ethnographic subject and we can talk about a growing body of road ethnographies.

This wealth of ethnographic material paves the way for a series of observations which can play a valuable role in the future development of an anthropology of the road. First of all, this newfound interest in roads has come about because societies and their practices have never before been so mobile and taken place over such extended distances. Similarly, never before have such frequent and long-range mobility and flows been embedded in the everyday life of such broad social classes (Urry 2007, 3–16). Nevertheless, these observations are only one side of the coin, as the majority of road ethnographies suggest. The other side of the increased mobility of the late twentieth and early twenty-first centuries is that never before have so many people been so deeply aware of the consequences of their exclusion from (auto)mobility and/or from accessing its infrastructures. Hence roads, together with the rest of mobility infrastructure, connect but they also disconnect, when they do not fulfill the promises embedded in a mobility infrastructure or, for example, when they violently alter existing sociomaterial orders (Dalakoglou and Harvey 2012).

Moreover, another idea that must be considered in an anthropology of the road is that, despite the common universal technical characteristics that determine a thing such as a highway or road, socioculturally, such things do not really exist as a universal category. Thus, although modern highways have a common material ancestry or obey similar international construction standards, any given road or highway is socioculturally many highways at the same time. As Lefebvre puts it in a celebrated quote: "The analysis of every space brings us up against the dialectical relationship between demand and command, along with its attendant questions: 'Who?', 'For Whom?', 'By Whose agency?', 'Why and How?'" (Lefebvre 1974, 116). Thus, attempting to conduct empirical qualitative social research on a given highway section will likely bring forth a number of very different explanations. Therefore, the Lefebvrian approach opens up a complex world with unlimited ethnographic possibilities, possibilities that were not implied by the early anthropological approaches to infrastructure such as those of Marvin Harris (1968) or Maurice Godelier (1978). In the programmatic contributions of Harris and Godelier, the necessary departure from the Marxist grand narrative toward ethnographic particularity and then back to theory did not happen in concrete and organized ways. On the one hand, these early anthropological perceptions of material infrastructures were groundbreaking in explicitly suggesting sociomaterial continuities in a manner that became popular after the cultural critique of the 1980s. On the other hand, the theoretical scheme "entrapped" such perceptions within its limits. If nothing else, a first limitation is the use of the grand category "infrastructure" which, within a materialist framework, determines everything else and simultaneously is too general to be defined empirically. This is not an effort to underestimate the Marxist perspective of infrastructures. Nevertheless, a purist Marxist perception of infrastructure does not leave much space for diversity. I do not mean only the diversity of representations by the different social and historical agents involved, but even the ontological diversity among the various dimensions of an infrastructure (e.g. the sociocultural, material, historical). By extension, the narrow limits of the theory prevent even the perception of diversity among the very different kinds of infrastructure(s): pipelines, roads, power grids, ports, landfills, or even hospitals, for example, are all labeled as infrastructure when they are radically different sociomaterial entities.

More specifically, regarding roads, the content of the Marxist scheme and its anthropological versions had to be stretched considerably in order to set the foundations for an anthropology of roads. If nothing else, there is a fundamental methodological problem in a potential purist

Marxist perception of the so-called (by Marx and Engels) communication (and not transport) infrastructures, namely, for historical reasons, most of the original references to these communication infrastructures were to canals and railways (de La Haye 1980).

Thus, the choice of the Lefebvrian perception is a very conscious decision for the current project. Lefebvre himself belongs to the school of Marxist authors who were critical of the high speeds of automobility and of the post-WWII West. The idea was that high speeds were crucial for the capitalist and industrial growth facilitating the exploitation of the working masses. The fast and mass production, transfer, and consumption of goods were transforming the Western working classes into simply consumers, alienating them from their production. Despite following this idea in principle, Lefebvre's poststructural reading of the original theoretical contribution allows us to resolve some of the limitations of Marxist theory, thus allowing for the renewal that is necessary for the ethnographic approach. Lefebvre's (2009 [1940], 88–102) historical materialist approach and his spatial analysis (1974) provide him with two methodological benefits. First, Lefebvre (2009 [1940], 1974), a theoretician, was not bound by the same compulsion to produce a scientific theory on which to base an empirical discipline—contrary to Harris and Godelier—and secondly, his main point of reference is *space*. In principle, he was analyzing an entity which may have tangible materiality, and at the same time may be relatively immaterial, yet qualitatively distinct: a concrete abstraction (Stanek 2008). As such, instead of seeing material infrastructures as a strictly materialist element that determines superstructure, he saw them as *spaces*. Furthermore, the Lefebvrian space is not neutral or objectively measured; it is a product of human action and thus a process. If space is always produced, it follows logically that it can also circulate and be consumed. In fact, the Lefebvrian space/infrastructure affords a similar analysis to the one afforded by any product of human labor. For example, its circulation is linked with its fetishization, and thus the social and economic relationships involved in spatial production are both embedded within the materiality of space/infrastructure and masked within the labyrinth of the circulation/consumption process. The users of a highway, for example, will never see the exploited migrant workers who constructed it.

The idea of an infrastructure as a product of human action easily leads to a perception of highways as technological artifacts. In this case, as is well known among scholars of science and technology studies (Khun 2012; Latour 1987; Latour and Woolgar 1979), technologies are not simply objectively and rationally created, but involve complex sociocultural, historical, and especially political dynamics, while simultaneously encapsulating what Michel Foucault called the micro-physics of power within their materiality. For instance, one of the most famous analyses from society and technology studies (Winner 2010)—which focused on transport infrastructure—manifests how bridges may have very explicit class and race perceptions incorporated within their design and within their materiality. However, such perspectives have far-reaching implications, well beyond the designers and creators, the users or the workers who built the actual infrastructures, beyond even those people who aspire, but never get the chance, to have a direct tangible experience of these infrastructures but who still have perceptions of them. For instance, Bruno Latour (1987, 248–9) used the case of road construction in the highlands of Crete in order to discuss the relationship between local communities and their aspirations for technological/infrastructural projects without having a tangible experience of them. As Heideggerian phenomenology (1971) would imply—again in reference to a bridge—just thinking or being aware of a built form automatically assumes the (virtual or material) existence of that form and thus the existence of certain "realities" related to the knowledge of that form.

Thus, it is perhaps here where Lefebvre, as a poststructuralist, comes in. The road product is open to social manipulations: it "kills" the authority (state, suprastate, the developer, etc.) in the same way that the Barthian (1967) poststructuralist perception of the text "killed" the author. The meanings of the road as a product are open to those who use it, experience its existence, are simply aware of its existence, or even just expect it or its rhythmic flows. It is possible to extend this approach even further, toward a more culturally relativistic approach: we cannot even be sure if a road we study is considered "space" or a "product" by the people who constructed it, use it, live by, work along, or even think of it. A road and its flows may promote hope or hopelessness, expectation or fear, love or hate, stability or instability, mobility, loss, suspicion, or subordination, to mention but a few of the ways roads are described within the related ethnographies. Such affective dimensions of roads are precisely the reason that anthropologists have coined new terms such as "imagineering," combining imagination with engineering (Löfgren 2004), or "road mythographies" grasping the close relationship between local narratives and roads (Masquilier 2002).

This is not to suggest a flat morphology neglecting social hierarchies similar to the one that notions such as that of *scapes* (Appadurai 2011) or actor-network (Latour 2007; Latour and Venn 2002) previously proposed. On the contrary, the morphology of the sociocultural entities around a road is evidently hierarchical and unequal. Even the way the roads are conceived is colonized by hegemonic (Gramsci 1995) rhetoric, which represents the perceptions of the classes in power. As Hansen and Stepputat (2001) or Foucault (2002 [1966]) suggested: the state itself is in fact a state of imagination and its infrastructures are imagined as much as they are built. Often they are just imagined and never built. Roads' multiplicity, however, is more complex and goes beyond the state. The fact that they comprise the tangible materialization of certain imaginations implies that the entire postmodern flexibility in meanings is met with certain implicit and explicit limitations. Especially in the case of a thing like a highway that carries so many political and historical meanings and ideas embedded within its materiality and more widely its historical existence. This is to say that roads—and by extension highways—are intertwined with the human mode of dwelling in the world (Heidegger 1971), as they originate from the archetypal human-made network of the bipedal mobile human subjects.

Thus overall, the parameters one has to take into account when deciding to study a road transcend most traditional social science scales (e.g. micro/macro, diachronic/synchronic, subject/object, proximate/distant, settled/nomadic, mobile/static, form/content). Perhaps this is the great methodological benefit of studying roads, and most likely this is precisely the reason that some of the most influential social science theories of late modernity try to think of the late modern world by employing the conceptualizations of networks (Castells 2010; Latour 1996). This is exactly the implications of an anthropology of the road: an anthropological approach which remains ethnographically rooted and simultaneously allows us to perceive some of the most static and traditional units of anthropological analysis such as the house, city, family, money, or architecture in direct reference to the infrastructural network's materiality and the flows on and of the road.

Note

1 The so-called asphalt lobby was already very powerful in the United States, gradually eliminating other paving technologies with the help of its political patrons (Holley 2005; MacNichol 2005).

2

The road to Albania

In nine days I reached Tepaleen, our journey was much prolonged by the torrents that had fallen from the mountains and intersected the roads. (Lord Byron, letter to his mother, November 12, 1809)

Ulysses' Gaze (1995) is a film by Theo Angelopoulos. It tells the story of a US-based film director, played by Harvey Keitel, who travels around the Balkans in the early 1990s, following in the footsteps of the Manaki Brothers, two pioneers of Balkan filmmaking who documented the people of the region via photographs and film in the early twentieth century. They were also typical of the multilingual, prenational Balkan subjects of their era, before the rise of nationalism and the tendency for people to identify with one national group over another. In *Ulysses' Gaze*, there is a scene in which the protagonist and a Greek taxi driver are trying to cross the border to Albania in an old vehicle. Along the snowy cross-border road, an old woman, who is standing alone, asks them in Greek if they could drive her to Albania because the taxi driver who brought her from Athens did not want to cross the border, "I am visiting my sister," she adds—in an allegoric manner. Meanwhile, a Greek police bus arrives at the border carrying young male migrants to be deported to Albania due to their lack of documents. They are heavily laden, carrying full bags back home. During the field research which led to this book, these scenes from the Albanian–Greek border kept running through my mind every time I crossed it.

This image implies the central idea of this book: when attempting to discuss post-cold war Europe, European borders, and in particular cross-border passages and infrastructures, are one of the best places to start—and, perhaps, to end. To some extent, this was precisely the case for most people I met in Gjirokastër who, while talking about things that initially sounded irrelevant to the road, employed the large cross-border road in their daily narratives. It was this common narrative that led to an on-the-spot transformation of my research project from an ethnography of the country's (post)socialist urban architecture and domestic materiality into an anthropology on and of the road. This statement partly answers the most typical question I received during my fieldwork in Albania and afterwards: "Why Albania?"

The (non)particularities of postsocialist Albania(ns)

The main ethnographic site of this book is the city of Gjirokastër in south Albania and a 29-kilometer highway linking the city with the cross-border passage of Kakavijë. Gjirokastër is a small city by international standards, yet in the southwest Balkans it is a significant urban center with an important geographic and historical position within the traveling routes of the region.

The boundary, the road, and the cross-boundary flows between Albania and Greece are ethnographically special, not because of their uniqueness but because they encapsulate processes typical of the recent past and present of Europe. Ethnographically, on and through the highway and its flows, it becomes possible, even necessary, to discuss a series of historical processes and sociocultural phenomena. These include the cold war capitalism–socialism divide and the postsocialist condition, as well as so-called European integration, migration within the continent, new social-class divisions, the construction fever of the economic boom, and the related crisis that followed. These processes are not only observable in a concentrated form along the cross-border highway—these flows of people and things have produced and continue to produce a new (post-1990) sociomaterial Europe both in the East and West of the continent.

Albania is one of the most stigmatized countries in Europe. The communist past and the much longer Islamic history were parts of Albania's Otherness. However, the majority of the post-1990 stigma is linked to the mass Albanian emigration following the end of socialism. Albania became the most migratory country in Europe, with approximately half of its population now living abroad. Indeed, as other authors have shown (e.g. Berger et al. 2010), in post-WWII Europe there is an entire "industry" of institutional marginalization of migrants and the countries of their origin. In the case of Albanians, there is a historical peculiarity, namely, most of them migrated to European countries that until the 1970s were migrant senders (Greece and Italy) and thus were, themselves, stigmatized until recently. Nevertheless, this did not lessen the process of institutional marginalization and stigmatization of Albanian immigrants within these two countries. By the early 1990s, both Greece and Italy were established members of the supposedly integrated EU. After many years of marginalization, they now belonged to the capitalist "West," the winners of the cold war, and they eagerly joined the other side of Europe: that of migrant-receiving countries in the 1990s.

The transformation from migrant-sending to migrant-receiving was one of the most precise markers of the sought-after "Westernization" and "modernization" that the governments of these two countries had aimed for during many decades. Thus, the application of xenophobic migratory policies, similar to those which Mediterranean migrants had experienced some decades previously, had enormous significance for the polities of the new destinations. This is a political significance, which implies a biopolitical condition, namely, the modernization of Italy and Greece, passed, and continues to pass, over the bodies of the non-EU immigrants who cross their borders (Dalakoglou 2013a).

In addition, the Italian and Greek migratory policies of the 1990s—which primarily victimized Albanians, and later other migrants—were not based merely on the respective governmental decisions but were part of the common EU migratory policies of Fortress Europe. Such policies were far more evident along the vulnerable peripheries of Europe, as with Greece, whose border was upgraded to an EU-external border. This was also the period when the old boundaries between North and South Europe became blurred due to the novel redetermination of the boundary between (post)socialist Eastern Europe and the rest of the continent. In other words, the gap between North and South EU member states began to narrow in the 1990s when the focus of comparison became postsocialist and nonsocialist states.

The European integration process started soon after the collapse of European socialism. This new European project originally concerned the twelve older EU members. It laid out criteria for the so-called modernization and Europeanization of the marginal Southern European countries. Later, when the boundaries were redrawn, both Greece and Italy were no longer marginalized but considered among the core. The reconfiguration of Europe and the new boundaries provided them with the archetypal necessary Other who was very deliberately embodied by the Albanian migrants. The Greek collective identity as modern and European became possible precisely through the portrayal and experience of the Albanian migrants next door as non-European and nonmodern. Thus, in terms of a scale of flows, the process of creating Otherness passed precisely via the cross-border highway. The implications of this then transferred to the cities and villages of Greece, creating an experience of boundary with respect to the Other in the neighborhood and thus allowing for a new collective superior self. There were now new marginal Europeans in the "European family"; Greeks were no longer at the bottom of the various pan-European statistic charts. By the early 1990s, they were scoring above most of the new additions: the postsocialist Europeans. Indeed, the flows on the border added further value toward such collective identities, since they facilitated the expansion of Greek capital toward the neighboring postsocialist states; Albania, Macedonia, Bulgaria, and Romania became new frontiers for Greek corporate economic development. The Greek governments of the time began portraying and promoting this so-called Powerful Greece as a broker of capitalist development in the postsocialist Balkans. This role was further encouraged by EU projects for cross-border collaboration with non-EU member countries.

Building the new Europe

The redrawing of boundaries within Europe and between Europe and its Others was merely one of the major, everyday sociopolitical processes on the continent during the 1990s and 2000s. Another defining characteristic of this period was the emergence of a new form of governance and respective political economy following the collapse of socialist regimes. This involved close collaboration between the first postsocialist governments and the EU leadership, together with other supranational organizations such as the World Bank, the IMF, the European Bank for Reconstruction and Development (EBRD) or later European Central Bank (ECB), which began to enforce neoliberal governance in Eastern European countries. This led to the formation of a system with minimal social provisions, precarious underpaid labor, public austerity, privatizations, mass emigration, and so on. The aggressive neoliberal governance that was applied in postsocialist countries during their—endless[1]— transition has also been applied to the periphery of West Europe[2] since the euro crisis of 2010. This process has meant yet another reconfiguration of the internal EU boundaries, increasing once again the gap between the South and the affluent North of the continent.

This new form of governance in postsocialist Europe has combined with a specific form of political economy with a spatial dimension, namely, the enormous boom in the construction sector witnessed throughout Europe in the 1990s and 2000s. The end of the cold war resulted (as most wars do) in a mass spatial expansion for the victors— occupying the territories and taking command of the resources of their enemies. In the case of the cold war, it was capitalism that triumphed over socialism, and thus most of the land, resources, and infrastructure of half of Europe was suddenly and cheaply transferred from public or state hands to private ones, ready to be consumed. In the early 1990s, developers—predominantly from the West or the Arabic world, but also the local new capitalist elites of postsocialist countries—benefited, massively, from this newly available, inexpensive resource, which allowed them to reconstruct the built environment. Construction, however, was not limited to former socialist territories, as the boom in the European construction sector soon expanded to the Western part of the continent, particularly the periphery, where mass construction (and a related privatization of public real estate) took place. It is these peripheral countries that were most affected by the so-called euro crisis of 2010 (Greece, Italy, Spain, Portugal, Ireland).

The same principle extends to the labor market. The newly integrated Eastern Europeans provided inexpensive labor both in their home countries and throughout the continent. The less developed Mediterranean countries of Western Europe relied on this new labor to gain acceptance into the Eurozone. This is clearly evident in Greece, where Albanian migrants bolstered the economy and (unexpectedly) allowed the country to meet the qualification criteria (see Katsoridas 2003).

It is possible to claim that, after 1990, Europe saw the largest production and renewal of the built environment since the reconstruction following WWII. Consider, for example, the reconstruction of East Berlin; the mass building of summer houses in Spain; Dublin's new satellite "suburbs" (now known locally as ghost estates); the pre-Olympics public works of London, Athens, and Barcelona; or the infrastructure developments in Albania and Romania along the natural gas pipelines of the Black Sea, to mention but a few. During the 1990s and 2000s, European construction became a huge simultaneous project which sometimes had tangible physical and material connections (e.g. trans-European highways or inter-European natural gas pipelines). Such connections, however, were not always so explicit, as this ethnographic study indicates.

In terms of political economy, the pan-European accumulation of built capital should be seen as part of the economic cycle (Harvey 1989, 2010). Within this cycle, each boom, by its very design, has systematically integrated the future bust. This is especially true when viewed in combination with the EU-fueled expansion of neoliberalism and the financialization of the 1990s–2000s (Lapavitsas 2014). This latter process led to a huge increase in virtual monetary capital which had the potential to acquire materiality via urban and infrastructural development and thus to acquire more real value via its transformation into the built environment through real estate and so on. At the same time, this process intensified the most typical cultural logics of real estate markets, such as the belief in unlimited inflation of property and other assets.

It consequently led to a reverse condition, namely, to a virtualization of the value of built capital into an almost immaterial capital with a flexible value. In reality, however, built capital is concrete and materially tangible, with a limited real value. Yet, ironically, a certain virtualization of the built environment did in fact take place due to the creation of a wasteland of unfinished infrastructural construction projects that now lie all across Europe. Such contradictions were intensified and facilitated by the speculation of banks and financial corporations in the European construction sector. Many such developments took place under the auspices of national governments all around Europe and indeed with the active support of various EU authorities. This produced exorbitant profits for those who knew their way around the markets and huge losses for almost everyone else, whether they were directly involved in those markets or not.

Furthermore, within that context and in terms of the political economy, large public works and major infrastructure projects became key vehicles for the advancement of this so-called European neoliberalization project. The end of socialism in Europe marked the end of public works constructed exclusively by the state, as international agents—donors or investors—entered the game. Thus, following Eastern Europe's integration, the former socialist countries and their Western counterparts witnessed a mass withdrawal by state authorities from infrastructure construction. In fact, for the most part, the state's role was reduced to that of a regulator. This explicitly paved the way for the emergence of large private European construction contractors and the privatization of public and state assets. The example of Greece clearly illustrates this process (Dalakoglou 2013b). The infrastructure projects of the 1990s–2000s can therefore be viewed as a major contributory part of the construction bubble.

From the road to the house and back: anthropology of Europe in new Europe

In terms of historical dialectics, the 1990s–2000s construction boom led to a new sociopolitical European condition. The question that first emerged within European anthropology in the early 1990s was how to understand, ethnographically, these multiscale processes, which interplay simultaneously and rapidly across the micro and macro levels of social analysis. This question has reemerged today, even more urgently, given the new European boundaries and the mass construction of the built environment. The temporality of these processes, their multiscale dimensions, and their mobile ontology pose a huge challenge for anthropology.

In a historical irony, while socialism, as a political system, collapsed due to its own contradictions, dialectic materialism has emerged as the best way to explain the sociomaterial transformations within Europe following the end of the cold war. The new political economy of post-Keynesian capitalism, the extreme neoliberalism that conquered the entire political spectrum, had its own material dimension built. In the same way that postwar reconstruction comprised the sociomaterial building of the two distinct, divided Europes, the end of socialism was met with the physical construction of the new unified Europe of victorious capitalism. Indeed, history not only failed to end in 1990 but on the contrary there was a desperate need both to signify and materialize the sociopolitical change and the new historical stage and determine its future evolution. What was sociomaterially constructed via the renewal of the built environment in the 1990s and 2000s was the postsocialist Europe; the Europe of the common currency, the so-called Europe of the common market, the Europe of loosened internal borders but fortified external ones; a Europe where the divisions between East, West, South, and North have been reconfigured. A Europe constructed by Eastern European and, later, non-European migrant laborers. A Europe with a new, postindustrial class division and middle-class lifestyles and cultural patterns based on the virtual economy of credit, remittances, and new opportunities provided by the (temporarily) thriving markets. A capitalist Europe which rapidly expanded and eventually gave birth to the extreme neoliberal governance we saw "eating" Eastern European societies, and which is now doing the same in the European South.

This in turn raises a number of questions: what are the details of this process? How does it work and what are its peculiarities and its paradoxes? How do people deal with it? And how does the continent look, following the end of socialism? In order to understand these processes ethnographically, this book focuses on a sector of the European mega (re)construction project: a cross-border road between an EU and a non-EU member state and the flows along the (dis)connections of this infrastructure. This is done in reference to the more conventional sociomaterial units of modern anthropological analysis (the city and the house).

Anthropology of Albania

Albania was the most closed of former socialist states (Schwandner-Sievers 2004b, 103). As the archaeologist Nicholas Hammond, after many decades spent conducting research on ancient Epirus (the area that is today South Albania/Northwest Greece), concluded, the limited

ability of foreign academics to access the country during the cold war
left its mark on every Western study of the area (Hammond 1989, 294).[3]
This was not always the case as for many centuries (up until 1913)
Northwest Greece and South Albania were one common sociohistorical and administrative unit. In fact, the boundary between the two
countries was only established in the 1940s. After this time, the governments involved made serious efforts to cut their common roots and the
routes between the two states, so much so that successive Greek governments remained hostile toward Albania for over forty years after WWII,
refusing to sign the respective peace treaty and claiming South Albania
as part of Greece. The Albanian authorities also shared some responsibility for the state of their relationship. A dogmatic misinterpretation of
Marxist theory on the transborder mobility of the workforce, combined
with an international isolationism adopted by the party's leadership in
the 1970s, contributed toward the sociohistorical division embodied
today in the Albanian–Greek border (see Green 2005; Nistiakos 2010;
Pusceddu 2013).[4]

The lack of nonnative anthropological studies in Albania after WWII
left a gap in knowledge of the area. Prior to this period, British and other
foreign ethnographers had conducted research in Albania, especially on
the Northern Albanian Ghegs,[5] yet the cold war, and particularly the
Corfu Straits incident,[6] interrupted the relationship between Albania
and the UK and several other governments. In fact, during this time—
within Anglo-Saxon anthropology—the post-WWII shift of focus
from sub-Saharan Africa to the Mediterranean, which passed through
Albania's neighboring countries, ignored Albania, leaving it out of the
anthropological map. Thus, contrary to neighboring places—such as
Greece (Campbell 1964)[7] or Yugoslavia (Halpern 1958)—an "Albano-
logical" legacy is only now beginning to be reshaped within English-
speaking anthropology.[8]

After 1990, this lacuna in academic and anthropological research
became evident as merely one dimension of the wider political process.
The lack of knowledge about Albania, its socialist past, its mass migratory present, and its people's stigmatization were crucial historical
factors in Southern Europe, which in turn played a crucial role in the
supposed European integration following the cold war. These processes
led to the Albanian migrants involuntarily becoming important historical actors both in the two main destination countries of their migratory
flow and, even more so, in the country of their origin. In this context,
what occurs along the largest highway linking Albania and Greece is
of particular significance as it is an examination of the entire European
border between postsocialism and capitalism. Simultaneously, the focus

becomes two of the most marginal European countries. Furthermore, it ethnographically emphasizes a very marginal margin between them. It is precisely along this margin that we may begin to understand the historical processes shaping our contemporary life, as other anthropologists have demonstrated in reference to both this particular border (Green 2005) and, more widely, the southeast margin of Europe (Herzfeld 1987).

The ethnographic site: Gjirokastër and South Albania

Having the largest citadel in the Balkans is testament to the major economic and military role that Gjirokastër city played from medieval times. The city's strategic importance continued long after this, and well into the twentieth century.

In Roman times, the city of Antigonea, located on the plateau of the Drinos River, was the most important settlement in the contemporary Gjirokastër area. The fortress that grew into the city of Gjirokastër dates back to the thirteenth century. The earliest known reference to Gjirokastër as a settlement was in 1336, under the name "Argyrokastron" (Silver Castle, in Greek) in the Byzantine chronicle of Ioannes Kantakouzenos (Riza 1981, 11). The Greeks continue to use the name Argyrokastro(n) today, and it was also used by foreigners during the nineteenth and early twentieth centuries (e.g. see Hasluck 2007 [1929], 541; Leake 1835; Pearson 2006). Until recently, both names were often used interchangeably, given the city's multiple ethnic groups, languages, and religions. The term Gjirokastër/Gjirokastra became the official Albanian name in the early twentieth century; an outward expression of nationalism coinciding with the struggle between the Albanian and Greek nation-states to annex the city and its surrounding area. As the Albanian term Gjirokastër is the official name of the town today, I use it throughout the book.

According to Emin Riza (1981), a historian of the city, after 1350 Argyrokastron was at the center of the feudal state of the Zenevisi clan, under the Byzantine crown. In 1419, it was occupied by the Ottoman army and subsequently annexed. In 1453, the Ottomans occupied Constantinople and made it the capital of their empire (1453). Gjirokastër was the capital city of the respective Ottoman *sandjak* (administrative unit). According to some of the earliest Ottoman fiscal archives of 1431–42, the city had 163 dwellings (Riza 1981).[9] The political center of the town during that period remained within the castle—with new fortifications being built up until the nineteenth century (Riza 1978; 1981, 30–5). Later in that period, a commercial center was developed around the wall of the citadel, in the urban district today called the Old Bazaar/Pazari i Vjeter (Riza 1978, 1981).

The city became one of the prime regional centers in the last century of Ottoman rule (1800–1913). Gjirokastër was particularly strong under the "Vylayet of Yannina,"[10] where it was the second largest city after Yannina.[11] This vylayet grew into one of the strongest of the empire during the early nineteenth century, so strong, in fact, that its legendary chief Ali Pasha claimed autonomy from the Sublime Porte, declaring a war against the Sultan which lasted until Ali Pasha's assassination in 1822 (Fleming 1999).

By the end of the nineteenth century, Gjirokastër was among the largest urban centers in the region, one containing diverse populations speaking Albanian and Greek, as well as Vlach, and people of both the Christian and Muslim faith. It became one of the focal points of the nationalist claims to the area. Following the end of the Second Balkan War in 1913, the Ottoman Empire lost its Balkan territories and the Albanian state was founded. Both Greece and the newly founded Albania claimed South Albania or, as the Greeks call it, North Epirus (see Green's 2005 work on the Epirotic question). After the Balkan Wars, the Greek army, which had occupied the Drinos River plateau, was ordered to abandon it. Despite being ordered to leave, local Greek politicians formed armed groups, and with the support of Athens they rebelled against the provisional Albanian government. The Albanian authorities were unable to protect the territorial integrity of the new state, and with the Protocol of Corfu (1914) the "Self-Governed State of North Epirus" was founded, which included most of contemporary South Albania, with Gjirokastër as its capital. The new state had a very short life; when WWI broke out in 1914, the Greek army occupied the Drinos plateau, southeastern Albania was occupied by the French army, and southwestern Albania by the Italian army. These foreign armies left the area at the end of the war when it was awarded to Albania, which was once again recognized as an independent state (Dalakoglou and Halili 2009a).

In the period between the two world wars, the newly formed state of Albania sought to develop modern institutions styled after those in the West. In reality, however, the feudal relations and institutions of the Ottoman era continued to play a dominant role in the country. Life for the people was difficult, with the vast majority living in abject poverty. In the late nineteenth century, many of those living in rural areas gradually migrated to the towns and cities, as the feudal system in the Ottoman and post-Ottoman periods did not explicitly force peasants to stay on the land (Stavrianos 1958). As such, the first micro-capitalist enterprises, which emerged in this period, developed in urban rather than rural areas. The inhabitants of the rural Gjirokastër area migrated locally to Gjirokastër or Ioannina, or farther afield to Salonica, Istanbul, and Tirana. Many also crossed the Atlantic, joining other international migrants to the USA. The Albanian migration to the USA was so large that during communism, the global center and the leadership of the predominant religion in the country, the Albanian Bektashi Islam, was based in Detroit.

At the beginning of the twentieth century, this new nation-state launched a modernization program that sought to encourage capitalist entrepreneurship. A civil service was established and craftsmanship and commercial activity increased, which in turn led to the emergence of a working class and a class of small-scale artisans made up of former peasants in the town of Gjirokastër. New social groups also began to emerge, such as the students who attended the city's French lycée. As a result, new ideas quickly began to conquer a changing city that was, itself, in a new and reconfigured central position within these new relationships.

Soon after receiving independence from the empire in 1913, Ahmet Zog (1895–1961) a landlord from Central Albania and former minister of the first Albanian government, staged a coup d'état and became the self-proclaimed King Zog of Albania. Under Zog's dictatorship (1925–39) which was inspired by fascist ideology, Albania became a political and economic protectorate of Mussolini's Italy. So, during the 1920s and 1930s an intensive modernization project was launched—which included roads, ports, irrigation systems, army, police, and public education—and it was the Italians who carried out and funded all of the high-profile public works (Fischer 1984). Aside from these public works, the Albanian fascist state and the governmental and business interventions of the Italian government did nothing to address the preexisting and newly emerging social inequalities, which widened considerably in this period.

However, while fascism dominated the country politically, influence from abroad in the form of returning migrant Albanians, as well as Italians and other foreigners, also brought leftist ideas to the country, with the first groups of communist and anarchist students and workers being formed in the late 1930s in various cities, including Gjirokastër. This leftist activity was concentrated mostly in the southern and northern cities due to the influence of the neighboring countries' communist groups (Dalakoglou and Hallili 2009b). The great turn in Albanian politics came with the military occupation of Albania by the Italian army in 1939 and the Italian invasion of Greece, which transformed south Albania into a battlefield.

Shortly after its foundation in 1942, the Communist Party of Albania was instructed by the Balkan section of the Comintern to carry out the anti-fascist resistance. The resistance received more support in South Albania than in other areas of the country; Gjirokastër became one of its centers, and the city was one of the first where partisans defeated the occupation forces and their collaborators. In December 1944, after a guerrilla war and a brief civil war, partisans seized Tirana and established a socialist regime. This was immediately followed by an extensive nationalization of the means of production and a process of intensive industrialization and urbanization, including the introduction of five-year economic plans and a large-scale social and economic modernization program. Within a couple of decades, Gjirokastër was transformed from an Ottoman feudal region into an industrial city, while the surrounding land was nationalized and agricultural cooperatives in the style of the Soviet *kolkhoz* were formed. In the case of Gjirokastër, every settlement on the s plateau became an agricultural cooperative with communal ownership of the land. This process led to the radical transformation of local hierarchies as the Islamic aristocracy of Gjirokastër lost most of their economic and political privileges. Despite this loss of status, in some cases the members of these families, even though they belonged to the feudal class, embraced communism. They saw a new form of political and social privilege replacing the preexistent ones.

In the first years of Albanian socialism, the country's leader, Enver Hoxha (1908–85) who was born and raised in Gjirokastër, kept the country within Yugoslavia's sphere of influence. Yet following the split between Stalin and Tito in 1948, Albania aligned with the Soviets. In the same year, the Communist Party of Albania was renamed the Party of Labor of Albania. After the death of Stalin in 1953, Soviet–Albanian relations deteriorated, as Hoxha considered himself to be the only true Stalinist and accused Khrushchev of revisionism. Hoxha soon aligned with Mao's China, a relationship that became stronger after 1961 when Albania and the USSR halted all forms of diplomatic cooperation. In 1967, Albania began its own cultural revolution, which entailed prohibitions on religious practices and activities, among many other things. In 1968, after the Soviet invasion of Czechoslovakia, Albania left the Warsaw Pact. Following the death of Mao in 1976, Hoxha's government began to criticize the new Chinese regime, leading to the complete cessation of relations and international aid from China in 1978. Without Chinese aid and export subsidies, the Albanian economy quickly began to falter, and by the 1980s the country was suffering financial crises and food shortages (Dalakoglou and Halili 2009b).

During the socialist period, the population of Gjirokastër grew in size, and the city also expanded spatially within the context of the country's industrialization and urbanization program. In 1985, the Kakavijë border checkpoint "opened," at least officially, and in 1987 the hostility that had existed between Albania and Greece since WWII finally came to an end. This led to a new chapter in the relationship between the two countries. In the summer of 1990, the people of Tirana began to rebel, demanding the provision of passports and the right to travel abroad; the crowd clashed with the police and entered foreign embassies. Soon, people started crossing the previously sealed borders on foot, leading the socialist government to introduce reforms and hold the country's first elections in 1991, which the Socialist Party—heir of the Party of Labor—won; the opposition Democratic Party came second, and "Omonia," the Greek minority party, came third (electing MPs in Gjirokastër).

Albania had severe economic problems: by 1992–93, most of its productive labor force was working abroad, the majority in Greece, and the country was struggling to restructure its economy. Gjirokastër, like most of South Albania, had exceptionally high percentages of emigration among the local population. In the elections of 1993, the Democratic Party came first, and it remained in power up until 1997 when the most important event since the fall of socialism occurred: the pyramid investment schemes collapsed. These were fake "investment schemes" which were promising remarkably high returns for the "investors" so literally the majority of the Albanian population did "invest" expecting the gifts that capitalism would bring them. The pyramids were closely linked with the Democratic Party's leader Sali Berisha and his IMF- and World Bank-sponsored reforms of the economy.[12] However, by the end of 1997 a huge number of Albanians witnessed their savings vanish overnight; chaos ensued, and the country descended into a short civil war. South Albania, including Gjirokastër, suffered the greatest from the collapse of these pyramid schemes, and it consequently became a major focal point during the ensuing armed clashes.

Geography and population

The city of Gjirokastër is located on the eastern slopes of the Mali i Gjerë (Wide Mountain, highest peak: 1,887 meters), overlooking the plateau formed by the Drinos River. It is the largest city on the plateau and, at almost three 300 meters above sea level, it is the settlement with the highest altitude; from its castle, almost the entire valley can be seen. As is to be expected of a city with such diverse ethnic roots, Gjirokastër has many ethnic and cultural–linguistic groups including Albanians (a sizeable majority) and several native minority groups such as Greeks, Aromanians (Vlachs), Roma, and Egyptians (which stands for a group

1 A Bektashi priest leaving the Tekke of Haliki, located between Gjirokastër city and Lazarat village. According to the 2011 census, 58 percent of Albanians are Muslims (both Sunni and Bektashi). Christianity is practiced by 16 percent of the population (both Orthodox and Catholic). The rest of the Albanian population is either secular or belongs to another religious group. Since the end of socialism, various missionaries have been active in the country.

usually called gypsies in other Balkan countries), and, of course, mixed ethnicities made up of any combination of these.

Official statistics on ethnic origin and language were available in the censuses of 1989 (*Vjetari Statistikor* 1991) and 2011 (INSTAT 2012), but not in the census of 2001. There are some official figures, but, given the vast migration abroad which heavily affected South Albania's demographics, these are more nominal rather than actual, as in many cases members of the households who were not present were declared. A common saying regarding the population was that "Gjirokastër city has thirty thousand residents 'half in—half out,'" meaning that half of these 30,000 are migrants, living abroad ("out"). Nonetheless, many newcomers to the city from surrounding villages and other poorer cities have, to some extent, replaced the pre-1990 population who migrated abroad. A personal estimation is that the city contained more than 40,000 actual residents at any given moment during the 2000s and 2010s (see Appendix 2).

In the presocialist past, people from all around the Balkans traveled there, as Gjirokastër Pazari was famous. During the socialist period, Yugoslavian, Soviet, and Chinese experts spent time in the city providing assistance on industrialization projects. In addition, following the end of the Greek Civil War (1946–49), partisans from the neighboring country fled to the city to avoid the anticommunist pogrom launched by the Greek authorities.

Today, there are Greek and foreign diplomats working for the Greek consulate, offices run by the Organization for Security and Co-operation in Europe (OSCE) or the United Nations Development Programme (UNDP) and so on, military personnel from Greece (from a Greek army hospital that operates within Gjirokastër's barracks as part of Greece's international aid program), tourists who come to see the urban architecture and the castle (a UNESCO monument), US Peace Corp volunteers, Christian and Islamic missionaries and teachers for the Greek Orthodox Christian Orthodox school or the madrasa, and even anthropologists and archaeologists.

Most of the area's Albanian majority identify as Muslim (both mainstream Sunni but also Bektashi Islam), whereas the Greek minority is exclusively Christian Orthodox. There are also some Albanian members of the Christian Orthodox Church. Today, they all belong to the Autocephalous Albanian Orthodox Church (which is headed by a Greek archbishop).

Notes

1 The notion of transition implies a state of exception, so rights and freedoms may be suspended, and austerity must be accepted, labor needs to be devalued, etc., supposedly for the sake of proper transition; in reality, this transitional state of exception became a permanent condition.

2 Any anthropologist who has research experience both in a postsocialist country and in the capitalist European periphery could not possibly fail to notice the resemblance between the structural adjustments that were implemented in postsocialist countries in the 1990s and those employed in the periphery of Western Europe after 2010—and indeed their similarity with, for example, the African case (Ferguson 2006). Nonetheless, there are differences: the governance of extreme neoliberalism in most of Eastern Europe was established during a rather optimistic and systemically transitional period when the people had just overthrown repressive regimes via popular revolts and were demanding a new system of government. On the contrary, since 2010 the rapid expansion of this form of governance toward other European countries is a much more enforced process.

3 This had to do with the Albanian socialist regime's suspicion of outsiders, which made it almost impossible for foreign anthropologists to conduct research in the country. While various anthropologists of socialism highlight the suspicion they faced from socialist regimes, Albania was unique. Acknowledging first of all that such suspicion for Western anthropologists was understandable, given the cold war, the Albanian authorities went the extra mile, refusing visas for long visits, while the few foreign researchers/journalists who were allowed to visit were closely controlled during the time they spent in the country. So, for example, despite the difficulties, Caroline Humphrey managed to get a visa to conduct her ethnography in the Soviet Union. However, Ruth Mandel, in personal communication with the author, told me how she was forced to abandon her planned research in Albania, as it was impossible for her to go. Nevertheless, as a member of a Greek Hoxhist group explained to me, membership of a foreign Hoxhist organization (or Maoist until the mid 1970s) could help in getting access into Albania.

4 For an in-depth explanation of this, see Chapters 4 and 5.

5 The Albanian language has a major division between South Albanian (Tosk) and North Albanian (Gheg). This division refers also to issues of sociocultural organization. For studies prior to WWII, see Margaret Hasluck (1932, 1933a, 1993b, 1938, 1939, 1946a, 1946b, 1948, 1949, 1950, 1954) and the work of her husband, the historian and archaeologist of the Ottoman Empire, F.W. Hasluck (1929 [2007]); see also Edith Durham's works (1904, 1905, 1920a, 1920b, 1923a, 1923b, 1923c, 1923d, 1923e, 1923f, 1923g, 1924, 1935, 1941, 2001). Archaeologists such as Hammond (1967) should also be mentioned. In German, see also the work of the Hungarian scholar of Albanian cultural life and language, Franz Nopcsa (1925), who assembled a large photographic collection available today in the Hungarian National History Museum.

6 British ships hit sea mines in Albanian waters in 1946. This incident led to a bitter dispute between the Albanian and UK governments. The communist Albanian state of 1946 claimed that the mines did not belong to Albania, but to the previous Italian/Albanian fascist regime. Britain refused to accept this. This issue must be seen as part of the cold war hostility between West and East. Britain did not support Albanian claims during the Peace Conference of WWII, and Albania was supported only by the USSR and Yugoslavia. The British Empire was aligned with the Greek monarchist government, which claimed that Albania should not be included among the winners of the war, but among the defeated, because it was part of Italy, and thus that Albania should lose its southern territories which would be awarded to Greece. This event provides one of the best preludes to the stories which will follow in this book.

7 John Campbell, in fact, was working with Sarakatsanoi semi-nomads in Epirus, just a few kilometers from the Albanian border.

8 Despite the lack of research by foreign anthropologists, there was (and still is) an Institute of Folk Culture [Instituti i kulturës popullore] in the Tirana Academy of Sciences. This was formally founded in 1979 out of the merging of the Folk Institute [Instituti popullore] and the Ethnological Department of the Academy. This epistemologically corresponds to the Volkskunde trend which focuses on the recording and classification of material culture, as well as recording "national Albanian traditions and customs." There were two major political aims of the institute (together with the Institutes of Monuments and Archaeology, and their journals *Monument* and *Illyria*): first, to establish a theory facilitating the cultural homogenization of the heterogeneous groups within the Albanian nation-state; and, second, to establish a theory supporting the long historical continuity of the "Albanian nation" within the related nation-state territories, via archaeological discoveries and their association with contemporary cultural elements in Albania (Vickers 1999, 1). In fact, the similarities between the Albanian and Greek Folklore Institutes, as the latter were presented by Herzfeld (1987), are striking regarding their political roles, and these have a significant social impact because the majority of the people in the two countries are convinced of their direct and clear-cut biological links with the ancient civilizations which lived in the territories of their nation-states in the ancient period. The Albanian Institute organized some expeditions and ethnographic field studies from a folklore perspective to the Albanian countryside, yet its Marxist orientation regularly added sociological and economic information to its publications. Today, these older volumes occasionally offer some valuable information on rural Albania (e.g. Gjergji et al. 1985). Since 1962, there have been seventeen published issues of the journal *Etnologjia Shqiptare* ["Albanian ethnology"], and the journal *Kultura popullore* ["Folk culture"] has been published since 1980. Both publications were disrupted after 1992, but *Kultura popullore* began to be published more regularly after 2002, as the academy was reorganized. Today, the ethnologists of the institute research themes such as customary

property conceptions (e.g. Bardhosi 2004), rural life in Albania (e.g. Muka 2003), and religion (e.g. Tirta 2006).

There are certainly a number of nonanthropological research studies, such as those in the historical or political science literature that are of value: e.g. Miranda Vickers and James Pettifer's books (1997, 2006) or Karl Kaser et al. (2002). Besides these, there are some Albanian scholars who study Albanian migration from different perspectives: e.g. Kosta Barjaba (2004a, 2004b); Hermine De Soto et al. (2002, 2005). There are also works by geographers such as Sjöberg (1990, 1991a, 1991b), and Hall (1994; 1999).

9 Each of these dwellings was a multi-floor, stone building which usually housed an extended kinship group, normally consisting of a conjugal couple, their male children with their own families, and the parents of the man from the original conjugal couple—this family structure remained the most common until WWII, after which the socialist modernization policies promoted the core family. In the 1940s, these large houses were confiscated; simultaneously, via its modernization policies, the socialist regime promoted the modern nuclear family, which led to a loosening of this aforesaid common structure.

10 Vylajet was an Ottoman administrative–geographical division.

11 Today, Ioannina/Yiannena is located in northwestern Greece.

12 It is important to mention that, in 1994, the head of the IMF considered Albania a perfect example of a proper economic transition to capitalism (IMF 1994).

3

The state(s) of the road

Now let us consider dominated (and dominant) space, which is to say a space transformed—and mediated—by technology, by practice. In the modern world, instances of such spaces are legion and immediately intelligible as such: one only has to think of a slab of concrete or a motorway. (Lefebvre 1991 [1974], 164)

The socialist utopia of the 19th century, like the democratic utopia of the ancient agora, was literally buried under the vast scaffolding of urban construction, obscuring the fundamental anthropological side of revolution, of proletarianization: the migratory phenomenon. (Virilio 2006 [1977], 32)

In 1921, US Brigadier General George Scriven wrote an article on the Albanian highways in the *Geographical Review*: "Of the minor events of the war whose effects have proved constructive rather than destructive ... [one] is the opening up of certain difficult and little known regions. ... [The roads in Albania] pass through scenes of rare beauty and attraction, among an interesting people, and by places which, though vividly historic and filled with an Old World charm, have been lost for centuries among their unapproaching hills" (Scriven 1921, 198). Writing in a similar vein ten years later, another American traveler in Albania remarked that "[at] least the war creates roads" (Chater 1931). According to the Albanian-American scholar Stavro Skendi et al. (1957), in 1912 and 1913, when the former Ottoman Empire lost most of its Balkan provinces and the Albanian nation-state was established, the new country inherited almost 160 kilometers of road network suitable for horse and vehicular traffic. The same author claims that the history of the more modern automobile roads began with WWI and the introduction of military automobiles. At that time, the Austro-Hungarian army occupied more than 70 percent of today's Albania. The Austro-Hungarian military administration carried out extensive construction and improvements of the existing roads so that, by the end of the war, more than 650 kilometers of road suitable for automobiles and 130 kilometers appropriate for lighter travel had been constructed. Prior to their evacuation, however, Austro-Hungarian military personnel carried out a broad road-destruction project. The Italian and French armies, which had occupied the southwest and southeast of Albania respectively, also constructed a number of roads—including highways able to carry heavy vehicles—such as the Durres–Tirana road and the road between Vlora and the Albanian border through Tepelena (Scriven 1921; Skendi et al. 1957).

The subsequent regime of the post-WWI state was not particularly effective in carrying out road construction. Internal instability, power struggles, foreign occupation, and local rebellion contributed to the inability of the temporary Albanian governments of the time to conduct public works effectively (see Puto and Pollo 1981, 171–216). Despite the construction of roads and the introduction of motorcars during the war, according to Skendi (1957) the best way to travel within most of Albania in 1920 (with some exceptions) was on foot or by horse and mule. According to some authors (Zickel and Inwaskiw 1994, 106 cited in O'Donnell 1999, 151), during that period in Albania:

> The trip from Tirana to Vlorë [Vlona] for example, involved a sea journey; and although Shkodër's tradesmen exported skins by boat to Italy, their compatriots from Gjirokastër had to cross the Straits of Otranto to buy them from the Italians ... There were also no roads across the Greek or Yugoslav border capable of handling commercial traffic.

In 1921, an older Ottoman law was revived requiring every adult Albanian man under the age of 58 to work, unpaid, on road construction for ten days per year or make a payment toward road maintenance (Skendi et al. 1957; also mentioned by Chater 1931). As a result, by 1925 some roads, including a few highways, had already been rehabilitated. Yet, according to the accounts of contemporary foreign travelers, the attempt to introduce unpaid compulsory labor was met with serious opposition, with some North Albanian highlanders, for instance, refusing to work outside what they considered their own territories (Swire 1937).

According to the traveler of the period Joseph Swire (1937), the vehicular roads across Albania were in a poor condition, and people who used more traditional means of transport continued to travel upon the older paths and routes, which did not appear on various road maps. It became a widespread practice for the new state apparatus to create new road maps ignoring previous routes. Nonetheless, in his *National Geographic* article on Albania (February 1931), Melville Chater dedicated the entire introduction to his surprise at the length of the roads he saw in Albania during his short visit. The Albanian diplomat who met him displayed a state-issued map depicting 1,000 kilometers of road, advising him to go by car and not by horse as he had planned. His travel experiences contradicted his poor expectations. His impressions were illustrated in the first photograph of his article, which pictured a car next to a group of donkey riders on the macadamed road near Vlora. In the caption, the stunned American states: "Due to the War ... Albania passed from horses to horse-power within one decade."

The regime of the Albanian dictator Ahmet Zog developed close ties with the Italian fascist regime prior to WWII. Mussolini's regime and its close links with the Italian car industry and building contractors played an instrumental role in the development of modern highways as we know them today. The regime not only built roads within Italy but also in the short-lived Italian colonies. Thus, between 1925 and 1939, the fascist Italian regime and Nazi Germany loaned 50 million gold francs for Albanian economic development (Fischer 1984, 91–2; Sjöberg 1991a, 23). The Association for the Economic Development of Albania administered most of this amount. Thanks to this fund, Albania had 2,224 kilometers of roads capable of accommodating motorized transport by 1937. There were also several kilometers of bridges and more than 600 kilometers of road under construction (Skendi et al. 1957, 239–42).

WWII and the resistance

In April 1939, two years after building thousands of kilometers of road for the sake of the country's economic development, the Italian army invaded Albania. Thanks to the roads, it took them just a few days to seize power. Count Ciano, the fascist minister of foreign affairs, and, at that time, the second most powerful man in Rome after the Duce, was explicit on the political value of Albania's infrastructure:

> It will be necessary quickly to carry out a program of public works. Only this way will we definitely link the people to us and destroy the authority of their chiefs, showing that only we are capable of doing what they have not been able or did not want to do. (Ciano 1953, cited in Fischer 1999, 65)

The fascist authorities also saw roads as being conducive to the economic exploitation of the country, as could be seen, for example, in the reports of Zenone Benini, Ciano's undersecretary for Albanian affairs. Benini wrote about the opportunities for financial gain and the need for infrastructure just a few months after the occupation (Fischer 1999). At the same time, the Italian fascists and their Albanian collaborators had promoted the foundation of the Albanian Road Agency

(Azienda Strada Albania), an Italian firm which immediately started to construct thousands of kilometers of roads (Fischer 1999, 66).

Just a month after the Italian occupation, on May 25, 1939, the Albanian fascist newspaper *Fashizmi* (later renamed *Tomori*) announced that 1,500 kilometers of road would be constructed within Albania by the end of 1941 (Fischer 1999, 67–8), for which 150 million Italian lire would be provided from Rome. In the summer of 1939, 17,000 Albanians and 500 Italian supervisors started to build or rehabilitate roads. According to the British Foreign Office, at the start of 1940 more than 30,000 people were working on road network construction projects. Mussolini ordered specific attention to be paid to the roads leading to the Greek border (Fischer 1999, 67–8). At that time, according to Gjirokastër oral history, the road, which connected the town with the Greek frontier, was repaired and surfaced. This ran almost parallel to, or intersected with, the current Kakavijë–Gjirokastër highway. A little before the invasion of Greece, the Italian state published the twenty-fifth volume of the tourist *Guide of Italy*, titled *Albania* (Consociazione Turistica Italiana, 1940).[1] According to the colored maps and the detailed description of the suggested tourist routes, Albania had a well-developed road system that was superior to those present in some regions of the country today; there was at least one road crossing the Greek border (between Permet and Konitsa), for example, which does not—officially—exist today.

These Italian-built roads facilitated a great part of the 140,000-man Italian invasion of Greece in October 1940. Following the invasion, road-building projects were seriously disrupted and large parts of roads were destroyed during the ensuing battles. In December 1940, Gjirokastër province came under the control of the Greek army following a counter-offensive, but this was not to last, as the arrival of the Wehrmacht in April 1941 to assist Mussolini in the Balkans meant that the Axis forces were able to annex Yugoslavia, Albania, and Greece in the space of a few weeks. The Italian road projects continued during the occupation. In 1943, the German diplomat Erich von Luckwald included a map in his book on Albania, which showed an extensive and surfaced road system. There are some doubts, however, as to its accuracy given the propaganda role of maps and the topographical mistakes it contained. Similar questions can be asked about the aforesaid 1940 tourist guide to Albania. A team of Albano-American experts led by Skendi seemed to agree (in the mid 1950s) that the zenith of Albanian road construction was in 1942 (Skendi et al. 1957, 243). However, this study was inspired by the anticommunism of the cold war, and it seems to run counter to local oral history. By late 1940, air and artillery strikes by forces seeking

Argirocastro - Municipio.

2 Postcard from the 1930s showing the municipality of Gjirokastër, then occupied by the Italian forces. The Italians came by sea to the west coast and proceeded to occupy the country via the roads they had built over the previous decade as part of the fascist regime's international development policy.

to bring the region under control, as well as effective and systematic sabotage by partisans, had caused serious damage to the infrastructure system. Much of the large-scale Italian construction project was left in a very poor condition. According to local oral history, by the time the Albanian communists came to power in November 1944, the transportation infrastructure had been almost entirely eliminated, including the road between Gjirokastër and Greece, which had suffered air bombardment and battles along its entire length.

The roads of state socialism
At the end of WWII, the Albanian Communist Party (ACP), which had organized most of the antifascist resistance, seized power after a brief civil war. By the summer of 1945, several major highways and bridges had already been reconstructed. The party authorities prioritized the country's modernization and urbanization; road and house construction became their primary focus. In the one-year state economic plan of 1948, more than 83 million Albanian lek were released for roads. In the following two-year economic plan (1949–50), even larger amounts were earmarked for the construction of highways. From 1951 (when the first Five-Year Economic Plan was introduced) to 1990 (when the last Five-

Year Plan was completed), "transport and communications" accounted for the highest levels of investment, after industry and agriculture.

This emphasis on infrastructural development resulted in a significant increase in the length of asphalt-surfaced highways in Albania, from 181 kilometers in 1950 to 2,850 kilometers in 1990. According to Albanian publications from the 1970s and 1980s, the total (surfaced and unsurfaced) automobile roads length was increased three times in comparison to the pre-war period (e.g. Anonymous 1984, 165; Marmullaku 1975, 101). Most of the roads in the country, however, were never surfaced with asphalt or any other hard material. The total length of metaled roads in 1950 was 2,919 kilometers, a figure which had increased to 4,600 kilometers by 1990. Such roads were made using crushed stone covered with gravel or sand (Skendi et al. 1957; *Vjetari Statistikor* 1991, 250–1, 269). Ironically, this combination of fragmented, unfastened materials was to become the perfect metaphor for the fragmented modernization project of the Albanian socialist regime.

Immobilities

This fragmented modernization, as far as roads were concerned, became even more evident through the contradiction in the relationship between road-building and people. Ordinary Albanians were forced to construct and surface roads despite having little or no access to them. Mobility via these roads, for the vast majority, was remarkably limited. Roads were economically and symbolically oriented rather than pragmatic or utilitarian. People recall walking to their workplaces even in the relatively privileged Gjirokastër, while the inhabitants of the less affluent surrounding villages were often forced to walk, sometimes for as much as three or four hours, in order to reach the capital of their prefecture.

Although the distances within the city were relatively short, as Gjirokastër is merely a town by international standards, this reflected a more general lack of spatial mobility. Private cars, for instance, were not allowed in socialist Albania until permission was finally granted on March 19, 1991 (*Fletorija Zyrtare* 1991, 122–4). In 1969, the entire country (with a population of more than two million people and 4,000 kilometers of highways), had no more than 2,700 passenger vehicles, plus 7,700 heavy vehicles (trucks and buses) (Marmullaku 1975, 101; *New Encyclopaedia Britannica* 1974, 191; *Vjetari Statistikor* 1991). Most of my interlocutors recalled that they traveled very little, if at all, by passenger car during the socialist period; if one considers the number of state officials and party nomenclature who had control over these few thousand passenger vehicles, one can probably grasp their scarcity for the rest of society.

Another dimension of spatial immobility was that passports were not available. In order to travel abroad, Albanians had to obtain a special one-page permission document—a temporary passport that was remarkably difficult to obtain. Potential escapees automatically condemned the families they left behind to a bad *"biografia,"* the regime's blacklist, leading, if nothing else, to serious difficulty in gaining access to tertiary education. This meant access only to bad jobs together with disdain and suspicion. In a *National Geographic* article, Mehmet Biber, one of the few journalists to obtain a visa to enter Albania in the early 1980s, described how

> No international highway crosses Albania, no railway crosses its frontier and no foreign airplane is allowed to fly across its airspace, the few commercial flights have to come from seaward and daylight hours only. (Biber 1980, 532)

During the socialist period, Albanian border guards had shoot-to-kill orders for those attempting to escape. This order led to some horrific incidents when it came into force, including the execution of people whose yards were divided by the obscured Albanian–Greek border. In later years, even internal migration became impossible as specific permission was required to leave one settlement for another.

Building the highways "voluntarily"

Despite the relatively large budget for transport infrastructure, and despite the practical limitations of road usage for most Albanians, these same people were both physically and ideologically forced to work on road-building without payment. The officially approved history of Albania, when it refers to the first postwar years, states:

> In the great burst of rebuilding, the reclaiming of the marsh, the cutting of irrigation-canals and the construction of roads to link the distant regions with the rest of the country were all set in motion on local and national scale. Voluntary, unpaid work was to play an important role, which was to be one of the most characteristic features of the reconstruction effort in the country. (Puto and Pollo 1981, 249)

This statement implies several things: unpaid road-building, economic modernization, postwar socialist reconstruction, ideals of a collective labor force, and, additionally, the integration of rural areas to the core of the nation-state. Regarding the last of these, the construction of a common material network would link the remote mountainous communities with the state authorities based in the cities, founding both a modern nation and a modern state. Such a link had not been achieved since 1913, when Albania was officially founded, as the vast majority of people in rural areas had remained distanced from urban ways of living and the events taking place in the cities.

It would be a mistake to consider Albanian socialism as one unique homogeneous historical period. The ethnographic evidence suggests that voluntary road construction made sense in the first years of liberation and socialism but not later. As an old partisan from Gjirokastër explained, "everyone [he looked around him and began to speak in a low voice], even some *Balistas* [members of Ballli Komptar: 'National Front,' the fascist armed collaborators] wanted to rebuild the ruined country." Moreover, theoretically, the roads had a role to play in the economy, and thus in the 1940s the idea was that the collective socialist economy needed the participation of every individual, and the government's economic plans called for their direct involvement. These ideological principles were condensed into a report by the editorial offices of the 1946 Constitution of the People's Republic of Albania: "People are not solidly supporting the democracy unless they grasp the economic problem in their own hands"—literally. This strategy was introduced during the socialist period with law no. 747/1949, which came into force on December 30, 1949, and dictated that it was compulsory for adult men, up to the age of 55, to work "voluntarily" during some of their holidays for road maintenance and construction (*Gazeta Zyrtare* 1949, 3–4). Such laws remained in force until the end of socialism. For example, in the late socialist period, the "Road Code of the People's Socialist Republic of Albania" of 1984 (*Gazeta Zyrtare* 1984, 85–115) was introduced. The law contained articles outlining the responsibility of rural people for the administration and maintenance of the roads within their villages. In addition to the volunteering, during the 1980s the regime also extended the policy of paid road maintenance, and several university students worked during their summer holidays on these paid road works. Nevertheless, volunteers undertook the majority of road works in Albania, even during the 1980s.

The practice of unpaid work for postwar reconstruction was a common phenomenon in many countries, especially those with socialist legacies. For instance, in other Southern European countries, where local communities used to offer voluntary labor for infrastructure before the war, this practice continued for decades after 1945 (e.g. see Roseman 1996 on roads in Spanish Galicia). Accordingly, forced voluntary labor for road-building was a characteristic of the prewar Albanian regimes. Nonetheless, socialist Albania is distinct from these. The most important distinction was in the gradual transformation of voluntary road-building into a standard measure for social oppression, similar to those employed by several colonial authorities against local populations, as was the case in Madagascar, for example (Thomas 2003, 378–9), or even Azande (Evans-Pritchard 1960, 311).

The ideological apparatus of road-building

These regulations resulted in a high proportion of the Albanian population working on road construction for free, and in the regime enforcing certain principles on almost everyone. First were the convicts who did systematic labor on roads and other public works; taking into account the number of political prisoners, road construction in their case facilitated the embedding of state-socialist principles. In addition to prisoners, the various youth unions, women's unions, unions of various nonmanual labor employees, local Democratic Fronts, cooperatives, and other groups (all under the party's control) organized expeditions of "voluntary" labor on public works, including roads. Students in secondary and higher education also "volunteered" for some road construction, usually having to spend some of their summer holidays working on roads and other public works (Anonymous 1984; Skendi et al. 1957, 246, 247).

As a Yugoslav–Albanian sociologist and Belgrade state official (Marmullaku 1975, 101–2) put it in the mid 1970s, "In Albania every citizen must spend one month taking part in work drives; even diplomats roll up their sleeves and give a hand in the work brigades when they are home on leave." In a later text, party intellectuals describe how "in Albania … you are liable to come across workers of the administration, people of intellectual pursuit who are working directly in production shoulder to shoulder with the workers and the peasants" (Anonymous 1984, 216). Even high-ranking cadres were supposed to participate in manual labor. Most importantly, however, both the aforesaid statements imply the ideological power of an apparatus that involved almost everyone. The collective building of roads may be considered as ideologically imposing as the universal and mandatory school education and military training programs of the regime. In addition to the very practical aspects of these activities (e.g. a literate and militarily ready population and free labor), the regime made vast political gains by imposing their principles both socially and physically on practically all citizens.

These three institutions—education, army, and road-building—were not only promoted by the regime but were combined very explicitly. As the propaganda texts explained, "In addition to classroom lessons and physical and military training, direct participation in production work is an essential component in our school curriculum too" (Anonymous 1984, 216). Generally, the militarization of society took place through pan-Albanian military training (which applied to both men and women from school age onwards). In addition to these drills, a two-year period of military service was compulsory for every man, and this service also involved strategic road construction; hence a slogan often heard in socialist Albania, "Let us found a socialist state with a pickaxe in one hand and a gun in the other" (Puto and Pollo 1981, 267) (this was also written on the façade of Gjirokastër University). A friend of mine once described his period of army service in the 1970s in the following way: "What guns? We were digging roads and holes in the mountain [bunkers], rather than learning army things."

It is estimated that more than 2,000 bunkers still exist on the plateau of Gjirokastër along the Kakavijë–Gjirokastër highway, erected to defend against a possible Greek invasion. A member of the Greek minority from Dervitsani village (just beside the cross-border highway) related how "the bunkers in our village have a window on the south side for Greece and another on the west side, for the highway." The strategic plans of the Albanian state indicate their belief that the enemy would invade Gjirokastër via the highway. A permission policy was strictly applied along the border zone, which began just a few kilometers south of the city. As such, Gjirokastrits, though unable to make practical use of the road for everyday life (due to the difficulty in obtaining the relevant permission), repaired and constructed this material ancestor of the Kakavijë–Gjirokastër highway. In fact, even with permission it was impossible to reach Kakavijë via the road as for most of the socialist period the last few kilometers were unsurfaced and had artificial hindrances in order to prevent the Greek army from using it in case of an invasion. It was a perfect example of a road leading to nowhere. Despite this, the rhetoric of fear regarding what the semi-cross-border road may bring from Greece was developed in official discourse and spread within the local communities, aided, of course, by the bunkers.

Building socialism as a road
This emphasis on roads stemmed from people's lack of mobility and these same people's systematic and intensive provision of labor for roads.

3 An image used in the 1970s in party publications regarding the economic development of the regime: trucks driving up and down a hillside road.

Thus, besides their economic purpose, why were these roads built? The first answer is relatively straightforward: if one paraphrases a statement by Katherine Verdery (1996, vii), who suggests that *socialism was the longest and most painful road from capitalism to capitalism*, then in the case of Albania this assertion was materialized literally through the labor of those who had to build many kilometers of road reflecting and symbolizing the achievements and ideology of Albanian socialism. This building of socialism in the form of roads requires further elaboration. Building socialism, as a road, first implied the building of modernization, second the building of a nation-state, and third the building of Albanian socialist subjects.

The order of modernization

One of the most significant principles integrated into road-building was modernization. The socialist Albanian official history states explicitly how "the ACP were hoping to make Albania, which until then had been the most backward country in Europe, a developed and modern state in the shortest possible period" (Puto and Pollo 1981, 251). These principles of modernization have to be considered along with the regime's urbanization projects.

Under socialism, the surfaced road had become a necessary element for the completion of the modernization process and, by extension, of socialism per se. People in Albania never fail to mention the roads as one of the successes of the socialist period. In a private conversation about the regime's record of modernization, Dino, a former low-ranking official in the Party of Labor, argued:

> Enver and the party made this place a country, before they had nothing here, you are young, but if you had been here you would have seen that Albania before the war was nothing because of Zog and the foreign interventions! Without state, without order, with poverty, without doctors—if you were sick you were dead! Finished! Illiteracy, so as to exploit the people easier, without big buildings, without electricity, without water,

4 Image from the party's periodical press of the 1970s showing women being trained in the use of rifles. During the socialist period, numerous gender equality measures were implemented, including universal military training.

without roads, without army, without police, without anything! N-o-t-
h-i-n-g! Everyone with a pickaxe, and very few clever ones with wealth,
and those that had, had it since the Turks. That was Albania. Eh, Hoxha
made some mistakes, but he took care of the country ... the party was in
order, today this, tomorrow that, slowly, slowly.

This statement alludes to a contradiction regarding roads, modernization, and a strong state order. Even those who did not support the
old regime admit, today, that socialism had "order" and infrastructure.
Ismail, who originates from a family that suffered under the political
clearance of the regime's enemies during Hoxha's era, explained:

Now we have capitalism and that evil over our heads has gone, now we
eat, we drink, we screw, we talk; everything is free; but I want to tell you,
Hoxha had many evils, but he made things. Hoxha made roads, hospitals,
schools, and above everything: quietness, no trouble, no theft, not like
now, now things do not always function properly, Hoxha had order. Eh,
we will be in order now as well.

Although the emphasis on order has its origin partly in linguistics, as the
most common Albanian term for "all right" and "OK" is literally translated as "in order" (*në rregull*), in the case of Albania, the enforcement of
state order via road construction is a statement with further significance.

This order, via roads, was accompanied by the building of a modern
state that was to have control over its spatial domain. A permanent
problem for the Ottoman and the previous Albanian authorities had
been the mountainous terrain of the country. That is to say, the authorities often had to deal with semi-isolated populations which refused to
exchange their older system for the new one. This disobedience was
regularly articulated as a refusal to build the roads for free, and, as
Joseph Swire (1937) explains, many local chiefs among the Catholic
clans of the North refused to allow participation in these projects.
The two prewar female ethnologists of North Albania (Durham
1928; Hasluck 1954) and other contemporary travelers (Swire 1937)
clearly depict the existence of an extensive, unwritten tribal law. This,
combined with a culture that associated masculinity with weapon use,
made any potential state intervention risky. Thus, prior to socialism,
the state was unable to control the rural territories completely. The
arrival of roads and the enforced building of the socialist state apparently fulfilled the objective of Zog's dictatorship and the Italian fascists:
to impose a state system on remote Albanian villagers that dissolved
their old sociopolitical system. This was translated in the first instance
as the universal spatial "penetration" of the nation-state mechanism
even to the most remote villages. State intellectuals expressed their
satisfaction: "Motor transport now penetrates deep into the mountain

regions of the interior which were inaccessible before" (Anonymous 1978). In contrast to previous regimes, which were unable to dissolve the existing local orders, the socialist state had very effective apparatuses for possible disobedience, as a man who is currently a migrant in Greece explained:

> We come from Shkodër [North]. When they brought the road to our village my grandfather, with some others, said that they would not build the road to its entire length, just the section around our plateau. For this, they and their entire families were exiled to the mountains down [South].

Thus the arrival of the road network spatially linked the various parts of Albania, networking the state. From a state, Albania became a nation. This process imposed a national identity upon people who had for decades neglected the concept of a nation-state. Local community structures further enforced this nation-statehood. The coming of the road brought with it land collectivization, party control, civil servants, police, mandatory military service, schools, and all the other elements which helped to cement this nation-state.

Ideology and socialist subjects on the road

Each aforesaid statement implies a relationship between individuals and the construction of surfaced roads. Each individual socialist subject shaped the roads of the socialist regime with his/her body and, conversely, the building of the road shaped the body, and hypothetically the psyche, of the same individual into a socialist one.

> That was the socialism of Hoxha, Enverism, all together working one next to the other, with our own hands, with our own sweat, to build Albania and to progress. We understood what it meant, how it is was created, not like now when you wake up in the morning and see a road ready, a square ready, a high block of flats ready, we knew well how things were made, how difficult it was and its importance.

Alqi, from Gjirokastër, complained in an interview that, in the 1980s, the state articulated the road construction as oppression, but he also added the actual illogical character of the building:

> That was Hoxha: "shut up and work." Sit here, break stone, build the road, build the wall and do not speak! They were above your head; they were guarding your mouth … if you would dare, speak! Say something! Complain about working! And see what would happen to you … what did they want the roads, without cars? Why did they have the roads? I will tell you; in order to see who was complaining, they were clever … to see who had people abroad, who watched television from Greece, and who knew that out there everybody had cars! Not like us, we made the roads without cars.

Arguably, even if private cars *had* been allowed and available in socialist Albania, very few people would have been able to buy them. Likewise, the picture Alqi had of Greece was one of Greece in the late 1980s, one he had seen, illegally, on his television. Private cars came into widespread use in Greece in the late 1970s and early 1980s, yet before this period most people could not afford them there either. In Greece, however, the lack of cars before the mid 1970s was a practical problem resulting from economic inequalities, as people could not afford to buy a car even though cars were officially available. The problem in Albania was not so much practical but theoretical, as the fact that private vehicles were forbidden was a very pragmatic limitation that visually highlighted the power of the state over individuals.

In the first instance, this process of building highways without permission to use them seemed illogical, but it had a very effective ideological effect. This was the new socialist logic of collective building and state-controlled collectivism via the instructed *communitas* of collaboration in manual labor. This process turned a completely anticapitalist principle on its head: according to the government, this unpaid labor was considered to be a pure anticapitalist action, as people did not turn their labor, and thus themselves, into a commodity (Anonymous 1984, 197).

In fact, as is clear from the aforesaid quotes, an important aspect of the collective road-building was its employment of both ideological and repressive state apparatuses (Althusser 1989, 170–86). There was a physical dimension, namely the individual's physical disposition to work on the road while being policed. Meanwhile, the ideological enforcement was implied in the implementation of a number of prescribed ideological principles through that process, such as, for example, the superiority of manual or so-called productive labor versus nonmanual labor or the hypothetical anticapitalism of unpaid labor. As a former party official explained to me, people were not transforming their labor into a commodity, and thus the volunteering for infrastructure construction was not alienating labor. Nevertheless, fear was ever-present as people ran the risk of being classified as anticommunist, and receiving a bad "*biografia,*" if they were not perceived to be participating willingly in the road works. The irrationality of building roads without being able to use them merely added more power to the process. This process echoed, in some ways, the convicts who broke rocks for the macadamed roads in the USA in the nineteenth century.

Some local members of the Albanian Party of Labor and a large number of socialist ideologists considered these kinds of practices to be at the core of a socialist lifestyle. In the summer of 2006, for instance, an old partisan named Flamur—who receives practically no pension today and has to work in his late seventies—mentioned in a coffeehouse in Gjirokastër:

> How nice it was when we were gathering the entire town and were going by the motor trucks to the villages to build the roads ... In the night we were staying under the trees or in tents and the truck was bringing food for everyone. Back in that time we were all together, we did not have "this is mine—this is yours," people were nice, now it is the money that makes order for everything. At that time we were all together, now ... [he moved his hand and head with disapproval].

The collective participation in the building and the consequent *communitas* was probably the most powerful ideological element in the process. Bearing in mind the example of four different Albanians, who, in four separate instances, told me (about the same road section in Gjirokastër)—"I built this road"—the direct identification of the self, the sense of belonging, the link between the people and infrastructure through the production of the road is clear. Today, the road section they referred to—and that all of them claim to have built—has been largely reconstructed and repaired since 1990, yet the strength of this identification was such that they continue to state it was they who built it. All Albanian men and women were, for a while, collectively transformed into wage-less road builders. This innovative experience was embodied through physical labor, which reproduced new collective identifications between the participants. One can draw similarities with "rites of passage" and *communitas* theory, particularly in the cases of the Party of Labor "*pionieri*" (analogous to the Soviet Komsomol), students and young soldiers who had to participate in this spatial road production at a particular point in their lives. This was a type of accreditation of the individual socialist and proletarian self. It was the passage from childhood to the real socialist adult, who got his hands dirty in a manual, productive, job. On the road, the creation of a new, complete socialist subject, both body and psyche, was achieved. If we consider that Albania, according to its constitution, was a country of the "dictatorship of the proletariat" (article 2 of the December 1976 Constitution), after building a road for one month a young person could claim his or her participation as one of the powerful (and dictatorial) proletarians, as each of them had become a "*shok*" or "*shoqe*" (comrade [male and female]). Manual labor in socialist Albania had a specific importance for the state authorities: "work was duty and honor" (Anonymous 1984, 202).

5 Propaganda collage published in the party's periodical press in the 1970s. Industrial chimneys, refineries, farmers, and children in costumes playing portray the progress that socialism brought to the country. In the foreground, a little child smiles.

From infrastructure to antistructure

Although phrases like "I built this road" clearly highlight individual identifications with the creation of socialist infrastructure, they simultaneously express a fragmented identification. People's identification was limited to building and was not expanded by usage. At the same time, their participation in the creation of this project was obligatorily organized and instructed by the central state apparatuses. This integration of individuality via a centrally directed and fragmented identification would eventually play a major role in the collapse of the regime. Through the assumption of this forced socialization, within three decades, the regime would become more and more alienated from the society that had initially supported it during the war and during the postwar reconstruction era. The emphasis would no longer be on the qualitative modernization of daily life but exclusively on economic figures. In the 1970s (and especially after the adoption of the 1976 Constitution), the Albanian state turned into a completely isolationist regime; moreover, it enforced ultimate collectivization, even at the level of small domestic livestock holdings and house yards. Despite such extreme measures, without international economic support and without small-scale decentralized food production it could no longer maintain the availability or variety of basic goods. Tirana officials would count the kilometers of new or surfaced roads and the numbers of people mobilized for each road construction project. This project of state-directed collective identification via infrastructure-building was, however, fragmented and semi-completed, which reflected the properties of the entire modernization project. Thus, although the state could not provide the people with the various elements of a potentially "pleasant" identification, such as adequate food or petrol stores or free mobility, it nevertheless expected them to undertake the "unpleasant" aspects of this identification such as unpaid road-building. In this sense, "voluntary" road construction as a socialist practice became a form of oppression and served to further enforce the growing popular perception of a state against society.

In addition to the social and political disappointment, this condition was eventually reflected in the materiality of infrastructure, as the road-building and maintenance became of increasingly poorer quality. Often people did not put great effort into the road construction, and thus an increasing disparity emerged between the state authorities and a society trying to negotiate the harsh reality of everyday life. The decadence is illustrated in the story narrated by Kosta that began with the announcement that someone important from Tirana was to visit his remote village to review their livestock cooperative in the 1980s. The local party authorities mobilized almost everyone, "even the dead ones," to work on the rapid maintenance of the worn-out road that the official's convoy would use. The VIP visitor from Tirana used the road to arrive at the time announced, but a storm forced him to stay overnight. The locals did their best to satisfy their visitor, who of course enjoyed his stay. The next morning, however, the new road was no longer there; the rain had washed it away.

The superstructural problem of infrastructures

Under socialism, road construction in Albania became one of the main priorities precisely because roads were the material entities that would tangibly and explicitly link—within an already familiar sociological realm—the central state with the people. The creation of new roads was intended to make people perceive the state not just as a modernizing force that brought electric light or other new technologies but one that explicitly changed existing daily material culture. Moreover, given the restrictions on movement (Dalakoglou 2010a), roads had little value as infrastructures of human mobility, yet they had enormous value as a political technology and material entity that was surfacing the land with the new lineal aesthetics of the socialist state. A new type of subjectivity was formed by producing these roads, since no particular technical knowledge was necessary in order for someone to work as a manual laborer in their construction.

The socialist regime prioritized material infrastructures and their economy over social relationships and individual subjectivity. The last two would be determined in reference to the first, which were forming a priori a socialist mode of production and thus a socialist mode of behavior and consciousness. The physical involvement of the people in the building and usage of infrastructure was considered necessary for the desired social organization to be produced; a situation that can be seen in the case of the most social of infrastructures: housing (see Buchli 1999; Dalakoglou 2009a, 2009b, 2010). In reality, however, although the roads under the Albanian socialist regime were initially supposed to be produced based on labor relationships organized according to a delineating model, the end result has been that the experience of the roads for the socialist masses evolved into a profoundly alienating project, particularly in the final years of the regime. By late socialism, the combination of road production with the rest of the material circumstances manifested a practical failure in the application of the theoretical principles. According to the textbook a certain kind of relationship in the production of the material world would lead into a particular human consciousness. However, it stopped having this result already in the 1960s. The internal contradiction of road construction versus extremely limited road usage resulted in an infrastructure fetishism, where infrastructures were produced for their own sake and failed to generate (via the labor relationships involved in their production) the desired human subjectivities. This process reduced the value of new highways to the level of a political emblem, like a monument of what socialism intended, but failed, to be. In fact, the combination of the spatial policies of the socialist state paved the way, both literally and figuratively, for the postsocialist spatial practices of Albanian society. Most strikingly, today in Albania, ownership of a car—*makinë*—has become one of the most explicit criteria for social and class distinction between the rich, the less rich, and the poor.

Thus, although the promises of the postsocialist dream are encapsulated in the new spatial practices, these are not necessarily dealienating for the majority. As with the spatial practices of socialism, the road-related spatial practices continue to be alienating for the majority, only in different ways.

According to several anthropologists of postsocialism (e.g. Alexander et al. 2007; Buchli 1999; Humphrey 2003; Verdery 1996), infrastructures in (post)socialist societies must be approached from a Marxist materialist perspective, namely, both as physical–material–economic entities, and, in a more abstract sense, as something onto which the sociocultural superstructure is erected. It is not only anthropologists who think this; the majority of people who were socialized under socialist regimes perceive infrastructure as a foundational system of reference for the entire society (Humphrey 2003). The inevitable analogy between infrastructure's materiality and social order is what causes ontological uncertainty and moral panic in postsocialist contexts, when infrastructures regularly break down due to neoliberal public cuts and the consequent collapse of the state apparatus (see Humphrey 2003). For

6 A young boy smiles as his father fixes his Mercedes-Benz in an abandoned former industrial facility.

most people, this material decay represents a wider social decay that has an immediate impact on individual personhood and contributes greatly to the uncertainties of everyday life.

The case of roads in Albania, however, appears to be distinct from other kinds of material infrastructures. For example, in the case of postsocialist Albania, substantial parts of the roads have either decayed or are in the process of decaying. Despite the moral panic involved in the increase of automobility, the new postsocialist usage of roads and the explicit inequalities in the way roads are used and accessed, there are no feelings of uncertainty linked with the materiality of collapsing roads as one would perhaps expect from a society largely socialized to approach the world in materialist terms. On the contrary, while the materiality of roads is an important subject of discussion in Albania today, and although the material decay of the roads in late socialism represented and was catalytic for the moral panic of that period, Albanians in the postsocialist period do not appear to be frightened or put off by the diverse or simply poor quality of their country's roads.

Note

1 *Volumes on Libya* (1937) and a work titled *Africa Orientale Italiana* (1938) had previously been published. Incorporating newly acquired lands into the core of the nation-state was very characteristic of the expansionist ethos of Italian fascism.

4

The city and the road

Each period, each mode of production, each particular society has engendered (produced) its own centrality. (Lefebvre 1991 [1974], 332)

This place is finished, as it was. What matters from now on is not the fields, not the mountains, but the road. There'll be no village, as a place on its own. There'll just be a name you pass through, houses along the road. And that's where you'll be living, mind. On a roadside. (Williams 1960, 242)

Urban metamorphosis

Today, the main cross-border highway of the Albanian–Greek border is the so-called Kakavijë–Gjirokastër road, which is named after the Kakavijë border station and the city of Gjirokastër, located 29 kilometers north of the border. Gjirokastër was the hometown of the Albanian communist leader Enver Hoxha[1] and has been one of the largest and most important urban centers in the region since the eighteenth century. In socialist times, it became a canvas for urban developers from the entire Eastern bloc, as well as China.

More generally, besides the construction of modern infrastructure, the other key dimension of modernization in socialist Albania was urbanization, which the regime-friendly literature emphasized as proof of the progress socialism brings: "Before the war, over 85 per cent of the population was rural and lived in backward and unhygienic conditions, with a high illiteracy rate. Since the revolution this ratio has been completely altered" (Marmullaku 1975, 107). A woman originally from a village near Gjirokastër described the day she received permission to move from her village to the city "with nice roads with asphalt, tall buildings and office jobs." Other publications around this time were also dominated by the same motif.

By 1975 the urban population made up 34.4 per cent of the population of the country, in comparison to just 15.4 per cent in 1938. The number of towns now is nearly threefold that of 1945. The old towns are being reconstructed, too, with wide, asphalted streets, multistoried modern buildings, cultural and sports institutions, parks and gardens. (Anonymous 1978)

Gjirokastër—as a city but also more generally—is in many ways unique. Gjirokastrits and non-Gjirokastrits alike stress its difference from the rest of Albania. People often note the differences, describing in detail the unique urban architecture or the major, regional historical events that have taken place in the city. Similarly, Gjirokastër's favored status before and under socialist rule, its famous residents, its proximity to Greece, and the presence of a Greek minority are just some of the frequently noted particularities attributed to the city. Moreover, among its specific characteristics, according to most other Albanians, the people who originate from the town are considered obnoxious. Most of the so-called "pure" (*puro*) Gjirokastrits who can trace their descent from families that lived in the city for many generations do not seem to defend themselves against such statements. Many of them often stress the "glorious" aesthetic value of their city or focus on the important historical figures who were born in Gjirokastër. In fact, the old part of the town is a UNESCO World Heritage Site. Additionally, it is not only the hometown of many significant historical figures, such as the previously mentioned Enver Hoxha, but also the hometown of the most famous Albanian novelist: Ismail Kadare. In 1970, Kadare published the *Chronicle in the Stone*, a memoir based on his childhood in the city. On the final page of this book, the author describes his physical, bodily, experience of Gjirokastër:

> My feet timidly trod the spine of its stone-paved streets. They bore me up. You recognized me, you stones. Often striding along wide lighted boulevards in foreign cities, I somehow stumble in places where no one ever trips. Passers-by turn in surprise, but I always know it's you. You emerge from the asphalt all of a sudden and then sink back down straight away. (Kadare 2007, 301)

Ismail Kadare left the town—and later Albania—long before the post-socialist metamorphosis of the city, and thus in his 1970 book he refers to an older urban materiality, and a physical experience of it that has rapidly changed over the last number of decades.

Today, the city of Gjirokastër is divided into three main parts: the pre-WWII "old town"; the postwar, socialist period urban complex; and the postsocialist section of the city. The old town was developed on the hills around a medieval citadel, the socialist section around these foothills, and the postsocialist section on the plateau. For the most part, the different materialities of the three blend into one another, except in most of the so-called museum zone or first zone[2] that includes the

7 Man walking on a street in the Pazari.

majority of the prewar town center together with several buildings on its periphery. These were classified as national monument sites by the Albanian authorities in 1961 and as such were preserved during the socialist period. The socialist regime promoted and applied a radical modernization program to the country, and thus a sense of nostalgia for the vanishing past also emerged during this period. This was phrased as an effort to preserve the craft of the "ancestral bricklayers and stone

8 The plaque celebrating the inclusion of Gjirokastër old town in the
UNESCO World Heritage list. It is located precisely where the asphalt road
ends and the cobbled street starts.

carvers" and directed by scholars of the newly founded Tirana University (1957), the powerful Institute for the Protection of the Monuments
of Culture, and the Institute for Folk Studies of Tirana Academy. The
specific urban architecture discourse was focused on the old sections of
two cities—Gjirokastër and Berat—which were classified as museum

9 This shop under construction is an extension of a socialist period block of flats.

cities. In 2005, more or less the same urban area that had been listed as the museum zone of Gjirokastër was relisted as a UNESCO World Heritage Site.

Today, it is not permitted to add new buildings in this part of the city, only to repair the existing ones. There is a second conservation zone, which includes the entire prewar urban sector, where certain restrictions are (again, officially) applied. Nevertheless, during the socialist period an equally important transformation began with the expansion of the city into a new terrain, out of the prewar district. An industrial zone was added to the city, along with modern public facilities and modernist blocks of flats and other dwellings. These were predominantly made from two new materials: cement and brick. Today, in the postsocialist period, these buildings are constantly being altered and expanded. Furthermore, the third—postsocialist—expansion, over the margins of the socialist urban plan, is rapidly occurring.

Relocating centrality

What is also called "the historic center" or "old center" of Gjirokastër town is the district called the Pazari (market, bazaar). It is situated on the hills of the north side of the town's medieval citadel and consists, for the most part, of a radial system of five cobbled streets and blocks of stone buildings used for retail.

Due to the sloping terrain, these blocks are erected in horizontal rows. The Pazari was, and mainly still is, separated from the residential sections of the town; hence very few permanent dwellings (if any at all) are located here. The plan and layout of the Pazari originated in the seventeenth and eighteenth centuries, although much of it was built out of wood until 1852. In that year, a fire destroyed the district and the Pazari was rebuilt, this time out of stone. In the nineteenth century, much of the city's activity left the citadel and the great majority of administrative, commercial, and artisan activities concentrated in the Pazari (Riza 1978, 1981). Today, the vernacular practices of Gjirokastrits have added two further, open-air, public spaces to the "old center." These are a spatial extension of the Pazari streets. The first one is Çerçiz Topulli Square, which lies at the southwest end of the Pazari and is named after the Gjirokastrit "Hero of People" who fought in the early twentieth century for the foundation of the Albanian nation-state.

The square today is the wide end of an asphalt-surfaced road in front of the entry to the cobbled streets of the main Pazari. It functions predominantly as a car park and taxi rank. The three most important buildings located there are the city hall, Hotel Cajupi (one of the hotels built in the socialist period), and the Greek consulate. In the past, another important building located on that square was the block of flats where much of the local party leadership used to live, whereas now there is a popular bar located in its basement. This is located on the eastern side of the square, behind the monument to Bule Naipi and Persefoni Kokëdhima, two young women who participated in the antifascist resistance and who were executed, on that spot, during WWII. Very close to this monument is the plaque, erected in 2005, which celebrates the classification of the old town as a UNESCO World Heritage Site. In the past, Çerçiz Topulli Square had a huge tree in the middle of it, but it burned down. Most of the Gjirokastrits of that time refer to the square as "rrapi" (plane tree). The 29-kilometer highway between the border and the city has two main entrances to the city: "18 September" Boulevard and an asphalted street that climbs up to the hills and ends in Çerçiz Topulli Square.

The second wide and flat open-air space is situated at the northwest side of the Pazari, on the edge of another steep hill at a higher altitude than the Pazari. This wide "square" is currently named "Fantasia" after the posh cafe-restaurant located there. In 2002, Fantasia replaced the building that used to house the "Palace of Culture," and the open space in front of the building became the car park for the customers of the expensive eatery. Today, this car park lies on the site where a statue of Enver Hoxha stood until 1991.

Historically, in the era of P.P.Sh (Partia e Punës e Shqipërisë) the nationalization of Pazari properties was one of the largest political

10 A school photo from the early 1980s in front of Enver Hoxha's statue. To the horror of some in the local community, the Palace of Culture—built during the 1970s—was partly demolished in 1986 to make space for the statue, which was in turn destroyed by a crowd celebrating the end of socialism in the early 1990s.

projects in the city. This was for symbolic as well as practical reasons. Before the socialist era, the so-called "domestic bourgeoisie and the semi-feudal landlords ... of the past" (Marmullaku 1975, 92) owned many of the Pazari properties. Real estate in the Pazari was a symbol of power for the wealthiest and most influential families of so-called pure (*puro*) Gjirokastrit origin. Most of these families also owned large plots of agricultural land on the Gjirokastër plateau.

When the Communist Party came to power, the new regime applied the relevant collectivization legislation that facilitated the nationalization of properties and commercial activities, including both farmland and urban properties. In November 1944, the party issued the first decrees for the control of domestic trade. This was the first step toward the control of commercial activities; the main economic activity in the Pazari. On December 15, 1944, a series of state laws were issued eliminating most private activities: law no. 19/1944 presupposed state control over industries and businesses; and law no. 24/1944 forced the registration of all commodities by the local authorities and dictated the quantities that a retailer could buy or sell without state permission, while also requiring the commandeering of food supplies, construction materials, and vehicles (which signified the end of privately owned cars in Albania until 1991). Moreover, law no. 25/1944 provided for the confiscation of the property of so-called political fugitives. This meant that almost everyone who had left the country during the war was

11 It is a historical irony that Enver Hoxha's statue's lower pedestal is now underneath the car park of the privatized Palace of Culture; one more high-profile project of the socialist period. This irony is further highlighted by the fact that Hoxha's regime was so dominated by anti-automobility principles.

under suspicion of being an anticommunist and enemy of the people, and his or her relatives who remained were in danger of losing all types of property, which was the case for some Pazari property owners. In January 1945, laws no. 3/1945 and 40/1945 officially came into force. The first provided for the taxation of war profits, and the second ordered the disposition of private retail properties. These laws allowed the state to establish control over most of the wholesale and retail units in the country, including the Pazari. Prior to WWII, all trade and retail activity was in the private sector, yet less than ten years after the war, by 1953, this figure had been drastically reduced to approximately 16 percent (Skendi et al. 1957, 205–10). Later still, in the 1960s, the "Foundation of the Enterprise of Crafts" led to the replacement of the private sector by cooperatives. Despite the implied cessation of official commercial activities, an unofficial economy of favors remained (Dalakoglou 2012).

In 1978, Gjirokastër's primary historian of architecture, Emin Riza, not only confirmed the central location of the Pazari but also the historical continuity of this centrality: "[a]t the outset of the 17th century, the construction of the new bazaar started on the area where it lies today, i.e. in the center of the city" (Riza 1978). It is important to note

12 A small corner of the old town, as seen from the castle.

that, despite the dramatic sociopolitical transitions, the new regime not only preserved the site's centrality but in fact strengthened it: the state administration—the city hall, the "Palace of Culture," regional government, public services, the post office, bank, and the party authorities—were all located here. In addition, the vast majority of retail facilities, including Magazina e Popullit (the shop of the people: where one could buy clothes), food stores, artisans, an open-air market (until the 1960s), public transport terminals, and even a cinema were all concentrated here. The combination of the Pazari's lack of dwellings in presocialist times, and the changes that socialism brought in use, ownership, and life in general, such as set working hours and, thus, leisure time, meant the Pazari could not be identified with any one person or function in particular but, on the contrary, with almost everyone in the city. Thus, under socialism, the Pazari became even more socialized and busy than before. The Pazari almost had a spatial "monopoly" over public life and it concentrated the city's social energy. In terms of everyday life, this meant that almost everyone in the city spent at least a few hours a week, if not a day, in the Pazari.

The relocation of the urban center

For the first time in two hundred years, today, in the postsocialist present, the urban centrality of Gjirokastër has relocated to a new site. The new center has become the roughly 1-kilometer-long asphalt-surfaced boulevard, running southeast to northwest and built, initially during socialism, as part of the regime's urbanization and modernization project. As well as building activity, everyday social activities have rapidly become concentrated around and along "Bulevardi 18 Shtatori" (18 September; it was named after the date when partisans entered the town in 1944). Prior to WWII, there were no buildings on the site of today's new center, only fields. The 18 September Boulevard was constructed after the war,[3] but it only acquired some social significance during late socialism, when it was asphalted and redesigned as a boulevard, with a roundabout at one end and trees planted between the two lanes.

The plateau where this boulevard stands lays outside the prewar urban complex; there were mostly "fields and flocks," as some pure (*puro*) Gjirokastrits joke when they try to emphasize the spatialization of their superiority compared with the newcomers to the town. The latter could be identified with the newer parts of the town but not the stone-made old city. The first building on the plateau near the boulevard was a hospital, built at the northeast end of the boulevard. The *spital* was built by the Yugoslav government in 1948 for the Albanian regime

13 Spoon-shaped garden fences, remnants of the metal factory.

who were, at that time, comrades. Many injured partisans from the Greek Civil War (1946–49) were allegedly hospitalized there during its early years. The urban complex expanded over the plateau during the socialist period, and especially during the 1960s and 1970s. In the early 1960s, a new power plant was added to the city; and an industrial zone developed on the southeast edge of the boulevard, near the highway. The largest factory, one producing metal goods, which is situated next to the southeast end of the boulevard, was built in 1964–66 with the support of the Chinese government. This factory produced "metal products" that became famous in the town's life as the greatest symbol of modernization and socialist industrial development.

Simultaneously, in the 1970s, the city expanded and new blocks of flats were built, not only in the direction of 18 Shtatori but also toward the low parts of the hills, like Lagje Puntore. In Albanian, these blocks are called *pallat/pallati* (indef. art./def. art.), which in this context stands for "edifice[s]." Although associated with the boulevard, these blocks were restricted to its southern side, at the foot of the old town, in an obvious continuation of the presocialist urban plan. They were dwellings for the socialist period's newcomers to the town, people who arrived from the surrounding villages or other towns. Most of the prewar inhabitants and their heirs, though forced to restrict their domestic spaces (e.g. many of the old towers were divided into apartments), usually remained within the prewar, urban residential areas: the stone-built core of old Gjirokastër.

These sociomaterial and spatial distinctions also relate to the historical formation of a locally specific—but important—social classification in Gjirokastër. This classification has become intertwined with the other social and local hierarchies (e.g. class, religious, and ethnic) that existed in each historical–ideological framework. This is the distinction between the aforesaid pure (*puro*) and the newcomers. Most of the former lived in the stone houses up (*lart*) on the hills, while most of the latter lived in the postwar cement and brick buildings lower down. There were exceptions, as many of the older Gjirokastrits, when they married, were allocated a dwelling unit in the newer part of the town. It is important to note that most of the city's higher-ranking party officials were living "up" in stone buildings made after the war, and not "down" in the new blocks of flats. Today, pure Gjirokastrits often use the term "peasants" (*fshatar*) to describe those who came to the town either from the countryside or other parts of Albania. This distinction has created certain tensions since the newcomers of the socialist period do not consider themselves the same as the newcomers of the postsocialist period; however, in the perception of the pure ones, both groups are considered newer to a city where their own families have allegedly resided for centuries. This distinction between pure and peasant is largely a historical expansion of prewar class distinctions. During the late Ottoman period and the early years of the nation-state, immigration from the smaller settlements to Gjirokastër had already begun. In the socialist period, a new wave of newcomers came; and certainly, although the prevalent idea was that "pure ones" were living on the hills and the "peasants" in the new block of flats, the situation was much more complex. Many of the so-called peasants had powerful positions in the new establishment and thus purity did not necessarily imply power; on the contrary, it could be dangerous to claim pure origin as this could mark someone out as a member of the prewar elite. The complexity of this situation is exemplified in cases where the prewar elites not only lost the ownership of their stone tower-houses (*kullas*) but also had to limit themselves to certain rooms or a portion of what had previously been their house. Most of these tower-houses were divided into smaller apartments, and often the people who moved in were "peasants." This situation was further exacerbated by the fact that not all members of the elite were aligned with the anticommunist forces. Thus, officially, they should have been happy with such arrangements; furthermore, there were sometimes exceptions to the house division rule,

14 The socialist part of the city: the Boulevard in the late 1970s. The University of Gjirokastër can be seen behind the stadium on the left or north side. The hospital is situated above the stadium. Across the road are the modern socialist blocks of flats, above which, in the background, on the right or south side of the boulevard, is the industrial zone.

usually based on the political affiliation of the residents.

During most of the socialist period, the cement-and-brick buildings did not "cross" to the northern side of the boulevard. Exceptions to this rule, however, include the hospital and some other public constructions that were erected there, which were elements of the regime-ordered modernization process. The most significant ones were the city's stadium (1968), the "Palace of Sports" (1973), the University of Gjirokastër (1970s), and other facilities considered to be for nonlocals, such as a hotel, and temporary lodging for military personnel whose service was in Gjirokastër.

In the 1980s, as the Albanian economy began to decline with the political system in disarray, the Pazari began to lose its symbolic and social centrality. From the late 1970s, and especially after the death of Enver Hoxha in 1985, the increasing levels of poverty and the consequent "attrition" of the regime were reflected in the social dynamic of the Pazari. People could no longer afford to socialize, there were almost no goods in the shops, and people had to queue for what goods there were. Thus, the Pazari started losing its previous collective perceptions. The more the economic depression came to dominate people's daily life, the more the state lost its social legitimacy and thus the more it resorted to security and surveillance tactics, which poisoned whatever social solidarity there had once been. Within that context, social interaction became increasingly (self-)disciplined and weaker within the key public space of the Pazari. By the late 1980s, some youngsters had begun spending time around the boulevard and the nearby university campus rather than in the Pazari, claiming they were trying to avoid the informal but strict control of their elders. This was partly true; however, at the same time, the Pazari had increasingly come to represent the unpleasant phenomena of queues and Sigurimi (the secret police). In addition to these practicalities, the movement of social activity to the new site came to challenge the established orders and spatial practices prevalent during socialism. Thus, the beginning of the boulevard, near the stadium area, gradually came to be included in the daily strolling (*xhiro*) of more and more people. When recalling his activities in the late 1980s, Flamur, a man in his late thirties, explained that: "[they] were all the time with the kids near the university; the girls, the students, were from other cities and we could flirt with them, which was an important thing." The first informal coffee shop on the boulevard opened in the late 1980s. Despite this, it was only after 1990, and especially after 1997, when construction, commercial, professional, and social activity expanded drastically and crossed to the north side of the boulevard.

If centrality is a form that is defined by the accumulation of whatever coexists in a given space (Lefebvre 1991 [1974], 331; Low 2000), then the new boulevard center seems to have won out over the old Pazari center in this struggle. Today, most of the retail shops are concentrated along the boulevard, as are most of the ready-made food and drink outlets. Moreover, some of the public services, such as the police department, tax office, and court of appeals, have also moved there. The daily

15 The boulevard today: a part of the postsocialist expansion of the city.

16 One of the bank branches on the boulevard; a Greek bank. The majority of the banking sector in the country is controlled by the Greek banking sector.

open-air market and the city's supermarkets are also located on the boulevard. A second post office was opened there along with five bank branches (in contrast to the single branch in the Pazari). Vehicle and pedestrian traffic is constant from about 7:30 a.m. to 2:30 p.m., when the market and public services close for the day and all of the shops (except some cafes and restaurants) close for a few hours. People go home for lunch, and perhaps a nap. Later, around 5 or 5:30 p.m., they reopen their stores—until 9 or 10 p.m.—or they just go out for the *xhiro*.

17 The uncle and the nephew. The former was convicted and executed by the People's Justice system in the 1940s; the latter reclaimed the family shop in the Pazari and put his uncle's photo on the wall.

A woman in her twenties who grew up in Gjirokastër described what this word means: "*Xhiro* means taking time to stroll slowly, in summer mostly, usually in the company of at least one person." *Xhiro* can best be described as a light stroll for the purposes of people-watching, gossiping, and social interaction. It is considered stress-relieving, and if tired, people often suggest "*dil dhe bej nje xhiro*" (let's go out to make a *xhiro*). In Gjirokastër, the location where people take their *xhiro* has changed. In the past, people would go for *xhiro* in Çerçiz Square, from where the UNESCO landmark stands today to the Greek consulate. Since the 1990s, the *xhiro* has taken place on the boulevard. In summer, every afternoon from 6 to 9 p.m., the road is blocked from the entrance to the city, at the end of the highway, so that people can take their *xhiro*.

Toward the new centrality

In 1993, after the relevant legislation passed, it became clear that the Pazari properties would go to—and would be symbolically and factually reidentified with—the families and religious institutes[4] who had owned them prior to their nationalization.[5] In these cases, the new owners (descendants of the presocialist ones) often reconfigured their properties aesthetically, confirming their historical victory, as for example with a coffee-shop owner who put a photograph of his uncle (convicted of antinationalist offences in the 1940s) on the wall of his reclaimed store.

Another person claimed that he painted the frame of the door in a particular color, one rarely seen in the Pazari, because that was the color of the door before the war. Aside from the process of making the properties feel materially familiar—properties that generally can be altered very little due to UNESCO regulations—such new aesthetics also highlight the dynamics of postsocialist real estate politics. These dynamics, among other things, imply the exclusion of the emerging elites from real estate ownership in the Pazari. These emerging wealthy classes include emigrants who have made money abroad and/or businessmen who have profited from the opportunities of the postsocialist market but who do not necessarily originate from the presocialist elite. Indeed, there are new rich who do happen to originate from the powerful families of the 1920s–1930s. In the case of Gjirokastër, since 1990, although the majority of these newly affluent people have bought or built properties within the city, only the prewar elites have had access to the property in the Pazari.

Most of the people in Gjirokastër are excluded from owning real estate in the Pazari, while in the post-1991 period, and especially after 1997, immobile property became a collective practical and symbolic priority. This increase in the social value of property originated from the violent events of 1997, when the popular pyramid banking schemes collapsed and $2 billion of people's savings vanished, leading the country to the brink of civil war. Following the crash, real estate values increased as property, a tangible entity, was seen as the most secure way to invest money. Albania is characterized historically by a social flexibility in the perception of monetary values; for example, people often orally quote prices ten times higher than the actual price of things, a habit linked to the 1,000 percent devaluation of the lek in 1968. Thus, the combination of the 1997 crash and the relatively recent devaluations of the Albanian lek, together with a historical lack of cash and chronic poverty, has had a huge effect on people's perception of money. Cash is viewed as something abstract and insecure, especially when compared with the security of immobile property.

Real estate consequently became more popular due to the social reaction to the financial mismanagement by the new capitalist state and financial sector. The aforesaid, migration-based, rapid rise to wealth of certain people had specific implications for the social identification of those who became wealthy. The migrant was transformed into a major income provider for her/his family. As a result, a new, more prestigious self emerged. This self was further shaped by the sociopolitical transition of the time. Thus, the sudden loss of this relative wealth had a tragic impact both individually and socially for all of those who had gambled their savings. People who had organized their lives around their remittances saw the promised interest increase dramatically (albeit fraudulently) during the pyramid fever. Many people even left their regular jobs, or sold their properties expecting to live off the high interest from the pyramid schemes. Suddenly everything vanished, causing widespread confusion and chaos for both the individuals involved and society as a whole.

From a social perspective, the most violent dimension of the 1997 "war" (*lufte*), as it is known, was not the violence that ensued but rather the massive return to poverty and subsequent alienation of what was considered the first tangible wealth of an entire society. This society now felt it had been cast back to pre-1990 poverty levels and in some cases beyond. This tragic "return" to poverty was exemplified by the various life stories of returned migrants who had to remigrate after 1997. Most of these people remembered with a kind of joy and even nostalgia their first exodus to migratory "freedom." Stories of police brutality or economic exploitation by employers had been narrated as positively as stories of those who were helpful and expressed their solidarity with the new immigrants. Yet, despite the fact that remigration was often easier logistically (e.g. legal visa documents, a network

18 An informal currency exchanger at the roundabout of the Boulevard Shtator, the new center of Gjirokastër. These exchangers offer much better rates than any formal bank. The background provides an idea of the heavy traffic, both of vehicles and people.

in Greece), those forced to go narrated their post-1997 remigration with deep sadness and trauma. The loss, then, was not just a monetary one but also a loss of a part of their new self. Thus, these same people formulated new practices of saving and investment after the catastrophe. These practices were much more closely linked with real estate, as I will show later in this book. Since the majority of those who could afford to buy real estate were still unable to obtain the socially exalted real estate of the Pazari district, there was an explosion of urban development after 1997.

The physical practicality of the new center, in terms of providing the suitable space and topography, led to its development. Gjirokastër's socialist civil architecture had kept large distances between buildings. Since 1990, and especially since 1997, the "free" spaces between buildings on the south side of the boulevard and the unbuilt space on the north side have been privatized and built upon. Thus, qualitatively they obtained monetary values, which quickly began to increase. Older, three-story socialist blocks of flats have now been hidden behind new high-rise blocks built of concrete and bricks, imported from Greece. These sometimes reach seven or eight stories and have ground and lower-ground floors that are designed for retail purposes. Furthermore, the socialist-era buildings have been modified with the expansion of retail units toward the road. This new undeveloped space on the north side of the boulevard became the sociomaterial tabula rasa where postsocialist conditions and powerful newly emerging social actors could create their own works on the postsocialist cityscape.

The practices of a displacing centrality

In the opening quote to this chapter, Ismail Kadare poetically described the tension between the physical techniques employed when walking on cobbled streets versus the surfaces of a boulevard abroad. In the poetics of postsocialist everyday life, there are several ways that people narrate and experience the same tension. Geni, a local friend, suggested some technical problems with the Pazari: "the Pazari is five narrow [...] *kalldrëm* [cobbled roads], the Pazari is good only for making your car break down!" Every time he passed through the Pazari, Geni, and many other drivers, would apply antievil-eye apotropaic techniques as apparently so many pairs of eyes overlooking you in such close proximity in the Pazari would cause you to have an accident sooner or later. Bledi, a man who spends most of the year in Greece, told me that two of his friends have had car crashes in the Pazari because the coffee-shops have so many tables outside and the space is so limited that everyone can stare at you, so it is easy for someone to put the evil eye on your car.

Although driving on the boulevard has become just as difficult as it is in the Pazari, due to the people, petrol fumes, and informal social control, it is apparent that the meanings and assumptions linked with being in, or passing by, the Pazari are still very different from being on or passing by the boulevard. This is not merely a matter of design and layout, but of spatial practices. The different corporeal experience of the two centers does not consist only of the different materialities of the "walking grounds" but also comprises different interactions between the human bodies and the machines (vehicle; *makina* in Albanian) and the social interactions dictated by the materialities and spatialities of the two sites. The daily *xhiro* remains a significant social practice, but the qualitative properties of *xhiro* today are changing: *xhiro* is not exclusively a walk (as was the case until 1991); today it may also involve vehicles. The (mostly male) drivers drive around slowly and interact with one another or even leave their cars close by, unlocked, and with windows or doors open while they have their drink in a cafe. For many young men in Gjirokastër, the car has become an extension of their bodies during *xhiro*.

Until 1991, vehicles were a privilege of the various elites in Albania.

19 Peak afternoon time in the Pazari's cobbled and narrow street.

At the same time, the lower classes were largely dependent on walking or animals for their movement. In the socialist past, there was an improvement in comparison to the presocialist past with the introduction of public transport, but passenger vehicles were still a monopoly held by the socialist nomenclature. As has been recorded in collective memory, the cars used by Albanian VIPs were all Mercedes-Benz cars with curtains in the windows. This partly explains the proportion of these cars in Albania today, a phenomenon often recorded in various tourist guides and which also attracts journalists' imagination, as for instance with the *New York Times* journalist who wrote: "In Poor Albania Mercedes Rules Road" (*New York Times*, November 10, 2002). The Pazari is looked upon negatively with respect to driving, but the asphalted boulevard, being the widest and straightest road in the city, is self-evidently a space of automobility. It is unsurprising, then, that with the exception of late night and the noon-siesta, the boulevard has a constant flow of traffic made up of thousands of cars, often the same ones passing through several times during the same afternoon.

The centrality and the openness of the road

It is important to note that in addition to the explosive growth of the city, the most defining spatial transformation of the postsocialist period (and the respective mode of production in Lefebvre's terms) is its own, new, centrality. The point of reference of the new centrality is a 1-kilometer boulevard, a road, located between the socialist and postsocialist urban sectors. Moreover, the city does not just grow materially in spatial response to the infrastructure of automobility but also socially through the new social practices that centralize mobility. This centralization of mobility is visible socially through the mass introduction of private vehicles and the parallel wave of migration abroad. Thus, the boulevard, being the city's main link with the 29-kilometer Albanian–Greek cross-border highway, takes on even further significance. The boulevard has become the ideal new center, as it facilitates *physically* and *socially* the centralization of automobility and migration.

The new postsocialist life has been spatially expressed in the urban topography and vice versa: the new urban topography has been defined by the postsocialist condition. This is analogous to the topographical transformations of the socialist period. Socialism as a new modern and modernizing political system was materialized via a new urban expansion. Besides stone, new materials (cement, brick) and new types of constructions (blocks of flats, factories, boulevard, etc.) were used in that spatialization–materialization of the new society. This spatial reformation had direct social consequences, as for example with the emphasis on new social formations, such as the nuclear family or new class structures, which were facilitated by the layout of the new dwellings, the urban landscape, and the introduction of new institutions such as the university, hospital, and so on. Accordingly, in terms of material metaphors and reflections, today the new center is the architectural phrasing of the new social emphases—automobility and migration.

This new postsocialist center has emerged in a new historical era, therefore in a new area, which is on the boundary between the second and third, historical, urban extensions. Similarly, the socialist plan extended from the presocialist one. The new center, having as a main point of reference a busy road, incorporates dynamism and transitional ontological properties that communicate—and eventually contribute to—the ambiguity and fluidity of the postsocialist worldview.

The centralization of the road ontologically represents, and at the same time is a formidable element of, the newfound mobility of Albanian society not only abroad (through emigration) but also internally: the introduction of private vehicles has mobilized the wealthier members of society, highlighting the new inequalities. In other words, the boulevard and the process of building around it became elements in the dialog between the small-scale cultural logics of everyday life in Gjirokastër and the larger-scale, transitional postsocialist Albania. The boulevard also became the element establishing continuity between the socialist past and the postsocialist present, as it was built during socialism as something new and this "newness" continues to extend itself into the current, post-1990 transnational condition.

The boulevard, however, not only represents newness but also fluidity at a time when fluidity is the archetypal phenomenon of the era, first and foremost in terms of its boundaries. Early in the fieldwork, I observed, among a group of middle-aged men, that when people say they are going to "boulevardi" they are, in fact, going near the boulevard, often without ever reaching the actual boulevard. I asked them to define which places people include when they refer to Boulevard 18 Shtatori. "Where the asphalt begins," Giorgo, told me. "No," said Pelub, "it is only the boulevard as such, the pavements and the area around the stadium and that's all," then Kujtim suggested something different, giving a number of spatial points which define where the boulevard starts. The argument over the different boundaries lasted almost thirty minutes. A similar situation occurred the next time I asked the same question, this time in a boulevard cafe, having overheard a similar discussion which I had not initiated. By contrast, people are much more precise and in agreement when they are asked to

20 & 21 The main street of Gjirokastër Pazari in the 1970s and today. These days there are no communist banners and the tower of the mosque has been rebuilt. Apart from these, there have been very few changes to the architecture. Beneath the stone façades, however, the dynamic of everyday relations and relationships has been drastically altered.

define where the Pazari begins and ends.

The boulevard's materialities are also much more fluid in comparison to the static materialities of the Pazari. The boulevard has been in a state of constant material transition since the fall of socialism. There is always something under construction on the road itself: asphalting, drainage works, paving, expansions, not to mention the buildings that surround the road, which are constantly being built or rebuilt. Over the same period, the most serious transformation in the materiality of the Pazari was the collapse of a wall from an abandoned building due to decay. The rhythm of construction works on the boulevard is such that, over the period of research for this book, some new addition to the cityscape would appear along it every month. Materially, the boulevard is both quantitatively and qualitatively different. Moreover, its dynamism is embedded in its own function as a mobility infrastructure; throughout the morning and afternoon, cars drive up and down it constantly. The necessity of traffic lights is ignored and illegal U-turns, stops to greet friends passing by, or even (by the mainly male drivers) to make comments to young women, are frequent. Correspondingly, the people on the pavement walk slowly due to the crowds and traffic. On warmer days, it usually takes double the amount of time to walk along the road due to pedestrians or the groups of youngsters who stand in front of the cafes and bars. While the rhythms of the boulevard are slower in comparison to the rhythms of the cross-border highway, the two are considered vernacular parts of the same whole. The third part, which completes this whole, is the border. This third place shares similar rhythms and spatial practices with the boulevard despite being situated at the far end of the 29-kilometer nexus, namely the Kakavijë border checkpoint. Thus, not only does the boulevard physically bridge Gjirokastër to Greece but in fact the entire city focuses its gaze on the neighboring country in several ways. The cross-border highway's materiality changed and came into broader use at precisely the same time as the centralization of the boulevard. Prior to this, during the socialist period, the boulevard was just a static element of urban planning rather than an infrastructure of mobility. Similarly, the cross-border highway was a monument of disconnection, scarcely reaching the forbidden zone of the borders. Although there exists diversity between the three parts of the system—boulevard, highway, and border crossing—the whole system is tied together by their common materiality, shared cultural logic, and political history.

22 Adding a floor to a socialist period building that stands in front of the roundabout on the boulevard.

23 The boulevard, as seen from the south side of the street, overlooking the new, postsocialist, expansion of the city. In the foreground is the bus connecting the upper and lower parts of the city. The background shows a Bank of Tirana branch (owned by a Greek bank), road construction works, and a large building under perpetual construction.

Notes

1 Enver Hoxha was the secretary of the Party of Labor of Albania, which ruled the country until 1991. Hoxha participated in the anti-fascist resistance during WWII and governed the country with the party from the end of the war up until his death in 1985.
2 Comprising the citadel, the Pazari, and its periphery, plus some several hundred individual dwellings.
3 It was a road that linked the lower part of the town, Varosh, with the fields and the old bridge over the Drinos. To its left was another road that linked the town with the Orthodox Church and the Teqeja up in the hills.
4 This has to do with the Islamic law that allowed for "vakuf," namely, property donated to religious institutes for the purposes of the common good. Under the Ottoman law, not only Islamic institutes or communities but also institutes and communities of other faiths had the right to vakuf.
5 However, ownership is not always clear and disputes over several properties of the Pazari have continued for decades now.

5

Fear of the road and the accident of postsocialism

> In the chronotope of the road, the unity of time and space markers is exhibited with exceptional precision and clarity. The importance of the chronotope of the road in literature is immense: it is a rare work that does not contain a variation of this motif, and many words are directly constructed on the road chronotope, and on road meetings and adventure.
> (Bakhtin 1982 [1930s], 98)

As is perhaps to be expected of a city that socially and spatially centralizes around mobility and its infrastructures, many of the most common narratives are those that locate their action precisely on the Kakavijë–Gjirokastër highway. Similarly, stories of car accidents, dangerous bandits, and the atrocities committed "out there" (*jushtë*), following the economic collapse and "the war" (*lufte*) of 1997, dominate the discourse of travelers crossing the border. In these stories, the highway emerges as the scene where the various episodes of an insecure daily life and a dynamic transition are located; the uncertainty and fluidity of the entire Albanian postsocialist transitional project. The stories narrate incidents from the near and distant past, personal experiences, and urban legends alike. Nevertheless, the road itself remains the constant throughout all the narratives; its topographical references are crucial for the orientation of the audience. The cross-border highway is often the only tangible and physical element of the stories that is in existence at the time when they are narrated. The storytellers, together with the incidents, narrate the road itself producing and reproducing the meanings of the space. In the following paragraphs, the three most prevalent narrative motifs of road stories in the Gjirokastër area will be presented and located within the current ethnographic and historical context.

Narrating the road

Crashes

Since the widespread introduction of privately owned vehicles in the early 1990s, driving in Albania has become a particularly risky activity. Automobility, being a new practice, meant that an entire country with little or no previous experience was suddenly driving. Almost immediately, high-speed driving emerged as a major pastime for young men. On January 12, 1999, the Albanian Telegraphic Agency (ATA) reported that Albania was listed as having one of the highest road-related fatality rates (2.2 deaths per 1,000 vehicles) in the world (ATA 1999a). In May 2007, the OSCE mission in Albania stated in a press release:

> Tired drivers, many of them Albanian emigrants returning home for the summer holidays, queue under the hot August sun to enter the country at the Kakavijë border crossing on the South Albanian/Greek border. As guards check passports, they also hand drivers leaflets asking them to drive carefully and reminding them that on average 25 people die every month on Albanian roads. (OSCE 2007)

Kakavijë is the largest and busiest border crossing in the country, and the highway between Gjirokastër and the border is one of the busiest roads in Albania. Thus it is to be expected that the great majority of accidents I heard about or witnessed occurred along these 29 kilometers. In fact, as soon as I began to ask questions about car accidents, almost everyone I knew had several stories to tell me. These stories included accidents they had personally witnessed or in which they had been a casualty, or crashes involving relatives or close friends. The amount of data I gathered on accidents reflects their incredible frequency. The following crash described by one of my interlocutors, Vangeli, includes many of the common motifs encountered in the discourse of young male drivers:

> I was driving, but it was not my fault, I know very well how to drive. My uncle gave me his car, I do not have one of my own yet, and my father is afraid so he does not give his to me. He [the uncle] had promised me that as soon as we entered Albania [the uncle is a migrant] I will be allowed to drive. He gave me the car in the evening and my brother, my cousin and I went out to the swimming pool [a luxurious club with a swimming pool on the s plateau, owned by a former chief of the Kakavijë border-crossing station]. I drunk two or three whiskeys, but this is OK. I am fine with two whiskeys as I do not feel anything and even if they had done an alcohol-test I would be clean! But there was oil on the roads, eh! I had floored it, I was going very fast and the car left the road. I held it! If it was not raised up, I would not have fallen off the road.

24 A small monument in Gjirokastër commemorating two women killed
during the 1997 conflict.

This story, as with almost all such stories, illustrates the typical irre-
proachability of the driver in causing the accident. Instead, the accident
is attributed to external factors, such as the oil on the road. Incidentally,
the car in the above story was destroyed; it remained upside down on
the side of the highway for weeks until it was picked up for scrap metal
by a local business owned by a Roma family.

   Another common motif in these stories is that of car accidents being
caused by supernatural beings. Some stories describe the appearance of

a Christian Orthodox priest or a Muslim dervish in the middle of the road, causing an accident, or conversely saving the life of the people involved. A Bektashi taxi driver, who used to keep excerpts of the Holy Koran hanging from the mirror of his vehicle, would toot his horn when passing a huge (4 meters tall) marble cross standing at the side of the Kakavijë–Gjirokastër highway, near a Greek minority village. Once, while driving me to the border, he explained how, a few years previously, he had an accident in the middle of the night near the location of the cross; a few minutes prior to the accident he had spotted a *papa* (Christian Orthodox priest) walking by the road. Since then, he believes that something related to the cross and the nearby monastery saved him from death. "Anyway I am with everyone, I have no problem, and all are good: Muslim, Christian, or a ghost ... the god is the same for all, yes or no?" he added.

The road and the "war" of 1997

During the violent events of 1997, widespread tales emerged of gangs of bandits who lurked on the highway between the city and the border. This was an emotionally and politically charged time in recent Albanian history. In fact, this period marked postsocialist Albanian history to such an extent that people in Albania divide local historical time into pre-1997 and post-1997 phases.

During the war, the limits of the city were clearly marked by the beginning of the boulevard linking the city with the Kakavijë–Gjirokastër highway. Within the city, the violence was relatively limited. However, outside the city-limits—"out to the road," as some people described it—violence, criminality, and killings were commonplace. For example, Klaudi, who lives permanently in Greece, told me about the 1997 war:

> Here in Gjirokastër we did not have too many killings and stuff like that ... eh all right, we had a few, people got guns and everything, but mostly for their protection ... some were killed by accident if someone did not know how to use the weapons well ... I mean that one tried to use the bazooka, but he held it the wrong way round and lost his head, but killings like in Vlorë [the city where the antiregime rebellion began and was based] did not happen too often, here we had only a little of that thing [killings]. Gjirokastrits were clever: they put a roadblock down on the entrance from the national road and were controlling whoever was coming around asking "who are you? What do you want here? Get out from here you have no business in here," and we did not have many killings, but out there, outside the city, down the road, hoo-hah!

In these narratives, the Kakavijë–Gjirokastër highway represents the "outside," the unfamiliar, the place where the violence and killings occurred, a motif relayed not only orally but also through other sources, such as newspapers, television, or other more official accounts. For example, on April 23, 1997, the ATA reported (original spelling has been retained):

> A grave incident occurred on Tuesday on the junction of the Kakavijë–Gjirokastër road. Armed persons, who were travelling as passengers on the bus, robbed and plundered the passengers and killed a young man because he did not follow their orders. (ATA 1997a)

Later, in June 1997, the news from ATA regarding killings on the road reflected an additional mystery (original spelling and grammar):

> Four people were killed on Tuesday at 17:30, on the national road, some 18 km to the south of Gjirokastër (Southern Albania). The victims, of whom only two have been identified, were found in a car of the type "Audi," with a number plate of Gjirokastër and were shot by a "Kalashnikov," according to the criminal experts. The motive of robbery is unclear, said one of the leaders of the criminal police, because the things and money they had with them was not touched. (ATA 1997b)

It is important to note that even the Albanian mass media calls the road "Kakavijë–Gjirokastër" rather than Gjirokastër–Kakavijë, although Gjirokastër is the capital of the county and Kakavijë is just a small village. This obscured topography will be analyzed subsequently with regard to hegemonic discourses and economic power on the road. Regarding the content of these stories, a major element that further contributes to the mythological dimension of these violent incidents was rumors about the identity of various malefactors. In some cases, the inhabitants of Lazarati, a nearby village, were accused; others claimed that the killers and robbers were agents of President Sali Berisha who had been sent to the South to establish a regime of terrorism and ruin the rebels' self-government. Some Gjirokastrits told me that the wrong-doers were Greek agents who came to cause a provocation and create a justification for the Greek army to occupy the south of Albania. Sali Berisha's government and supporters claimed that the criminals of the road were pawns of the socialist party, who had initially rebelled against the state and then turned to robbing travelers. Others claimed that the highway robbers were the agents of the pseudo-banks' pyramid schemes who were causing social anxiety and helping the pseudo-banks to take their time exporting the "lost" money abroad. Police officers were also blamed for taking part in the roadblocks, as were the Albanian "mafiozi." Nevertheless, the latter probably had bigger business to take care of at that time (such as smuggling weapons and petrol), rather than robbing vehicle passengers; on the contrary, organized crime groups in South

Albania seem to prefer periods of state-established order. There is even a theory that one of the reasons why the situation calmed down in the South is that big business (including both mafia and legal multinational companies) wanted order for the proper functioning of their work in the area. In this sense, the newly emerged opportunist petty criminal gangs, which were formed in 1997, were opposed by the older established mafia, and this may also explain some of the killings, when two opposed groups with similar inclinations encountered each other. Last but not least, in the "1997" mythology of Gjirokastër, blame was laid upon the people from North Albania for ambushes on the motorway. This accusation was based on the typical scheme of accusing the outsiders who are the most similar to the collective self. Yet, according to local belief, they, as outsiders, had no compunction in what they did to the poor passersby.

The cross-border highway, being one of the few legal entrances to the country and located in the troubled South, had a number of temporary roadblocks where armed men demanded money for passage. A professional driver who used to ride this road during the "war" explained: "It depended on the roadblock, some thieves were putting up a hand to stop you, if you stopped, and they did not like you, they may rob you. If you did not stop, they did not care to follow or shoot you or other things. The professionals yes, they were bad, but some others were just for fun."

In 2006, I met a group of unlicensed taxi drivers at the Kakavijë border checkpoint. One of them explained to me how during the "war" the few motorists who waited for journalists or returnees in Kakavijë were armed themselves, and usually accompanied by one heavily armed man as an escort, "with hand grenades and everything." The taxi fare from the border was extremely high at that time, due to the scarcity of taxis, but also due to the cost of the escort and the "toll" to the roadblock keepers. Unarmed returnee migrants with their remittances and the scores of foreign journalists who had rushed in to cover what seemed like the start of a civil war were easy targets for the old and new gangs. Edvin, who claimed to have been one of the first people to buy a private car in Gjirokastër, has worked as a taxi driver in Kakavijë since the early 1990s. He recalled the bands of armed youngsters who stopped him on his way to the frontier and threatened to shoot the children in the car if they did not give them money.

The Kakavijë checkpoint at the very beginning of the 29-kilometer section of highway was where much of the armed activity occurred, as was reported in another ATA article:

At the border checkpoint of Kakavijë, which connects Greece with Albania, criminal gangs continue to rob and exercise violence against Albanians who travel through this point. These gangs continued systematic robberies on Tuesday and were confronted with forces deployed to establish order, as a result of this, the policemen Maksi Aani and Genci Mullai were injured ... the border checkpoint of Kakavijë is under the complete control of gangs. Several days ago they gravely injured a 13-year old girl from Delvina, as well as violating an Albanian citizen who was coming from Greece. Robbery and terror were also exercised against the vehicles and buses in the axis of the road Kakavijë–Ballsh. (ATA 1997c)

Moreover, a tragic story, narrated by a former police officer who worked at the border checkpoint for many years, provides a vivid illustration of the extreme risk associated with using the road at the time:

In 1997, from one point on, fewer and fewer people were crossing the border to Albania. We were hidden, with Kalashnikovs in hands all of the time, and we did not have lights on, but they still shot us! You never knew. From behind, from the road we heard volleys of fire. Once, a guy passed during the night. When he climbed out to the road they shot him. Riddled with bullets, he ran again in to us with his bowels in his hands, we put him in the ambulance to Ioannina [Greece] to the hospital. But he died before reaching the hospital. These guys [the killers] were from the North; Berisha sent them to commit terrorism in the South because the people here were against him.

It is important to note the classic "in/out" motif associated with the highway: the road is "out" (*jashtë*); the border checkpoint is "in" (*magin*). The place where the bullets flew was described as being "out on the road" (*jashtë në rrugët*) not "on the plateau," or "in Dropoli," or "the fields" or in any village. The evils lie outside—on the highway. In addition, the last story highlights the major tensions between North and South Albanians. The policeman, as a Southerner, attributes the criminality to the people from the North of the country (outsiders) who are considered dangerous, sinister, and unfamiliar.

During the 1997 unrest, the strategic importance of the road became evident in the sheer number of attempts to blow up the bridges that mark the entrance to the s plateau. In the second half of May 1997, almost a dozen explosions on highway bridges, especially the "Urë e Kardhikit" (Kardhiki) and "Viroi" bridges were reported. Fundamentally, it would appear that these explosions formed part of a direct effort to prevent pro-Berisha forces gaining control of the Kakavijë–Gjirokastër highway. Thus, the road per se appears to have played a specific role in the political anxiety of 1997. From a military point of view, the Kakavijë–Gjirokastër highway was considered one of the most important roads in South Albania. In addition to the gang violence and robberies (mostly organized by opportunist criminals on the road), there was also an ordered conflict between sections of the armed forces. This consisted of skirmishes between those faithful to the right-wing president, Sali Berisha, and organized groups of socialist-oriented Southern rebels on the other. These groups took names such as "People's Committees," "Salvation Committees," and "Plurality Committees," and were very well armed, having looted army barracks. Many ex-militants, fired by the Democratic Party regime, participated in these committees, including the famous "General Agim Ghozita" in Gjirokastër.

The conflict between these two groups was a semi-formed civil war, and within that framework, control of the road was crucial. Miranda Vickers and James Pettifer (2006, 26), experts on Albanian issues, state in reference to the 1997 conflict in South Albania, the importance that was attributed to the control of highways as it had happened in the rest of the previous Balkan conflicts. The mountainous terrain of the Balkan Peninsula made the construction of new routes relatively difficult, meaning that many battles to conquer road routes have taken place since ancient times. In addition, the involvement of members of the Greek minority in the South's uprising against the Tirana government, in combination with a concentration of Greek army infantry around the border area, proved extremely alarming for the already anti-Greek Berisha government. The section of the highway between Gjirokastër and the border, passing through the main Greek minority area of the s plateau, became extremely important for the faltering Tirana government. As such, Gjirokastër became the center of attention in the rebellious South. Berisha's government realized the town's strategic importance in gaining and maintaining control over the highway. Accordingly, they kept Gjirokastër under state control for as long as possible and fought hard to reoccupy it after they lost it. The conditions of the state of emergency placed the mass media under direct government control, implying a pro-Berisha affiliation. Nonetheless, they were still able to provide a certain amount of information about military movements and conditions on the highway. On March 4, 1997, the ATA reported tension over the control of this 29-kilometer long section of the highway (original spelling):

> In Jergucat (18 km far from the city and near the border with Greece), a key point in the whole zone of Dropull, and in Vrisera, the rebellious forces looted two shops two days ago. A rumor was spread that two trucks with criminals came on Tuesday to Gjirokastër, which was not true. The tanks of the Albanian Army have moved on the Jergucat–Tepelene road.[1] There is no armored vehicle deployed in the city of Gjirokastër. The roadblock of Jergucat, reinforced with armored vehicles, makes it impossible for the criminals to come from Saranda and Delvina into the zone of Dropull. (ATA 1997d)

In reality, the truth was less positive for Sali Berisha's government. Although people generally avoid discussing the events of 1997, thus casting out the "madness" and the "evil," incidents from that time are sometimes recounted. According to oral history in the city, the situation became increasingly unstable and the army unit deployed in Gjirokastër was almost isolated and not sufficient to defend itself. On March 8, 1997, in a vain final attempt to keep control, helicopters carrying Special Forces soldiers flew in to secure the city. That was the start of the well-reported dramatic rebellion in the last Southern town under state quasi-control. The police department was looted and set alight; the city hall was attacked; barricades were erected at strategic points; and the last remaining soldiers of the garrison abandoned their positions, allowing the crowd to seize the contents of the barracks. In the hands of the rebels, these arms (including tanks and antiaircraft mortars) forced the masked men of the Special Forces to retreat back to their helicopters and fly away. By the evening of March 9, Tirana forces had lost total control of the town and the highway (Pettifer and Vickers 2006, 19–36).

The dangerous village by the road

The road is the physical place where narratives about criminal activity are located. Narratives of smuggling, drugs, weapons, money laundering, trafficking, illegal emigration, and, more generally, outflows and inflows, all locate their action on this particular cross-border highway. Despite this, in the local taxonomic system such activities are classified as less important and less negative in comparison to physical violence against human beings.

The people of Gjirokastër and the other surrounding villages often blame the residents of Lazarat village for the majority of violent incidents that occur on the road. Lazarat is located on the west side of the highway, less than 1 kilometer south of the Gjirokastër periphery. In the area, it is sometimes referred to as the village of "marginal criminals." Once, while returning from Greece (Ioannina market) with Gjony and his cousin, in a minivan packed with goods for his grocery shop in Gjirokastër, I suggested having a coffee in Lazarat. Both men laughed and asked me if I wanted our car to be emptied; "they are dangerous," one said.

The motif of the outsider, the "incoming," and the unfamiliar can again be seen in the narration of the following story by a woman from the city. In my experience, hers largely represents the opinion held by most Gjirokastrits of their neighbors:

> These people were always robbers and Turks! And it is them who organized every evil back then in the war [1997]! What do you want me to

mention first, that they marry only among themselves? Because nobody else wants them! That they were soldiers of fortune for the Turks? That Ali Pasha was using them to massacre the whole of Albania? Hoxha had them locked into the village! Lazarat was the jail of old Gjirokastrits! Beasts! They are not from here.

During my fieldwork, the Albanian police organized several raids on the entire village of Lazarat. They arrested several inhabitants for drugs offenses, accusing them of cultivating cannabis. Other stories told in Gjirokastër include that of an Albanian police helicopter that was allegedly shot at while flying above the village.

Another story I recorded in Gjirokastër concerned the kidnapping of a Gjirokastër prefect in September 1998 by an armed gang from Lazarat. This prefect was a Greek Orthodox Christian from Dervitsani, one of the largest Greek minority villages on the plateau (located 1 kilometer south of Lazarat). Lazarat is the most consciously faithful Muslim settlement in the religiously mixed prefecture of Gjirokastër, and as a Lazarat friend told me, his village is the only "purely Albanian" village along the highway south of Gjirokastër. Although the background to the incident was complex, it seems that it had both political (between the main Albanian political parties) and nationalist motivations, including land ownership disputes and local antagonisms. The event provoked much tension, which soon spread, and the fear of potential ethnopolitical violence between the villagers of the two settlements, Dervitsani and Lazarat, was very tangible. Eventually, after political interventions, the prefect was released on the highway between the two villages where an armed band of his fellow villagers were waiting for him.

In January 1999, a mission from Lazarat went to Tirana to meet with the prime minister as, according to journalists, the conditions in the village had become unbearable due to the criminal gangs active there. The ATA stated in their report:

> After the terrible events in the spring of '97, when the army depots were opened and arms were robbed, a group of teenagers from this village [Lazarat] posed a serious threat to the passengers passing on the national road, near the village. According to police statistics, some 200 lootings of passengers and goods were registered in this village in 1998. 7 members of the police force were wounded during an initiative to apprehend those responsible last autumn. These things as well as the apathy of the local government have meant Lazarat is now considered a "looting village," having previously been considered by the communist regime as "Ballist" (supporters of the National Front) village. (ATA 1999b)

Previous research in Dervitsan (Mantzios 2007) reports that, during the early 2000s, several members of the Greek minority were accustomed to firing volleys of Kalashnikov gunfire in the direction of Lazarat. The Dervitsan people claimed this was done in order to scare off wolves and protect their flocks; however, there is no forest on the plateau, and the last time wolves were reported in the area was before WWII.

In the socialist period, levels of criminality were extremely low for a range of different reasons, perhaps because, originally, the regime ensured a certain level of social peace by providing for almost everyone or perhaps because strict law enforcement was practiced. Following the collapse of socialism, migration, remittances, private businesses, and its associated inequalities have led to an increase in everyday petty crime. At the same time, large-scale organized crime began to replace the absent state apparatuses.

Narratives of the road

The aforesaid road narratives of the new postsocialist condition built upon existing narrative schemes. Traditionally, the roads in Balkan folklore were associated with dangerous creatures and dangerous people who attacked lonely travelers, especially on junctions, bridges, and crossroads that were often seen as charged with ill fate. For example, transport infrastructure was often considered haunted due to gruesome human sacrifices. Allegedly, the practice of walling-in women and children occurred in the past in order to "fasten up" the newly built bridges of the transport networks. The Balkan ballad of Arta Bridge (located in Epirus) is a famous example of that motif (Beaton 1996). There is also an Albanian version of Rozafati Bridge (Skendi 1954, 50–5). This motif is further repeated in other traditions such as the Jewish one (Shai 1976). These ballads describe how walled-in people return to haunt the infrastructure, causing accidents, harming travelers, and so on. Besides these supernatural stories, historically and legendarily, one finds stories of road bandits (similar to the Anglo-Saxon highwaymen) throughout the Balkans, who violently demand payment from travelers in order to pass. During the Ottoman period, groups of mercenaries, often in league with robbers, were employed by local leaders to guard road passages. During the same period, merchants' caravans were reportedly accompanied by armed escorts to protect them from highway robbers (see Dimitriadis et al. 1998; Holland 1815, 81).

Narrative schemes similar to those describing the Kakavijë–Gjirokastër highway today are not a monopoly of the Balkans. Contemporary anthropology suggests a qualitative change in local oral discourse, which is associated with newly built or newly extended and newly opened highways throughout the world. Ethnographic surveys traditionally take place in "stateless" regions and in the remote corners of states; consequently, ethnographers often witnessed the arrival of highway networks in those communities. Almost every ethnologist who has studied highways[2] reports that roads trigger people's imaginations and are frequently incorporated into the tales and stories of those who travel on or live close to them. For instance, Luise White (1993) discusses the introduction of vehicles and vehicular roads in central Africa; this inspired local mythography, so that there are stories about vampires who drive fire engines or other vehicles and kidnap the people to drink their blood. Giles-Vernick (1996, 259) writes of the short bush spirits, along the big road built by European colonialists, who harm travelers and people living across the road. Adeline Masquelier (1992, 2002) provides us with accounts of the dangerous "Doguawa" and the "Takwa Darko" or other road spirits and "sirens" that have caused deaths and car crashes in postcolonial Niger. In addition to such stories, more earthly narrative themes of danger can also be discerned. Robberies, violence, and witchcraft or car accidents and other stories of travelers who "set off on the road" but never return also emerge for example in Papua New Guinea (Hayano 1990; and Stewart and Strathern 1999).

It is impossible for infrastructures such as new roads to be introduced into the space and life of a community without causing major socio-cultural transformations, which are then reflected in local narratives. Sometimes, newly constructed or extended roads are imported violently, as with highways in Palestine (Selwyn 2001). In other cases, the local population requests new roads, like Hayano (1990) reported in Papua New Guinea. Although there are radical differences regarding road-related experiences, new roads emerge as a novel, alien, element that inspire poetical and literary responses by those who attempt to make sense of them. This process may take on multiple dimensions depending on who is narrating the road; thus, for example, the Palestinian road can be interpreted as either Israeli state colonialism or a connection with the rest of the world and progress. In either case, the roads are included in local narratives. In fact, newly built roads divide and break existing social and spatial continuums and orders while, at the same time, affording new, far-reaching possibilities. It is important to stress that the supposed modernization that comes with highway construction is not the only theme associated with the modern road narratives; on the contrary, though new roads may officially be presented as places of ease and progress, they simultaneously appear as a source of both fear and danger. Moreover, the ways roads are described may change signifi-cantly over time. Where written historical accounts are available, local stories often contradict the official versions of history intended to be incorporated into local narratives. Roseman (1996) notes how Galician villagers in Spain poetically manipulate oral narratives concerning the building of a particular road in favor of the local politics of memory. In Santiago de Carreira, official historical documents recount forced labor for road-building, while later oral narrations not only omit the forced participation of such labor but, in fact, maintain the road was built through a combination of volunteering and active political lobbying by the locals. Over the course of the three decades since its construction, the road has transformed from something that locals disliked to being internalized and adopted by them. Similarly, Cole (1998) reports local narratives from postcolonial East Madagascar that incorporate roads, built by the colonizers, into local community history.

Moreover, there are even cases where lineal historical thinking was introduced together with the roads. João Pina-Cabral (1987) suggests, in his ethnography, that the construction of the new paved road in Alto-Minho in northwestern Portugal introduced a new perception of time, and of the concept of history, alongside the preexistent means of perceiving time. In this case, the disregard of the older paths in favor of the new surfaced roads provoked a shift in the way people perceived their own spaces and sense of time, and eventually their entire past (Pina-Cabral 1987, 732).

Highway-related narratives are not a monopoly of rural and non-Western communities. For example, Orvar Löfgren (2004) describes the emblematic relationship between road-bridge engineering and narrative imagination he recorded in reference to the bridge connecting two Scandinavian capital cities, suggesting a term which combines both: "*imagineering.*" Even within the most Western of the West, in the United States—the land of freeways that inspired Jean Baudrillard (1988)— road mythography has been generated through various mythographic means such as cinematography, music, fiction, literature, and urban legends. Thus, it is not the introduction of automobility and the unease of previously automobile-less people that triggers road mythographies. With or without automobility, human societies have generated many narratives about roads and events that take place on or around them. In fact, both ancient Greek and biblical mythology contain motifs that display striking similarities to contemporary highway mythography. For example, two main "heroes" of ancient Greek mythology had decisive encounters with their enemies and destiny on the roads. Hercules had to decide how he would use his vast physical power on the junction between the path of vice and the path of virtue. As for Theseus, when he took the road from Troezin to Athens to find his father and become king, it seems that the only things he met on the side of the road were three horrific malefactors, who tested his intelligence and fighting skills. Moreover, the motif of danger on the inland traffic systems is followed up in the story of the Sphinx, who lay in ambush on the road to Thebes; if passersby did not know the answer to her riddle she strangled them (Morford and Lenardon 2006). Biblical mythology includes another motif of the road, that of mystery. The now popular urban folklore motif of the vanishing hitchhiker can be found in the New Testament where an Ethiopian chamberlain picked up the "hitch-hiker" apostle Philip in his chariot. After baptizing the Ethiopian, Philip disappeared (New Testament, Acts of the Apostles 8:26–39). The contemporary "urban legend" tells of a driver picking up a hitchhiker who vanishes from the car mysteriously; in some versions of the story, the driver later finds out that the hitchhiker was someone who had died years ago (Brunvand 1981, 1999).

Some of the most iconic modern road narratives are characterized in US fiction, both cinematic and printed. The diversity of these narra-tives is again evident: some of them are stories of beatnik or middle-class fascination with automobility, while others are the sad stories of the abandoned social landscapes left behind after the construction of the so-called Dwight D. Eisenhower National System of Interstate and Defense Highways in the 1950s. This massive infrastructural project was spurred on by the cold war, the logic being that in the case of a Soviet attack the cities would have to be evacuated quickly. The cities were partly evacuated, but this was articulated as a new social and economic trend among the higher classes, toward the suburbs, around highways. Hence new semi-urban districts were built around new roads.[3] This new road system left behind a great portion of semi-abandoned old road network and the neglected landscape that went with it. The old road landscape underwent a radical transformation and a new category of decrepit, almost uninhabited wasteland was created around the old road network. That landscape became the location where most of the post-WWII road fiction was set (see Olsen 2004; Polster and Patton 1997). One of the most characteristic road ethnographies: "A Space on the Side of the Road" (Stewart 1996) discusses the places and the people in the United States that have been left behind by the new road network.

In his text "The Forms of Time and Chronotope in the Novel," from *Dialogic Imagination*, Mikhail Bakhtin (2010, 98, 243–6) argues that the theme of the road is one of the most prevalent in European novels.[4] The road is the perfect place for random encounters. It is the chrono-tope on which social and economic distinctions are eliminated; it is a hybrid place where people and creatures of all types, who normally live in *social distance*, may come into direct contact with unpredicted results. The road is the space where events are governed by chance and fluidity (Bakhtin 1981, 243–6). Most importantly, Bakhtin explains how in European fictional narratives the road becomes the definitive chronotope where time melts and becomes one with space. This is very much the case for the stories told of and along the Kakavijë–Gjirokastër road. The historical temporality melts into the limited spatiality of the 29-kilometer-long highway. It becomes the chronotope where the twenty-five postsocialist years merge with the collective memory and experiences of four decades of socialism and are expressed via three kinds of narrative schemes: car accidents, the war of 1997, and criminal activity along the road.

Despite all its drawbacks and shortages, the majority of Albanians I spoke to over the period of research for this book expressed a somewhat paradoxical nostalgia for socialism. Although Albanian socialism changed its character many times in its brief history, from Yugoslav-friendly to Stalinist, to Maoist, and eventually to Hoxhist, daily life is generally described as having been relatively stable. For the most part, people agree that for the majority of the socialist period they encountered known systems of reference that had explicit principles. If nothing else, the construction of public works by the people themselves cemented certain forms of relationships and expressed the presence of the state. The frenetic pace of life introduced with automobility and the use of the cross-border highway, together with the journey abroad and so on, implied, among other things, the arrival of the car crash, and by extension, risk, the unexpected and instability (Beck 1992; Douglas 2003). Thus, the introduction of this new technology implied the intro-duction of car accidents, similar to the original Virilian accident, where the invention of each new technology, is synonymous to the invention of its failure (Virilio 2007). Similarly, the introduction of a capitalist market-centered economy implied the sudden and unexpected financial collapse of 1997 and, more widely, the threat of crises. Moreover, the introduction of private property, profit, and neoliberal statecraft was closely linked to the rise of organized crime and violence. Together, these phenomena became the main characteristics of the postsocialist condi-tion and simultaneously the main motifs in the narration of the road in postsocialist Gjirokastër.

Notes

1 Again the road flows from Greece to Albania and its name runs from the South to the North—an issue I will analyze extensively in the following pages.

2 For example, Niger (Masquelier 1992, 2002), Scandinavia (Löfgren 2004), the Highlands of Papua New Guinea (Hayano 1990; O'Hanlon and Frankland 2003; Stewart and Strathern 1999), Peru (Harvey 2005), Portugal (Pina-Cabral 1987), or Spain (Roseman 1996), Bosnia-Herzegovina (Coles 2002), Madagascar (Cole 1998; Thomas 2002), the Central African Republic (Giles-Vernick 1996), Laos (Trankell 1993), or Palestine (Selwyn 2001). I would also include Merriman (2007) in this list, although he is not an anthropologist.

3 This was the most expensive road network ever constructed and the largest public works scheme ever completed; beginning in the 1950s and finishing in the 1990s. It comprised 41,000 miles of new surfaced road infrastructure, traversing the United States and passing through the major urban centers (MacNichol 2005; see also Weingroft 2006).

4 The word chronotope, coined by Bakhtin, is a literary theoretic one. It is defined as how configurations of time and space are represented in language and discourse.

6

The road of/on transition

The myth is certainly related to given facts, but not as a representation of them. The relationship is of a dialectic kind, and the institutions described in the myths can be the very opposite of the real institutions ... this conception of the relation of the myth to reality no doubt limits the use of the former as a documentary source. But it opens the way for other possibilities; for, in abandoning the 'search for a constantly accurate picture of ethnographic reality in the myth, we gain, on occasions, a means of reaching unconscious categories. (Levi-Strauss 1976, 172, 173)

Two more road stories

Two road myths provide perhaps the greatest insights into postsocialist, transnational, everyday life in Gjirokastër. One is a tale of loss, the other of uninvited gain. These are the stories about what flows into and out of Albania to and from Greece via the Kakavijë–Gjirokastër highway. I intend to recount the mythology, and to seek its associations with the broader materiality of the highway and the sociopolitical system of reference within which it is embedded (including the highway's role within the mythology). I claim that these two myths are part of the same process, expressing three major sociopolitical phenomena: (1) a new form of Balkan nationalism; (2) a Balkan version of neoliberal globalization from above; and (3) the everyday migratory life which is accompanied by transnationalism from below. The last of these will be elaborated upon in the following chapter, where I examine the case of the houses that migrants build in Albania, although they do not reside there.

The outflow of Albanian wealth to Greece

As previously explained, the violence in 1997 was triggered by the pyramid investment schemes scandal and the broad disappointment with Sali Berisha's regime. The majority of Albanians had invested their money in these pseudo-banks and most of them lost their savings. For most Albanians, it was a tragic experience; some of them sold their recently gained real estate in order to "wager" the cash in the pyramid schemes, while others "played" their migratory remittances. Following this loss, they also faced the fear of civil war. Today, almost twenty years on, it is still extremely commonplace to hear discussions about "1997" and the pyramid crisis in Albania. It has left an indelible mark on the collective identifications of Albanians. The greatest mystery related to this so-called war of 1997 is what happened to the $2 billion that vanished (Pettifer and Vickers 2006, 5).

One of the most popular stories explaining the fate of the lost money claims that the money "escaped" to Greece along the highway in question. The various versions of this story all situate the action along the 29-kilometer section of the national road between Gjirokastër and the border checkpoint (Kakavijë). Marenglen, a "*puro*" Gjirokastrit, told me the most common version of this story:

> A friend of mine, who works down in the petrol station next to Kakavijë ... and others also saw it ... the friend told me that in December 1996, one Christmas Eve late at night, a long convoy of armored lorries, with army, masked police, and helicopters, without lights on, came and passed quickly through Kakavijë and were not searched by anybody, by anybody! And so then, what were they? What did they have in these vehicles? Why did they pass in the night? Why without lights? You study Albania; tell me! What is your opinion? Was it the money from the pyramid, which went to Greece, or not?

The incoming of national danger from Greece

It is also widely believed that the highway was not only used in order to carry away the stolen money but that it also facilitated the inflow of what one could call national dangers. There are numerous stories which refer to the (imagined or perhaps real) activities of the Greek state's intelligence service KIP (ΚΥΠ).

One version of a story narrated by a talented storyteller went as follows:

> BERDI: In 1994, in 1995, and in 1996 the bodies of dead Albanians arrived in Kakavijë nonstop. Perhaps, if you will go and open the documents you will find ten dead people per day, but where is the truth behind it? What was happening there?
>
> ME: Who killed them?
>
> BERDI: They were dying! I do not know ... in the building sites where they worked they were falling from the scaffolding and that kind of thing ... One day the most superior customs officer wondered: why are these coffins sealed? What do they have inside? He sent a letter to the president saying "Mr. President so and so, I have worked

here many years and have done other kind of things ..." In the end
he wrote "I observed this and that, and I want to open a coffin." In
the first letter the president said "no," in the second again "no." In
the third letter the president did as he was legally bound to and let
the officer open one. And he took a hammer and opened one coffin
... and what it was in there? What did they find? It is me who will
tell you! They only opened one but if they would have opened a
hundred, in my opinion, 90 percent would be like this. Inside there
were crosses, books, and many other ancient things of that kind.
That was so the Greeks could tell us in a hundred or two hundred
years' time that Greece was big, as far as here, and this kind of
thing. The wood and the human beings will disappear but the
archaeologists will find these things and the Greeks will say "this
was a Greek place." I tell you the truth, are you getting the trick?

Perhaps these two stories about incoming national dangers and outflows
of Albanian wealth are based on facts, perhaps not; the point of this
ethnography is not the "truth behind the myths" but the fact that these
stories exist, narrated and reproduced for future generations. They are
used as exegeses of current political and social conditions. These two
stories do not locate their action on the Kakavijë–Gjirokastër highway
without reason. There is an internal logic in them: they tell us a number
of things about the highway and its links with the sociopolitical situation and the economics of postsocialism within which it is embedded. As
such, this section of highway incorporates the three major characteristics of the daily experience of postsocialism in Gjirokastër and the fears
associated with it, namely: a "revival" of nationalism; the transition to a
market economy in the age of globalization; and migration. All of these
phenomena simultaneously imply the contradictory elements of loss and
gain, both uninvited and invited; they imply the simultaneous loss and
gain of the present age. Prior to considering these three issues, however,
I will now provide some information on the everyday experience and
materiality of the Kakavijë–Gjirokastër highway as it is today.

The inflowing materiality of the "Kakavijë–Gjirokastër" highway

The Kakavijë–Gjirokastër road has a "phenomenological" limit,
as emerges through local practice; it is considered to end where the
"Albanian" part of the highway network begins. In practice, the division
between the Greek road system extending to Gjirokastër and what lies
thereafter is a much more explicit one than the border itself. In February
2006, for example, Fredi and I were bringing a door (the fourth such
door during my fieldwork) from Athens, where he has lived for the last
fifteen years, to his village in North Albania, where he was "making" his

four-story house. We began the trip around ten o'clock at night. Almost eight hours later, we crossed the Kakavijë border checkpoint with the door secured to the roof of the car. My friend bribed the Albanian customs officers to avoid taxation for the new door. The policeman who was responsible for the metal barrier asked for 200 lek, the usual "fee" for Albanians (foreigners are exempt from this unofficial fee). We then crossed under the half-open rusty barrier and entered Albania.

Twenty-nine kilometers past the border, immediately after Gjirokastër, the car started to rock due to the poor road surface; he slowed down and parked on the right-hand side of the national road. "Mitso … [a common Greek alternative for Dimitris], let's just sleep a little, for half an hour, before going on, because we have road in front of us [a long way to go]." Soon I realized that twenty meters in front of the parked car there was a metal plaque with the EU flag on it; I left the car to take a closer look. It was a public works announcement for the repair of the highway section between Gjirokastër and Tepelena, the town a few kilometers to the north. I realized that the only long break, the only break for a nap during the fifteen-hour trip, came at the very end of the repaired and recently surfaced Kakavijë–Gjirokastër highway section, the location where the events of the local myths take place. After this highway section, the Albanian highway system proper begins. It is characterized by old, poor-quality roads. The difficulty in negotiating the poor roads stands in stark contrast to the ease of negotiating the border checkpoint, and thus it is natural that a rest is needed here rather than at the border or other points along the journey. My friend, who has been carrying the building materials for his house from Greece to Albania for seven years, possesses a personal cartography of his route; this map contains a limit at the end of the road section linking Gjirokastër with the border. He is not the only one: I often saw other drivers taking breaks in precisely the same place—in front of the metal plaque. This is an unofficial rest place; there are no roadside facilities, such as parking spaces, a canteen, petrol station, or anything similar. Thus, this 29-kilometer section of the highway where the afore-said stories are set is a distinctive feature in the mental cartographies of Albanian returnees who use this busy route.

The practice of taking a break at this particular point and the claim that this good Greek road constitutes a Greek inflow into Albania has a very material dimension. During my fieldwork in 2005–6, the 29 kilometers of the highway between the Greek border and Gjirokastër (which ended where my friend had a rest) was a distinct material entity in comparison to the surrounding Albanian highway network. Indeed, it was the material expansion of the Greek highway system right up to the city of Gjirokastër, explicitly inflowing from Greece to Albania. Materially, these 29 kilometers represent a Greek surfacing of Albanian territory.

Over the period of research for this book, the surface of the highway changed dramatically after the twenty-ninth kilometer: it had breaks and rough-and-ready repairs. The four-lane highway was transformed into a road one and a half lanes wide. Furthermore, while the inflowing "Greek" road was elevated and treeless, the old socialist Albanian section was at ground level, passing by picturesque streams and lined on both sides by trees.

The materiality of the surface was not accidental. In early September 1997, as soon as the situation in Albania had stabilized and the new regime of Fatos Nano had been established—a regime more willing to collaborate with the Greek side—a Greek governmental delegation went to Tirana and arranged the Kakavijë–Gjirokastër project to promote Greek private construction companies. The Kakavijë–Gjirokastër highway was designed and constructed between 1997 and 2001 by Greek firms using "Greek" techniques. The engineering surveys, blueprints, all came from Greece. The diverse construction materials used in building the road provide a good example of this inflow as they were exclusively imported via or from Greece and are the same materials which are used for roads in the neighboring country: for instance, the expansion joints, named "Algaflex T-160," which were used for the Kakavijë–Gjirokastër road, were imported from Italy by an Athens-based company called "ELEMKA S.A." Since 1996, ELEMKA has been part of "Mytilinaios S.A.," which was one of the largest public works construction firms in Greece. A Greek contractor named "ETEP-METON S.A.," under the surveying and engineering supervision of another Greek company named "DOMOS S.A.," installed these expansion joints. In the same year, 2001, ELEMKA provided the expansion joints for at least thirty-six Greek highway construction projects. This means that most of the highways under construction in Greece—at that time—used the same expansion joints as those used on the Kakavijë–Gjirokastër highway.

Another example is the engineering survey and design of the Kakavijë–Gjirokastër highway. A Greek company named "Aronis–Drettas–Karlaftis Consulting Engineers S.A.," based in Athens since the 1960s, conducted the entire technical survey, studies, and design between 1997 and 2000. This project, titled the "Road Link of Kakavia–Girokastra," was financed by the Greek state as a gift to the Albanian government. The project involved topographic surveys; a detailed design of the road alignment; geotechnical and geological studies; hydraulic and drainage studies; a design for the widening and repair of the existing road; the design of slip roads and crossings for housing compounds; the design for connecting the Kakavijë customs office to the road; a study on adjusting the Drinos River bank; detailed studies of the structures; a study for the repair of the existing road by covering and linking it to the new layer; and the preparation of tender documents. In other words, the entire roadwork project was designed in Athens. At the same time, between 1997 and 2000, the same firm also designed two dozen similar road projects which were located in Greece.

It is important to note that both construction companies titled their separate road projects "Kakavijë–Gjirokastër"; in other words, they considered the project as beginning from the border and going toward the interior, despite the fact that Gjirokastër is the capital of the prefecture and Kakavijë is no more than a tiny village. It is also interesting to note that ELEMKA S.A. includes "The Repair and Reconstruction of the North–South Corridor Road Kakavia–Gjirokastër" in its *Greek* projects report and not in the list of its international projects. It is not only Greek contractors who perceive this section of road as extending from Greece. Albanians also believe the road is an inflow from Greece, as is evident from local discourses. In terms of road mythography, the road is perceived as a Greek intervention, or more precisely as the vehicle that brings national dangers from Greece.

Nationalism

National dangers and underground
The story of the postsocialist construction and usage of Kakavijë–Gjirokastër makes further sense when examined in the context of the revival of nationalism in the region where this road runs. It is not an exaggeration to say that WWII between Albania and Greece only came to a complete end in 1987. In that year, the state of belligerence ended and both governments formally recognized the border between the two countries. The checkpoint (Kakavijë) had already been open since 1985, but successive Greek governments had refused to sign documents formally ending WWII and recognizing South Albania as part of Albania. Both the Greek and Albanian states had claimed these territories since 1913, including a claim over the s plateau where the Kakavijë–Gjirokastër road runs today. In fact, this road runs over the nationally charged territory of North Epirus or South Albania, a land which causes a great deal of turbulence in contemporary Balkan relations. In the 1990s, after the end of socialism, several violent incidents took place in this region; though these did not escalate to a dangerous degree, they nonetheless indicate the potential dangers of nationalism.

In Albania, the organizations which emerged from local partisan groups after WWII were named Democratic Fronts. The Gjirokastër Democratic Front (GDF) had a significant level of Greek participation as most of the Greek minority were active in the resistance and had Communist Party affiliations. In 1991, "Omonoia," the party of the ethnic Greek minority, which became the third largest party in Albania after the first national elections, emerged from this Democratic Front. In 1993 and 1994, however, severe violence broke out. Greek minority activists claimed they were being subjected to police oppression, while the Albanian state claimed that several Greek minority activists were seeking regional autonomy, as was the case with the Albanians of Kosovo. The most serious incident involved the deportation of the Greek archbishop of Gjirokastër, which was followed by the deportation of the Greek consul and an invasion, by uniformed men, of the Gjirokastër-region barracks next to the border. This invasion resulted in the deaths of some of the Albanian militants and their weaponry being looted. The next day, a statement about the incident was sent to the Greek press signed by the Front for the Liberation of North Epirus (MABH=MAVI). The Albanian government arrested several Greek minority politicians and jailed them for the incident, while Greek nationalist ministers (including Stelios Papathemelis) and the Albanian president Sali Berisha, a nationalist himself, even began to discuss the possibility of war. The situation reached its apogee when approximately 60,000 Albanian migrants who were living in Greece without the relevant documents were violently deported from the country. This was a simple task for the Greek government to do, as the migration law of 1991 did not include a green-card policy that would enable them to stay in the country legally, and thus, even if the Albanian migrants wanted to hold legal documents, such documents did not exist. On the other side, the Albanian authorities stepped-up the violence and pressure against Greek minority villages and Greek activists, and an increasing number of Greeks were fired from their jobs in the Albanian public sector. Since this time, every year there have been a number of reports about breaches of minority rights in the region of Gjirokastër. In addition, there are also a significant number of Greek politicians in the area who talk openly about the liberation or autonomy of North Epirus (South Albania).

The dual and contradictory history of the over-ground territory of South Albania has an underground dimension, expressed clearly in the story of Greek spies hiding ancient Greek artifacts in the coffins of dead Albanian migrants to fool the archaeologists of the future. Today, the nationalist conflict on the surface is linked to what is buried beneath the surface of the ground. The following event illustrates this association and provides us with some striking similarities with Catherine Verdery's argument in the *Political Lives of Dead Bodies* (1999). During my field-work, in early June 2006, I was placed in a difficult position when several people asked for my opinion about a great "anthropological" conflict that had emerged regarding the activities of a local Greek priest in the village of Kosinë of the Përmet district in the Gjirokastër prefecture. The Greek priest involved, Vassil Thomollari, claimed that some of the tombs in the cemetery of his church belonged to Greek soldiers who had died there during battles with the Italian army in WWII. As a result, with the permission and collaboration of some relatives of the deceased, he ordered the remains to be exhumed[1] and reburied together under a newly erected monument for Greek soldiers. The Albanian Muslims of the village claimed that most of these bones belonged to their own ancestors and not to Greek soldiers. The argument grew, with some people claiming that the Greek army had never gone there and others simply claiming that the poorly maintained cemetery contained both the remains of Greek soldiers and local civilians. The tensions generated in the local communities and the discussions regarding typical "Greek" or "Albanian" facial characteristics visible in the skulls were talking points for some time. Beyond the skulls' characteristics, however, the issue soon took on political dimensions. The local archbishop and politicians became involved; police intervened in the church where the bones were stored, and news reporters mobilized members of the Albanian government who publicly insulted the head of the Albanian Church, who was Greek. A diplomatic incident occurred; Albanian television dedicated long reports to the story, and bitter arguments were exchanged for almost a month. Even President Berisha commented on the issue. Eventually, the decision was to be made according to a DNA examination of the remains (see Koleka-Reuters June 2, 2006).[2] Although the real issue for most of the villagers and the relatives of the Greek soldiers was to discover the bones of their people, the political dimension had little to do with the actual human remains and much more to do with the land where they were buried.

This question is ever present in the everyday life of Gjirokastër, where many Greek minority members and most Albanians claim they are the rightful heirs of these territories. A further example of the underground questions directly linked with the myth of ancient and Christian artifacts hidden in the coffins is the question of the ancient city of Antigonea. Antigonea was the most important city on the s plateau section of the Roman Via Egnatia during the Classical and most of the Byzantine period (500 BC–1500 AD); it was located almost 5 kilometers to the east of contemporary Gjirokastër. Archaeological findings from

1966–71 suggest that the city's fortification dates back to at least the third century BC. The city was well known in historical and archaeological literature (e.g. Hammond 1966, 1967; Hughes 1830, 134) due to its role in the Second Macedonian War (197–200 BC) and the references to it by the Roman historian Livy (1823). The site as we know it today was discovered, excavated, and confirmed as Antigonea in the late 1960s by two Albanian archaeologists (Prendi and Budina 1970); this excavation continues today. Since Antigonea's discovery by the national Albanian archaeologists, a discussion on the actual origin of its ancient inhabitants has ensued. Despite the most common theory that Antigonea and, more generally, Epirus was part of the ancient Greek world (e.g. Borza 1992; Crew 1982; Hammond 1994), since the 1970s, Albanians and later foreign archaeologists have classified the city and other parts of Epirus as part of the Illyrian civilization (Prendi and Budina 1970).

Beyond archaeological discussion, the same themes emerge in everyday conversations in Gjirokastër today. I frequently found myself in company where the discussion focused on what the language of the inhabitants of Antigonea had been, or when exactly the Illyrians occupied Antigonea, or who had really laid the foundation stone of Antigonea, or even more anachronistically, which ethnic group had been in the majority in the Antigonea of antiquity. The aim of this discourse is of course to lay a contemporary political claim on the area based on a historical discussion of the past. Antigonea is only a small part of the argument over the historical territory, which was called Epirus, and is today shared between Albania and Greece. The nationalists of Greece and Albania both locate their claims temporally in reference to the ancient world, but spatially to the contemporary one. According to Greek nationalists, the Epirus of ancient Greece extended more or less to the areas that Greece has claimed as its own since 1913. On the other hand, according to Albanian nationalists, the sites of ancient Illyrian invasions and settlements are located up to the areas which Albanian nationalists would include in the so-called Great Albania (see Kola 2003).

Folk studies and archaeological institutes were introduced in both countries which were oriented toward proving the respective ethnic groups' historical presence on the territories where their nation-states are located (Kyriakidou-Nestoros 2001; Vickers 1999, 1). They also aimed to ground their national claims to territories of their neighboring nation-states. Thus, they created clear-cut historical schemes constructing contemporary Albanians as directly linked with Illyrians (see Kola 2003; Schwandner-Sievers and Fischer 2002) and contemporary Greeks as directly linked with ancient Greeks (see Herzfeld 1982,

1987). Today, such archaeological discussions are much more relevant in everyday social life than one would expect. In the case of my research, most of the Greek minority populations in South Albania declare that they are the direct descendants of ancient Greek Epirots, considering themselves the original inhabitants of the area. Regarding their Albanian neighbors, they believe that the Albanians who live in Gjirokastër today came south during the Ottoman period and are an ethnic mixture of Turks, Greeks, Albanians, and Gypsies, or that they were Greeks who were Islamized and Albanized during the "Turkocracy." Conversely, most Albanians in the region consider themselves the direct descendants of the Illyrians, and argue that everyone in ancient Epirus was Illyrian. They postulate that the Greeks came to the area as workers on the agricultural land of Albanian Beys (leaders) during the Ottoman period or that they are Albanians who were Hellenized by the Greek Orthodox Church. In other words, both opposing groups consider the other a newcomer who has fewer rights over the land they inhabit.

Both Greek and Albanian nationalists search for elements to assist their claims to the territories of South Albania and maintain that many of these elements lie underground. Within this atmosphere of nationalism, disputed territory, dual history, and minor everyday "wars" lies the related road myth of the inflow of national dangers, in the form of ancient Greek artifacts, via the Kakavijë–Gjirokastër highway. Under socialism, the Kakavijë–Gjirokastër road led nowhere: the last few kilometers leading to the border were unsurfaced and there were obstacles preventing access to the borders. In the postsocialist period, the opening of the highway came together with the revival of nationalism among those who lived near or along it. Both the "opening" of the highway and its later repair became parts of the nationalist conflict, but they also had an impact on these people's everyday lives. In *The Production of Space* (1991 [1974]), Henri Lefebvre viewed highways as the emblematic element of dominance over a landscape. It is therefore not an exaggeration to consider the Kakavijë–Gjirokastër highway a dominant element over the landscape of Gjirokastër but with implications and attributions of Greekness. That is to say, it is a Greek road on land that was awarded to Albania but which still causes disputes between the two countries.

In fact, the Kakavijë–Gjirokastër road is situated in a region which, by its very nature, is ethnically mixed. Moreover, after 1990, this road section, which was already a central point of reference for the local communities, also became a central part of and major influence on the newly emerging nationalism. For instance, it is frequently considered a highway built by Greeks for Greeks. This "new nice road" (as a man from Dervitsani village described it) is built in an area where one of the largest concentrations of Greek minority citizens in Albania resides and it ends precisely where the purely Albanian settlements start. Deliberately or otherwise, the exclusion of Albanian-speaking settlements led to the formation of a "Greek road," a fact that local people are acutely aware of. Many Greek minority members refer to this 29-kilometer section as "our road." When I asked for clarification, both the fact that this road runs next to "their" villages and that Greek firms and the Greek state have built it were put forth. Another man, Enver, an Albanian Muslim from the city (who was convinced for a while that I was a Greek spy), explained:

> Here in Gjirokastër, Greece is in command, look at the consulate, it is above our heads [referring to the position of the building high above the square where we were having our coffee] look, they only brought the asphalt up as far as the consulate yard, after that they left it as it was.

Enver was referring to the cobbled street that begins a few meters after the asphalt-surfaced road. Although this asphalt-surfaced road linking the consulate with the Kakavijë–Gjirokastër highway was repaired during a different period and by the municipality, not the central state

25 Road signs entering the cross-border highway from a Greek minority village, signs in Greek have been covered with paint.

(unlike the highway), the asphalt surface gives a sense of continuity from the highway up to the Greek consulate, further expanding its perception as a "Greek road."

One major phenomenon that emerged in the postsocialist period was the nationalist tension in Gjirokastër. Today, nationalism is also located explicitly on the road. Along the highway between Gjirokastër and Kakavijë, for example, the road signs are bilingual, in both Albanian and Greek (for the sake of the Greek minority), but the Greek language has been painted over with black paint.

This covering of the Greek signs with black is a symbolic response to the covering of Albanian territory with black Greek asphalt.[3] Given the sealant properties of asphalt, the Greek surfacing material seals and steals a strip of 29 kilometers of Albanian territory. In addition to the signs, some of the petrol stations or *lavazho* (car wash) stores located along the last few kilometers of the Kakavijë–Gjirokastër road

26 The cobbled street of Pazari meets the asphalt. The Kakavijë–Gjirokastër highway blueprints, from the webpage of the private Greek public works consultants ADK Engineers SA.

section, owned by Albanians, fly the Albanian or even the Turkish flag. Following discussions with some of the *lavazho* owners, one of them explained that he had a Turkish flag because when Greece wanted to occupy Gjirokastër in 1997, Turkey was the only country that protected Albania. Moreover, very visibly, several of these *lavazho* are "stealing" some centimeters (or more) from the highway's edge, expanding their cement-surfaced yards over the road surface. In light of the aforesaid discussion, they are not hijacking Albanian but in fact "Greek" public property, in retaliation for the "Albanian" space which had previously been hijacked from them. The expansion of the yards over the highway follows the same logic as the painting over of the road signs; it is an Albanian covering of the Greek covering of a disputed territory.

The transition to capitalism

A further reason this particular road section is considered Greek is that it is financed by or via the Greek government; yet this fragment of Greekness is supplemented through the new economic principles of the market economy. From above, it is considered part of a larger project for embedding neoliberal market principles, but from below it is theorized within discourses such as the inflow/outflow myths. In addition to a newly formed expression of old nationalism, these stories also consti-tute a local expression of anxiety and an effort to come to terms with the ethos of the new market as represented by the new method of road construction, which is so radically opposed to that employed during the socialist period. For decades, Albanian society was socialized within a system that constantly criticized the market economy. Today, however, following rapid reforms to introduce a capitalist economy, ordinary people's experience involves both the anxiety associated with such enormous change and the practices they use to cope with it. This phenomenon has already been observed in other postsocialist societies (Humphrey and Mandel 2002); here I will elaborate on the Albanian case in reference to the specific cross-border highway.

In October 1997, ATA reported:

> A routine Greek–Albanian commission, which monitors the PHARE and INTERREG programs, decided late on Friday in Athens to award 10 million ECUs to Albania for 1997–1998. Some 7.2 million ECU will be used to rehabilitate the Kakavija–Gjirokastra road, 2.4 million ECU to construct new border checkpoints in Konispol and Tre Urat, and 0.4 million to administer these projects. (ATA 1997e)

In total, according to an EC report titled 'EU Interventions in the Trans-port Sector between 1994 and 2001', the EU provided €13 million for two projects on the Kakavijë–Gjirokastër road (ADE 2004, Annex 3, 23).

The main sponsors of infrastructure in Albania are international organizations, supranational authorities, and banks. Together they provide Albanian governments with financial aid and loans. Road construction projects have been variously financed by organizations and agencies such as the European Commission, the European Investment Bank, the World Bank, the Italian, Swedish, and Dutch states, the Kuwaiti Fund for Arab Economic Development, the EBRD, the Islamic Development Bank and so on (ADE 2004, Annex 3). Between 1995 and 2001, the European Commission allocated more than $133 million for traffic projects in Albania. A major part was from the PHARE program.[4] From 1992 to 1999, among a total of eleven PHARE projects in Albania, the largest one (€63.3 million) was for the infrastructure program (transport, energy, and telecommunications). Additionally, within the PHARE framework an extra €104 million was dedicated to the PHARE cross-border cooperation program, which among other things provided for the repair of cross-border roads and border checkpoints (PHARE 1999). Following the completion of PHARE, the INTERREG program (2001–6) part of the "INTERREG III A–Greece–Albania Neighborhood Program" offered more than €64 million to improve transport infrastructure around the border.

As well as PHARE and INTERREG aid, the EBRD has given Albanian governments more than €90 million in loans for road construction and rehabilitation. In addition, according to press releases, the World Bank offered a $25 million loan in June 2008 for a new road reconstruction project (World Bank 2008) and in February 2007 it offered a further $20 million (World Bank 2007).

The motivation behind providing such a large amount of money for road projects is to instill new principles and a new ethos into Albanian politics and society. Loans and aid are not unconditional; on the contrary, they must be seen within the framework of general intervention and international dependency. In the 1930s, the Italian fascist government built highways in Albania in order to use them during the war, while the socialist regime built roads for the sake of its own economic and ideological aims. Just as every previous political entity tried to establish power over Albanian society through the development and maintenance of roads, a new power game is taking place via the construction of roads today. The end of the previous politico-economic regime, in combination with the new forms of "place-less powers," has transformed contemporary Albania into a fertile territory for road-aid politics. In the past, the "invisible" central socialist power used to make itself tangible via material interventions into everyday life, such as the forced construction of roads. During the socialist period, nobody complained about the roads, most likely because people were forced to work on them with their own hands, and as such they did not dare to complain about their condition or demand better infrastructure because they themselves would be called upon to build it. In addition, the road network of the socialist period was more than sufficient given the tiny number of vehicles. In this way, if nothing else, socialism was highly successful in using roads to establish state power over society.

During the first postsocialist years, Albania experienced very difficult conditions as Albanian wealth, as per the aforesaid myth, flowed abroad in the form of the migration of the most productive cohorts. The socialist state's ideological emphasis on "honored labor" (Albanian Constitution 1976) had a practical dimension: labor was probably the most productive sector of the Albanian economy. Hence migration, together with the instability of the state, shut down almost all production. The country's economy had been built for five decades on a quasi-autarky, which was, to a great extent, based on the people's labor, especially the free construction of public works. Hence the economy was almost completely paralyzed when the majority of the "work force" migrated abroad. During the 1990s, the government based its economic semi-sufficiency on international economic aid and on migrants' remittances. Simultaneously, political instability and power struggles intensified and politicians consciously overlooked their duties. As a result, the road network in the early 1990s suffered due to neglect and general poverty; in 2004, the World Bank reported that only 10 percent of Albanian roadbeds were in good condition (ADE 2004, 9).

Nonetheless, socialism had established a close link between the notions of progress, modernization, and the extended road construction; additionally, the presence of newly surfaced highways was taken for granted. These schemes still dominate the political life of Albania today, especially now that people have private cars. Under capitalism, the number of cars has increased dramatically, from no private cars in 1990 to almost 300,000 by 2007, and the labor market has replaced forced labor; hence, today, people complain about roads. Nowadays, the provision of infrastructure seems to be a significant political criterion for Albanian society. In February 2007, during the local elections, the voters' primary request and the prospective leaders' major promise was the provision of infrastructure, mainly electricity and roads. Despite these two criteria, it appears as though blackouts annoy Albanian people much less than poor road surfaces. The various Albanian authorities must now find the resources to meet the need for an extensive reconstruction of the road system without overtaxing the taxpayers who vote for them. Given that roads are now in demand and more necessary than ever before, international aid and loans have appeared like the *deus ex machina* saving the politicians from a dead end. Following the collapse of democratic republics, the new capitalist democracies, unable to follow the example of the previous regime and use free labor, need economic resources. In the case of Albania, this is collected from abroad in the form of aid and migrant remittances. The cultural logic of the market, however, implies that it is impossible for anything to be offered without some form of exchange.

First of all, as with all loans, interest must be paid, which guarantees the long-term dependency of the Albanian state on its creditors: banks, foreign governments, and suprastate authorities. This dependency became evident in 1994 when two Albanian militants were murdered (most probably by Greek nationalists): the Berisha government in Albania arrested five famous Greek minority rights activists and accused them of involvement in the assassination. They were eventually jailed by a kangaroo court, to which Greece responded by freezing several million ECU (the accounting unit used by the EU prior to Euro) in the EU's pipeline of aid to Albania (Greek Helsinki Monitor 1994). Furthermore, Greece also deported tens of thousands of undocumented Albanian migrants, causing economic hardship for their families and serious consequences for the Albanian economy, which is dependent on these international flows of money.

Although aid and remittances flow into Albania, often they also flow back out to Greece or to EU firms. For example, via the Greek government, the EU was the primary financier of the Kakavijë–Gjirokastër project: Greek companies were appointed to construct it, and thus they received the aid. Moreover, given the remarkably low levels of production in Albania, most products consumed there, especially in Gjirokastër, are imported from Greece. It is easy for Albanian business owners to gain a merchant's visa, meaning they can enter Greece for twenty-four hours in order to buy supplies for their businesses; the route they use is the Kakavijë–Gjirokastër highway. As such, the highway, both in construction and use, is the artery where money allocated to the Albanian government and Albanian society flows out to Greece. Metaphorically, this echoes the people's belief that their $2 billion flowed out to Greece in 1997.

Albania's politico-economic dependency is deepened further by the new economic measures (and new political morality) that Albanian governments must apply to secure finance. Just as, during socialist times, roads were a way to embed new socialist principles in the daily lives of Albanians, the aim of road construction in the age of the market economy is to embed the core tenets of the free market of neoliberalist principles. I will mention two indicative examples: the Council of the European Union and the European Bank for Reconstruction and Development.

On January 30, 2006, the Council of the European Union—a major sponsor of international aid, including roads—published a document titled "Council Decision on the Principles, Priorities and Conditions Contained in the European Partnership with Albania" (EUC 2006). This document provides guidelines with regard to every aspect of the Albanian government's political and financial policies (EUC 2006), including the requirement that the Albanian government should take care of the country's traffic infrastructure (EUC 2006, 6, 16, 19). The purpose of this requirement was to facilitate the "free movement of goods" within Albania and to assist the "free movement of [EU] persons and right of establishment" on its territories (EUC 2006, 6–7). "Persons," incidentally, refers to both physical and legal persons (firms). Additionally, another duty of the Albanian government is to safeguard the "free movement of capital" (EUC 2006, 6–7). Given that Albania today produces very little in comparison to the past, and its most productive economic sectors (e.g. telecommunications, Balsh petroleum, sea ports) have been privatized and placed in the hands of EU (primarily Greek and Italian) firms, the circulation of goods, persons, and capital necessarily refers in part to these firms' economic interests. Moreover, keeping in mind the generally limited productivity of the Albanian economy and the much higher percentage of imports from the EU in comparison to exports, this circulation is also related to the goods that EU-based companies sell to Albanian customers. Albanian consumers are acceptable as consumers of EU goods, but they are considered unacceptable as common EU citizens or even in their eligibility to obtain an EU visa to travel on the roads outside their country, some of which are a continuation of the roads within their country. Most of those who want visas never obtain them, and thus legally they should not use the roads along the borders of their country or cross these borders illegally via the hills or fields which surround them. In other words, the roads should help the circulation of EU products and citizens into and through Albania but not the circulation of Albanian citizens into the EU. Moreover, a great proportion of this consumption of EU products in Albania is facilitated by the migratory remittances. Hence, put simply, Albanians work for EU employers, send their money to their relatives in order for them to consume EU products, and eventually return these same remittances back to the countries from where they came. This shares striking similarities with the road myth that narrates the outflow of the Albanian wealth in 1997: first comes the outflow of the most productive cohorts of the Albanian population and secondly the outflow of their remittances to the EU, which in the case of Gjirokastër is Greece, where a third of Gjirokastrits reside. At the same time, the merchants of Gjirokastër consider the city of Ioannina their "capital," where they can easily obtain temporary merchants' visas and buy all their supplies. In Gjirokastër, the convenience store and supermarkets look identical to any supermarket in any rural Greek town. The same (Greek or imported) goods that can be found in Greece with labels in Greek are to be found on supermarket shelves in Gjirokastër, where it is also possible to purchase them with euros rather than Albanian lek.

Another criterion placed on the Albanian government by the Council of the EU—linked with the cross-border highway—is described under the section titled "Visas, Border Control, Asylum and Migration" (2006, 10). According to this section, the Albanian government is required to "focus increased financial and human resources on addressing human trafficking and illegal migration" (EUC 2006, 10); evidently, "illegal" migration implies that of Albanians into EU territories. Via this last instruction, a key political principle of Fortress Europe rhetoric is enforced on the victims of this policy: non-EU citizens. In addition, no distinction is made between human trafficking and crossing the border without documents, despite the two being completely different processes. For example, after meeting a London-based Albanian "migrant" in the summer of 2006 in Gjirokastër's cafe Fantasia, our mutual friend later explained that: "My cousin is not a very good person, he has done four fake weddings with four young girls in Albanian villages and exported them to brothels in London, one of them returned with her throat slashed for her mother to bury her. He told her father that she cheated on him and that he had divorced her and had no idea what happened to her afterwards." According to the EU, this man belongs to the same category as the Gjirokastër university students who go to Greece every summer to work in various manual jobs trying to meet their winter expenses.

Human trafficking, and other hard-core illegal activities, take place via the Kakavijë–Gjirokastër highway (with the participation of policemen and customs officers from both sides) or with legal visas, acquired through marriage to an EU citizen, as revealed by the case of the cousin and many others I witnessed and heard about. The soft-core and debatably "illegal" migration of workers largely occurs in the mountains and hills, along narrow high-altitude paths, where the border is unguarded. I had the chance to observe this "illegal" crossing of the borders in the summer of 2006 together with some men of my own age from the north of the country. Border crossing along the highway can only be achieved with the proper EU visas, and more often than not, the Kakavijë–Gjirokastër highway is the location of most major criminal activity in the area.[5] It is the route of the free market, both the legal and illegal one. By comparison, the mountainous paths of migration are used very little by smugglers, and those who do use them are small-time; the organized crime flows take place on the highway in plain view of the border guards. Perhaps the story of the escape of Albanian money down the highway is based on this knowledge. It would certainly appear that the highway allows any kind of inflow, but only limited outflows. Most of the poor and powerless of Albania, who constitute the mass of aspiring migrants, are denied the right to a visa and are excluded from using this highway. This is reflected in the road myths: everything can inflow, even the national dangers, but only a convoy of armored trucks in the night can outflow, and this outflow, in fact, is a loss, like the loss of the girl who only returned in a coffin.

The principles enforced by the EBRD, which has sponsored road construction, are another example of an authoritative mechanism behind road-building which aims to enforce a new political and economic logic in Albania. The EBRD's first priority is privatization and helping the country to move closer to a full market economy. Regarding roads, the bank states in its strategy document on Albania that,

> Supporting the rehabilitation and restructuring of the transport and energy sectors, particularly within a regional context, will remain the main focus of the Bank. Where possible, the Bank will endeavor to channel long-term finance to private public partnership schemes, subject to open and transparent tender procedures. The Bank will pay particular attention to the implementation of projects in the energy and transport sectors. The Bank will continue its policy dialogue on the privatization of utilities and will make it available to support viable privatization schemes.

The EBRD states clearly that the neoliberal privatization of the public sector and particularly of "utilities" encompasses road rehabilitation. The economic avant-garde of the former first world, the banks, ensure that these Balkan neophytes will correctly implement every aspect of the dominant political system through their new roads. It is a process similar to what Count Ciano, Mussolini's minister of foreign affairs, described in his diary during WWII. The new political powers want to make it clear to Albanian society that *they* can build these grand public works that the old regime could not. At the same time, these highways facilitate the economic and political interests of their sponsors.

In addition to neoliberal ideology, the EU is also trying to legitimize these roads ideologically by attributing a desired Europeanness

27 One of the largest Greek public works companies constructing a road in Gjirokastër.

to Albanians. This is made evident by the inclusion of many Albanian roads in the so-called Pan-European Corridors: Albania is crossed by Corridor VIII (Durres–Black Sea), which meets Corridor X (Salzburg–Thessaloniki) and Corridor IV (Berlin–Prague–Vienna–Sofia–Thessaloniki–Istanbul). Some sectors of the Albanian vehicular network are secondary to other major European corridors, such as the modern "Via Egnatia," which, through historic acrobatics, moved south to Greece, and connects the Ionian Sea to Istanbul.[6] In theory, these corridors are uniting Europe, and hence Albanians, who consider themselves the oldest people in the European continent, respond favorably to their inclusion by the EU in its trans-European common identification infrastructure projects. Despite this, ideological apparatuses aside, in everyday terms most Albanians cannot cross the boundaries of their country. Hence a specter looms over the newly constructed traffic infrastructure of Albania, best illustrated by a question a woman once posed in relation to socialist road policies but which applies even more so today, in the postsocialist period: "for whom are these new highways being built?"

Postsocialist daily road politics

During the socialist period, the building of roads was one of the key elements in the relationship between society and its roads; use of the road, in contrast, had little or no significance due to the lack of vehicles and the restrictions on mobility. Today, private cars are legal and their number is rapidly increasing. In the postsocialist period, a counter-phenomenon is gradually emerging, where the majority of Albanians are completely alienated from road production. Albanians now claim a new relationship with the road through its usage, not its construction. Socialism led society into a fragmented relationship with its roads exactly because it alienated them from road usage; however, today there are new forms of fragmented inclusions or total exclusion from road-related practices. For example, the poor in Albania do not own cars. In addition, there are many who are partially excluded from road usage. This is to say that Albanian roads are theoretically included into European networks but people cannot, for the most part, cross the borders into the EU. At least socialism allowed for the totalitarian and all-encompassing involvement of society in roads by forcing people to build them; now, several groups are being excluded completely from the highway, both as users and producers. Identification with "communist Albanianness," through the road, used to be a possibility; today, identification with "Albanian Europeanness" through the highways has in effect become a complex project of exclusions and economic asymmetry. There is, however, a category of people in Gjirokastër who do not experience the fragmented identifications and relationships surrounding road usage because they use them along their entire length and most of them are able to buy cars. This sizeable category consists of the migrants, who in fact reclaim and familiarize themselves with the roads via their practices and discourse. In other words, there is an additional dimension to all of the above, which is reflected in the aforesaid inflow/outflow myths and is linked with actual inflows/outflows from below.

In comparison to the single socialist state of the past, in the era of neoliberalism multiple and diverse powers and authorities—often with conflicting interests—are involved in road production, enforcing new orders which are then embedded within society. The multiple and sometimes conflicting interests can be demonstrated by the example of the Greek state, whose own nationalist aspirations are filtered through neoliberal globalization policies using EU money and the neoliberal aims of the EBRD. These elements are all incorporated within road production. The contradictory and complex tensions in the relationship between roads and Albanian society in the postsocialist period are partly recoded and resolved by Albanians in their everyday life, not only via a mythology articulated in terms of old nationalism and hostility but also in terms of new postsocialist sociocultural codes. Arguably, the most representative and characteristic phenomenon of postsocialism is migration, which is also associated with the road network, and particularly with the 29-kilometer Kakavijë–Gjirokastër highway because this is the largest entrance to South Albania and has shaped Gjirokastër's society as it is today. Migration should be seen within this framework of road usage, adding an extra dimension to the road, which on the one hand resolves the fluidity and tensions involved in road production while reflecting it on the other.

Albanian migration and transnationalism

Migration: outflows and inflows

Among the stories of inflows of unwanted dangers and outflows of Albanian wealth, there are some desired outflows and welcomed inflows via the Kakavijë–Gjirokastër highway. Nonetheless, contradictions exist even within these desired flows in which migration is the desired outflow and remittances and foreign goods the desired inflows. According to statistical data (Vullnetari and King 2008), at least a third of Gjirokastrits are living as migrants in Greece, yet informal everyday estimations put this figure much higher. The stories about migration reflect two positive aspects to this process: First, the right to free migration abroad, which was a long-standing and collective demand of Albanian society under socialism. Secondly, the remittances and frequent gifts from migrants to their relatives, who remain in Albania, provide salvation from poverty. Nonetheless, although they may save people from

28 Tire and oil technicians at a truck stop on the Gjirokastër–Kakavijë highway.

poverty on the microlevel, remittances and articles sent or brought from Greece are part of a relationship of uneven international dependency, as the Albanian economy has come to depend on them. Thus, the positive aspects of migration have a negative effect at a macroeconomic level for the country. As with the road myth of the outflow of the $2 billion during the 1997 events, today the outflow is the macroeconomic loss in the form of a brain-drain and loss of the most productive cohorts in Albanian society. Hence the short-term economic security provided at an individual and state level by the inflow of remittances contains within it an inflow of threat and insecurity for the people in Albania, as with the artifacts which inflow in the coffins of the dead Albanian migrants.

Migration and material culture

The collapse of Albanian state socialism is closely linked to the growth of Albanian migration, and both migration and the end of state socialism are directly associated with material culture. In most of the socialist countries, the antiregime rebellions and the violent events of the transition took place in squares, universities, on the streets, or in governmental buildings. In the case of Albania, the locations where people challenged the socialist regime were the foreign embassies. The violent transition to a multiparty state actually took place on Skenderbej Street, a barred street in Tirana where several foreign embassies were based. On May 10, 1990, among the transformations triggered by the European crisis of socialism, the national assembly of Albania authorized the issuance of passports, which had previously been restricted documents. By June, however, this decision had still not been put into effect. Although there was agitation and public disappointment, there was no particular popular reaction. Nonetheless, on July 2, 1990, a crowd of hundreds of youngsters in Tirana invaded the foreign embassies. The number of "invaders" gradually increased; the crowd tried to claim asylum "abroad," and to jump over the fences into the embassies' enclosures, to "migrate" symbolically. These rebellious and ambitious migrants clashed with policemen who tried to prevent the "outflow" (Vickers and Pettifer 1997). This form of rebellion reflected the increasing pressure to open the border and to provide passports and visas.

Before 1990, the labor of citizens was the largest and most effective means of production, and thus the regime could not allow it to migrate abroad. The elevation of this exigency to an ideology can be seen in the emphasis on "labor" within the formal discourse. For instance, in the 1950 Albanian Constitution, labor was considered a matter of honor for every able-bodied citizen. Skender, who is originally from Gjirokastër and is currently a migrant in Greece, explained:

Two things I learned well in Albania, Marxism-Leninism and to work like a dog. What kind of work would you like me to do? Everything, I can do everything, build a house, collect cotton, dig a canal, carry sacks, and I had a diploma from the institute [degree of higher education]. I will tell you and make you laugh when you see what I mean: when I came to Greece I knew only three words: Eh, ok, "Marxismos" is the same but I knew how to say "bread" and "work," you know why? Because of the minority people that I met while I was working, those were all the Greek words I learned after working with them so many times, because we were doing nothing else, just eating in order not to die, a bit of bread and work.

As well as the economic emphasis on labor, Marxist-Leninist ideology, which views migrants as a "reserve army of Labor" (Marx 1993a, 46–72), prohibited migration and simultaneously reinforced that prohibition. According to classical Marxist thinking, migration benefits bourgeois masters. The argument is simple: the surplus of imported labor migrants offer brings a balance of lower than normal wages for every proletarian within an economic system, and dramatically decreases the negotiating power proletarians have in relation to their employers. Consequently, the socialist state could not allow migration due to the ideological restrictions of Marxist-Leninist theory and because migration would have a negative effect on the economy.

Another aspect of migration was the fact that many of those opposed to the socialist regime left the country just before their defeat in 1944. Most members of their families and extended kinship group, however, stayed behind and faced the antimigratory attitude of the regime. The problem was that under the new socialist administration, inquiries were conducted into everyone who had left the country. Many people who had left Albania during or even before the war were considered to be spies, or anticommunist traitors or enemies of the people because they had not remained to fight for the liberation of the country. Hence, they lost their lands, which were usually common family property, and thus their family, who stayed behind, faced harassment and the appropriation of their property. In many cases, those who left and were blacklisted by the socialist regime had had nothing to do with the anticommunist and collaborative Albanian "National Front" (Balli Kombëtar) and were, in fact, simply continuing a long tradition of Albanian migration (Barjaba and King 2005).

Regardless of this, fear of migration was very much a characteristic feeling of the socialist period. As one of the unlucky ones left behind, a man in his fifties, told me: "We had a bad *biografia* [reputation] because we had the uncle in America, I had to try a lot to fix my *biografia* and I even managed to become a member of the party in the village, but it took a long time."

From the late 1960s onwards, this antimigratory policy was characterized by widespread propaganda against migration. Halil, who has lived in Greece since he was twenty years old, recalled the antimigratory mentality in Albania:

> Television in Albania was showing documentaries from Biafra, with children dying and pictures from occupied [Nazi] Greece with children dying from starvation, and they were saying that here is capitalism, we are the best country in the world, we should be happy to live here, in Greece they are starving, we are giving them food to eat.

Typical examples of this rhetoric can be seen in the many photographs and articles, in the various prints published by the ruling Party of Labor, and, by extension, the state. These images of queues of unhappy migrants were accompanied by captions such as: "These Migrants from Various Countries Are Looking for Work in the Capitalist West" (*Laiko Vima* June 6, 1974). In the very late socialist period, when the migration current was at its peak, headlines such as the following would appear in the party press: "Our Home is Becoming Empty, People Come Back" (*Laiko Vima* January 20, 1991); "At the Kakavijë Crossing: 2309 Albanian Citizens Returned" (*Laiko Vima* January 27, 1991); and "The Tragic Fate of Albanian Migrants in Greece" (*Laiko Vima* February 17, 1991).

In 1990, the entire, once sealed, South Albanian border to Greece was transformed into a vast crossing. This Albanian exodus to the South began after the invasions of the embassies in Tirana in the summer of 1990, and peaked in the winter of the same year. The symbolic migration to the embassies, and the asylum offered by Italy and later other countries to the embassies' occupiers, made people realize it was possible to cross the prohibited border. A Gjirokastrit recalled his first encounter with migrants on the highway:

> — What did we know? Newspapers and television said nothing. But those from Tiranë knew, they had seen what was going on, they were the first to go and the next ones were the minority when they saw the first people from Tirana passing through their villages and going, they emptied entire villages in one week. One afternoon in 1990 I was waiting for the bus, and I saw two guys walking down quickly.
> — Who were they?
> — Wait, I will tell you: "Oh guys," I called [to] them, "how are you, where are you going?" They just said that they had relatives down in Goranxhi [a Greek minority village], but they were lying because I wished them "to have a good trip" in Greek, [showing] that I knew the how to say it [=the phrase in Greek], and they did not know how to answer. Later we saw many others, every day more and more, and at night you could hear them walking through. At that time the night

shootings along the border increased a lot. Slowly we [Gjirokastrits] learned it too and started going to Greece, every day more and more kids [young men] were missing from their jobs. In a while it became like [the] sea, people were walking … running. The place filled up with people walking out; thousands. In the beginning they were lying but then they were telling you, "we go out to Greece," who could stop them? They were so many.

The size of the initial Albanian migration has been recorded quantitatively. According to a report (de Zwager et al. 2005) by the International Organization of Migration's Tirana office, more than eight hundred Albanian citizens crossed the Greek–Albanian border on the night of December 30 and 31, 1990 alone. Other statistics are even more impressive: according to the Italian Ministry of Internal Affairs, more than 25,000 Albanians crossed the sea straits between the two countries in March 1991 (Meksi 1996 in de Zwager et al. 2005). Today, Albania is the most mobile society in Europe: in 2000, it was estimated that around 800,000 Albanians were migrants, in comparison to the 2.5 million living within the country (Barjaba and King 2005, 3). The 2001 Greek census estimated that more than 430,000 Albanian migrants are living in Greece. In 2004, Kosta Barjaba compared different sources and estimated that 200,000 Albanians were living in Italy and almost 600,000 in Greece. They are the largest migratory groups in both countries (Barjaba 2004a; de Zwager et al. 2005).

Albanian migrants often say that "half of Albania is in Greece," and some of the more nationalist among them sometimes add that "half of Greeks are Albanians," referring to the Albanian-speaking communities (Arvanites) who have lived in the country since the Ottoman period when the boundaries established after the foundation of the nation-state did not exist. The question, however, is not so much the quantity of migratory flows, as everyone agrees that migration from Albania is unprecedented in comparison to the country's total population, but a qualitative question: What exactly does this vast migratory flow mean for the migrants themselves, and how have they articulated their migratory experiences?

The material culture of poverty

Research on Albanian migrants has demonstrated that people articulate a discourse based on material culture (about contemporary definitions of material culture, see Tilley 2004), something encapsulated by an expression often used in the country: "In here we had nothing, out there you had everything!" The Albanian socialist regime had a very specific and restricted material culture. Albanian socialism was not only a political and economic mechanism but also, most significantly, a cultural and social organism which determined people's everyday lives and personal axes of reference for almost five decades. Under socialism, Albania pursued a policy of strict economic isolationism, which in turn led to frequent crises surrounding the scarcity of commodities such as foodstuffs, water, electricity, and petrol, particularly in the regime's final years. Petrol shortages also led to food shortages because almost the entire population had at least one type of petrol-based cooking apparatus.

Indeed, in 1990, in one of the last publications it ever issued, even the Central Committee of the Party of Labor stated that "nothing can justify the shortages of vegetables, milk, even of meat at the market of any city" (8 Nentori 1990, cited in Vickers and Pettifer 1997, 22). The main characteristic of the Albanian socialist economy was that the state controlled production and thus, in a sense, these deficiencies in the variety and availability of goods demonstrated its ability to control people's everyday life.

In addition to this, the shortages assigned a specific character to the economy of Albanian socialism. Private property, for example, was very limited; this not only applied to accommodation but also basic personal items such as clothes. Almost everything that could somehow be considered a means of production, such as the gardens of the houses where people cultivated vegetables for personal consumption, was declared state property in the late 1960s. This is reflected in a Gjirokastrit woman's words:

> The end of your house was where the water from the roof dribbled. Outside that mark was the state sector. Even inside was the state sector if your neighbor was communist, because they were eavesdropping through the walls.

The materiality of everyday life in the late socialist period was very limited for the great majority. In an interview, Halil recalled the way they created "homemade" pencils out of coal when he was a student in the late 1980s. Someone else in the same discussion added that he had had only one pair of trousers for a couple of years, and most of his schoolmates were in the same position. Yet, what is more important is not that they had only one pair of trousers but the related restrictions about the type of trousers which were considered legitimate dress. Blue jeans, for instance, were out of the question. A woman in her twenties who graduated from secondary school in the mid 1980s recalled that her uncle as a prewar migrant to the United States had sent two pairs of denim trousers to her and her sister. When she wore them for the first time, the chief of the local youth wing of the party, who was her schoolmate (and during my fieldwork in 2005–6 the mayor of the city) publicly accused her of "bringing *petite bourgeois* habits from America to Albania," adding "you behave like we have capitalism" and warning her to be more careful about what she was wearing. A teacher at her school who knew her family visited the house the next afternoon and advised her father not to allow his daughter to cause provocation and get a "bad name," yet the girl had no other pairs of trousers, only skirts. One can see the "proper" fashion for young ladies of the early 1980s in a typical photograph of female Tirana university students practicing for the Liberation Day march. All two-dozen girls are dressed in similar knee-length skirts and very similar sandals produced in only two colors—white and red (Biber 1980, 546). This conformity was a result of the concentration of the means of production. The central state Five-Year Plan of production dominated the lives of everyone. By the late 1980s, Albania was the poorest country in Europe (see Hall 1994; Vickers 1999; Vickers and Pettifer 1997).

Poverty, however, should be considered in sociocultural terms, not just economic ones, as the main problem was not that people did not have money. Rural Albania was very poor before socialism and it suffered from extreme inequalities; the majority of the population had serious economic problems and had faced worse shortages before socialism. Yet, during the socialist period, there was also an inability to perform cultural and social duties such as marriages, baptisms, or funerals properly, or to clothe the dependents of the family in a proper way (King and Vullnetari 2003). Nikolaqi, from Gjirokastër, recalled the lack of coffee when his mother passed away. Coffee is a necessary element of the correct funeral, and the lack of it was considered a great shame as it is customary to offer it to the people who visit the night before the funeral and after the funeral service:

> When mother died, in 1972, with the brothers we did not have coffee to serve to the people. Eh anyway we had a bad biography [reputation] and people were afraid to come for condolences ... but can you think of it? Not to have coffee for the funeral! We borrowed from the neighbors and the relatives. Because at the end a lot of people came, although they were afraid, they did like us. But I want to tell you: not to have coffee for the funerals, there was no shop with coffee in the whole of Gjirokastër, no coffee, can you believe it? And some coffee shops had the coffee scant, counted, they could not give it to me, they would have trouble. If I was communist, perhaps, but no coffee for the mother's funeral?

A few months later, the same person mentioned that even bread had been scarce in the village in Gjirokastër district where he grew up prior to the war:

— Our mother once per week was making loaves of bread, she was putting them high above the fireplace so we could not reach them, we were a lot of children [boys] and no girls and we were falling on the loaves when she was bringing them out of the fire, we were so hungry that we were burning our hands and throwing the hot bread from one hand to the other and afterwards they were all red, our palms.

— Did anyone ever die when you were a child, I mean from the family, any old relative?

— Oh yes, our great-grandfather and ...

— And what happened with coffee, what did you do at that time, who was selling coffee in the village?

— Ah nobody, from time to time someone was coming with the wagon, or if someone from our people went to the city he bought some. When grandfather died someone came to Gjirokastër to buy coffee, on the list [on credit].

Nikolaqi's stories show that at the level of ideology the major difference between the poverty of the presocialist and late socialist periods was that in the presocialist past people felt as if they had an absolute responsibility to fulfil their social duties. Even if they had to buy something on credit due to extreme poverty they could somehow arrange its provision in case of emergency. Under socialism, however, a state-patron who was claiming to control everyday life was charged with the responsibility of confronting these problems; its inability to make things available and provide the necessary quantities in cases of emergency was determinant for people. Albania's "prewar feudal capitalism" (as it was called by the socialist authorities) masked the relationships of inequality, blurring the actual politicosocial conditions in a very effective way. Later, the socialist state took particular care to teach Marxist and Leninist sociology systematically. Consequently, the "masses" learned about concepts such as "commodity fetishism" and "primary accumulation," and Albanians could see that during the years of the party, although there was no lack of bread, they were being exploited in a very similar way to the way they were exploited in the past, only by a very different kind of master and within a different ideological framework. Hence the poverty of socialism was a particular type of poverty due to the general sociocultural framework and the way this was perceived by the people themselves.

The principal economic strategy pursued by the Albanian regime involved entering into temporary relationships with other socialist countries (Yugoslavia, the USSR, and China). These relationships usually ended in conflict with criticism of the respective regime's revisionism and ultimately in diplomatic isolationism. This system of temporary foreign relationships is illustrated by the geographical distribution of exports and imports. For example, in 1950, 62.7 percent of total Albanian exports went to the USSR; in 1960, that percentage declined to 49.9 percent, and from the mid 1960s until 1990 Albania never again exported or imported anything to or from the USSR. In 1970, the major country of export was China (25.9 percent). From the 1970s to 1990, China was no longer a major importer of Albanian production. In fact, we see that in 1980 China imported no Albanian products at all. In 1980, Yugoslavia was the major importer (16.9 percent) together with Greece (11.5 percent), which appears as an importer for the first time in that period alongside Romania (10.5 percent). From 1980 to 1990, Czechoslovakia and Yugoslavia, Bulgaria and Romania were also importers of Albanian produce. Very similar figures dictate imports to Albania from the various countries. The major exporter to Albania until 1960 (56.3 percent) was the USSR. In 1970, the USSR disappears from importation figures, and in 1970 it seems that China (56.9 percent) replaced the USSR completely in imports. Later, after 1970, the imports are very fragmented for various countries, as is also the case for the figures on exports (*Vjetari Statistikor* 1991, 312–13, 324–5). The dogma of isolationism and the critical eye to other socialist states can be seen in the classification of these statistical figures, where Yugoslavia and China are both included in the "Developing Countries" (*Vendet ne zhvillim*).

The analysis in percentages belies the fact that the Enverist dogma was always "autarky," even in the various periods when Albania was a satellite of China or the USSR. The country produced according only to its own productive abilities: the aim was to import as little as possible, and to import only raw materials and know-how in order that the end product could be produced in Albania. In the 1970s, most of the products the country was consuming—from television and radio sets to fridges, from tractors to clothes—were made in Albania. As the regime literature states:

> Today light industry and agriculture ensure about 90 per cent of the needs of the population for foodstuffs and other mass consumer goods. The remainder is secured from imports of essential goods and these imports are completely covered by our exports. (Shkodra and Ganiu 1984, 17)

Yet, this emphasis on self-reliance resulted in a production-centric economic system, which caused shortages in everyday consumer goods. In the first instance, the scarcity of goods for individual consumption involved scarcities in variety and availability. Scarcity, in terms of quantity, mainly appeared later, in the 1980s. The political consequence of the scarcity in the availability and variety of goods was obvious: the state was controlling production and so it made its power over everyday

29 The main device used for cooking until the early 1990s was this petrol-based stove.

life tangible by providing, for example, only one kind of shoe, or one type of fabric for shirts or other clothing, one type of pasta, of bread, and so forth. In addition, these products were made available only when the plan determined. Through this method, the state was able to demonstrate its ability to control people's everyday lives while dramatically limiting the possibilities for individual self-determination that goods can provide (see Verdery 1996).

Albanian migrants and the new material culture

The poverty in Albania, in combination with the ban on migration, had become the norm of everyday life for Albanians—a rule of limitations, both in terms of goods and mobility. Eventually, these conditions were directly linked to the rebellion and transition to postsocialism. According to the discourse of migrants themselves, as emerges from their oral narrations but also from their observed practice, migration was inextricably and explicitly linked with the challenge to the material dimensions of the old regime (Mai and Schwandner-Sievers 2002, 942). Almost all migrants agree that the poverty in the country, combined with the, real or imagined, affluence abroad, led them to migrate. Miranda Vickers and James Pettifer (1997, 40, 41), who witnessed the initial outflow to North Greece, describe the wide-eyed reactions of Albanians on their first encounters with the (for them) unbelievably prosperous society abroad. In the literature where there are direct narrations from Albanian immigrants to Greece (King et al. 1998; Nitsiakos 2003) almost every interviewee frames their first experience of the country in absolutely material terms. As it was mentioned earlier, a dominant and repeated narrative feature is: "In there [Albania] we had nothing; out here [Greece] you have everything." In the same sense, another migrant recalled his first thoughts when he entered Greece: he realized how poor he had been all his life (King et al. 1998, 160, 168).

From the outset of the postsocialist flow from Albania, one of the first concerns was the dispatch of money and objects back to relatives. Automobiles full of consumables queuing at the Kakavijë border post became a familiar sight. Initially, the flow of goods and remittances, from the migrants to their families in Albania, came to replace the market and labor mechanisms, which had been paralyzed. Yet semiotically this flow of goods constituted the social network, which explains why these flows have continued and still exist today, at a time when the market functions properly at the level of consumption. In other words, the most significant transition in Albania was not the transition from socialism to capitalism but from a closed, sealed, xenophobic society to a society with open borders. The unusual geographic distance (in comparison to the pre-1990 years) led to a renegotiation of the networks that previously existed, and thus new practices of network constitution emerged via the flows of objects. The importance of familial, friendship, or community networks was not eliminated; the nexuses were simply refashioned according to the new migratory pragmatics. In addition to the practical abandonment of the socialist productive and consumption model, the flows of material goods constituted a practice of remote networking between the members of various groups. On the one hand, there was the geographic distance that suddenly emerged; on the other hand, the desire to preserve relationships beyond borders led to the transnational materialization of the social bond. That is to say, that individuals manufactured social webs immune to the distances and the governmentally-imposed boundaries of human mobility. A man in his forties confirmed this practice:

> Others stayed but me: no. Everything I had was back here in Albania. If I would not dispatch anything back, what would I have? Nothing. Human beings are like this, they need the other, Aristotle said it, not me. In Greece they do not want you, in Albania if you do not send things, you do not call, what will become [of you]? Even your mother will forget you if you go far away.

From the very first months of the flow, and given the newfound mobility, Albanian migrants returned from Greece to Albania carrying various objects for their families and houses. The nature of these objects ranged from foods that were scarce in the first years of capitalism in Albania (e.g. soft and alcoholic drinks, chocolate) to cars, cellphones, foreign clothes, and shoes, as well as household devices such as electric cookers, fridges, heaters, and furniture. Migrants frequently collected enough in Greece to buy a vehicle, which they gradually filled and used to carry all these things to Albania. In addition, it was commonplace to see migrants carrying building materials from Greece in order to renovate or build a new house. A young Albanian girl who is now living and studying in a Greek university described how,

> When my dad came for the first time to the village [back to Albania] from here [Greece] I was young but I will never forget it, very early in the morning I saw a truck full of everything you can ever imagine, coming up the hill, but I did not know that this was my dad because he did not let us know. At that time, people had started to return and everyone was back with cars stuffed with things and we thought that this was for someone else. He [my father] and someone else from the village hired the truck in Greece and they came together to Albania and the truck stopped first at the other guy's house, which was lower down the hill and we thought that everything was for them, then I went to school and the other children let me know that my father was back and had brought things, I left school and I found them ... everyone in front of the house carrying the things indoors.

Sometimes the experience of return was not a positive one:

> The first time they caught us, I did not have the time to buy anything. I was saving money, I was living in a hotel in the Larissis station [a major railway station in Athens] area with some other kids [men] and I even left some of the money in the room, because they caught us [while] waiting for the patron in the square [a typical job-seeking practice for Albanian migrants

at that time]. I was not annoyed at the beating, nor for kicking me out, I had no papers anyway, but the shame is that I did not bring anything back for the children, just like this, something, they were small and were waiting for me to return to bring something, and I brought nothing, not even a chocolate. At that time I did not know and in the *klouva* [police bus] when stopped I asked to go down for one minute to buy chocolates and the policemen laughed at me, "later, later" they told me.

Road poetics

In the case of southern Niger, Adeline Masquelier (2002, 834) rightly argues that stories about dangers and risk on roads in the global (or in our case European) periphery cannot be reduced to a simple critique of automobility, nor should they be attributed solely to the traditional behavior of "indigenous people" who have lost their previous social, political, and economic orders with the arrival of new highways in "their" territories. Instead, she suggests that these stories are creative and poetical schemes through which people perceive and make sense of the complex global economy and of daily life in the age of fast and widespread mobility, migration, and transnationalism within which highway construction projects are embedded. Poetics, however, is not confined to oral narratives. The anthropological notion of "poetics" usually includes and goes beyond the oral creativity of storytelling to include the collective nonverbal improvisation and "performance" of, for example, spaces and identities. In this sense, it refers back to the original etymology of the term poetics, namely, to the notion of creation and construction. In the Albanian case, I refer to the poetics that comprise both the narrations of the Kakavijë–Gjirokastër highway and the spatial practices on the highway that lead to the creation of local road-related history. These translate and integrate the road into the new conditions of daily life. This situation is similar to that analyzed ethnographically by Sharon Roseman in "How We Built the Road" (1996), in which Galician villagers in Spain poetically manipulate oral narratives about the building of a road in favor of the local politics of memory. In the Santiago de Carreira version of the road's history, forced labor for road-building became, in later local narrations, volunteering and active political lobbying by the villagers. After three decades, the road went from being something alien that locals disliked to being internalized in local discourse. It was claimed and adopted by the villagers, who have metaphorically and rhetorically constructed a new road, related to, but different from, the one physically built.

Overall, the politico-economic framework of the road stories, together with the narratives and the spatial poetics of its daily use, reveal how people negotiate the tensions of a complex and transitional postsocialist everyday life in reference to the Kakavijë–Gjirokastër highway. Via their practices and narratives, they go beyond the macropolitical and macro-economic implications of their road-related daily activities (migrating, returning, consuming, and remitting), and reclaim their own agency in perceiving and socially constructing the road and, more generally, the conditions of their everyday lives. These road poetics potentially resolve the contradictions of postsocialism, at least in part. Similarly, the inhabitants of the West Virginia miners' settlements that Kathleen Stewart (1996) studied and the villagers of Roseman's (1996) Santiago de Carreira, although conventionally and initially appearing peripheral and left behind by road modernization projects, reclaim, through their poetics, their centrality to their own version of road modernization. Nevertheless, as Masquelier (2002) suggests, within the road's poetics, the contradictions of neoliberal globalization remain: the same practices that give agency and dealienate the society are part of the bigger picture of an asymmetric globalization of sovereignty.

Notes

1 On the importance of exhumation in Greece, see Seremetakis's work on death in Mani, in the south of the Greek mainland (1991).
2 Reproduced online in the English edition of *Kathimerini*, June 15, 2006. See also a related article reflecting a Greek-oriented interpretation, published in *TA NEA* on July 9, 2002.
3 This inflowing materiality is visually observable in cartography. Maps of Northwest Greece and South Albania clearly show the continuation of the Greek state's national road across the border as far as Gjirokastër.
4 The EU established the PHARE (Pologne, Hongrie Assistance à la Recon-struction Economique) program in 1989 to provide financial assistance to former socialist countries. PHARE was one of the major programs of finan-cial assistance from the EU to Albania during the 1990s. From 2001, it was replaced by the CARDS (Community Assistance for Reconstruction, Development and Stabilization) program, and from 1999 onwards trans-port infrastructure projects were financed by the ISPA (Instrument for Struc-tural Pre-Accession) or other programs.
5 Between 2003 and 2006, customs officers discovered only ten stolen vehicles. In 2006, a number of Greek customs authorities were accused of corrup-tion and fired, and between mid 2006 and mid 2008 the new authorities discovered thirty-two stolen cars at the Kakavijë checkpoint. Nonetheless, a few months in Gjirokastër are enough to understand that these numbers are ridiculously low.
6 The Roman Via Egnatia linked Dyrachium (today Durrës, Albania) with Byzantium (today Istanbul), yet the contemporary Via Egnatia links Igoume-nitsa (Greece) with the Greek–Turkish border.

7

Domesticating the road

Time, as it were, fuses together with space and flows in it (forming the road); this is the source of the rich metaphorical expansion on the image of the road as a course: "the course of a life," "to set out on a new course," "the course of history" and so on; varied and multi-leveled are the ways in which road is turned into a metaphor, but its fundamental pivot is the flow of time. (Bakhtin 1981, 244)

However paradoxical it may initially sound, it is possible to claim that houses are the main inflow along the Albanian–Greek cross-border highway. Migrants themselves bring them in the form of materials from Greece. Thus, the houses of postsocialist Albania not only flow on the road but are a continuation of the materiality and ontology of the road itself.

The importance of building houses in their home country, despite not being in residence there, is well documented in the case of Albanian migrants (e.g. Dalakoglou 2009a, 2010a; King and Vullnetari 2003; Nitsiakos 2003). Houses migrants build are a frequently reported ethnographic phenomenon in other migratory countries such as Jamaica (Horst 2004; Miller 2010) and Greece (Friedl 1962; Herzfeld 1991, 41). This ethnographic chapter intends to provide an insight into this phenomenon in Albania. It begins by examining the socialist background of housebuilding, which was distinct in comparison to other socialist countries: in Albania, private houses outnumbered state-built ones, a practice which paved the way for the strong postsocialist identifications with houses. Despite the difficulties involved in housebuilding under socialism, the social emphasis on houses facilitated the transnational links between migrants and their people. These transnational links are much more important than the complications they involved, and thus people neglect the pragmatic difficulties and the related anxieties. Moreover, the complexities and anxieties involved in the house-making of Albanian migrants are the general anxieties of Albanian postsocialism and transition which are involved in all of everyday life, including road usage and perceptions.

In building these houses, Albanians familiarize and perhaps partly resolve the contradictions and controversies of what we could call postsocialism on a macroscale, something which is evident in the road-related narratives. In fact, house-making brings what we abstractly call postsocialism, transnationalism, and globalization or international dependency down to the familiar and affective sphere of home. These large-scale phenomena, which were examined earlier in reference to the roads, are condensed into the familiar sphere of domestic material culture and are reconfigured accordingly. House-making and road poetics have similar properties in providing a way for people to make sense of, familiarize with, and negotiate a fluid and dynamic everyday life.

Building houses in socialism

Following the end of WWII, Albania had undergone a transformation in the materiality of its landscape and the material culture of everyday life as a result of construction work. Highways, houses, bunkers, ports, stadiums, power plants, dams, industries, and mines are only a few examples of the large-scale projects that were undertaken by the socialist regime. Politically, this focus can be seen in the founding of a "Ministry of Constructions" in June 1955; however, this ministry was only responsible for a portion of the total projects. In all the Five-Year Plans throughout the socialist period (i.e. between 1951 and 1990), constructions and installations received the greatest amount of state investment. Over time, the Albanian socialist state spent between 34 percent and 51 percent of its total investments on "constructions and installations." According to the economic plans, the construction of roads and dwellings was the third and fourth largest state investment after industry and agriculture (*Vjetari Statistikor* 1991, 250–1). In the case of roads, however, the state had a monopoly over organizing and administering construction, while citizens had the "monopoly" over actually building them for free. On the other hand, in the case of domestic spaces, the state had only partial participation in their production, leaving a great part of the organizing and administering of the housebuilding process to the individuals themselves and even accepting some very private practices. From the 1960s, there were two main ways for a dwelling to be built in Albania: either privately or by the state. The state-built houses were either built by volunteers or by builders' cooperatives.

In absolute numbers, the dwellings built quasi-privately or, as the regime termed it, "by people themselves" (*nga vete populli*), between 1945 and 1990 account for more than 50 percent of all dwellings built at that time (266,078 out of a total 469,725). In actual fact, these houses were private projects for individuals or families, yet the regime deliberately used the charged socialist term "people" in an effort to integrate this practice into socialist terminology. Of the approximately 202,000 state-built dwellings, 78,000 were built by "volunteers" (*Vjetari Statistikor* 1991, 260). I refer to them as "quasi-private" simply because everything else involved in the housebuilding process, such as building material loans or permissions, was closely controlled by the state, making this kind of housebuilding a partially private project.

This limitation of state-built houses was related to urban–rural differences, as the great majority of dwellings built "by the people themselves" were in the countryside.[1] By contrast, in the cities, the great majority of the new, socialist period dwellings, mostly blocks of flats, were constructed by the state. Nonetheless, even the cities contained several houses built by individuals. In addition, many presocialist houses were renovated and some were divided into smaller apartments, but they were all still considered private properties. In the case of state-built dwellings, in the 1960s the Albanian government used a type of voluntary labor to construct houses that was very similar to that used for roads. These volunteer house-builders were made up of various groupings under the control of the party, such as students who had to do manual work as part of their curricula, local Democratic Fronts, or various unions (e.g. of artists or white-collar workers) who spent a few weeks per year in manual jobs. These "manual labor holidays" were their participation in so-called productive work, as people who were not workers or farmers were considered nonprime producers. The houses, however, had one important difference in comparison to the roads in that these voluntarily built dwellings included those built by the "*kontribut*" method, whereby people in need of a house could spend their afternoons working on the construction of a block of flats and, upon completion, they were able to move into one of the flats.

Although Albanian socialism applied an extended project of nationalization to almost every kind of immobile property, such as agricultural land and retail property, it did not treat housing in the same way. According to the 1946 Albanian Constitution (article 5), the economy had three sectors: (1) cooperatives (2) the state sector, and (3) the private sector. This last sector was most definitely not encouraged or favored. Thus in 1953, less than ten years after the end of the war, this had fallen to less than 16 percent and later it vanished completely (Skendi et al. 1957, 205–10), at least officially (unofficially, semi-illegal commercial activities still existed). At the same time, a similar condition characterized agricultural land, which, within ten years, came under the complete control of the state and cooperative sectors (Skendi et al. 1957). As such, many large houses owned by the "feudo-bourgeois classes" or other "enemies of the people" *were* confiscated. Some were subdivided into smaller apartments, or sold by their owners in anticipation of their seizure. Nevertheless, most houses in Albania remained, for all intents and purposes, private property. In fact, private housing was ostensibly encouraged by the socialist state, which even offered incentives for private ownership from the 1950s on, when credits from the Bank of Albania became available to help pay for the construction, refurbishment, and repair of houses (this policy changed slightly in the 1980s when the 20,000 lek loans for the construction of new houses, repayable in twenty years, were available only to rural populations) (Postoli 1983, 176–7).

The private house was one of the very few private property rights recognized in socialist Albania for both state-built and privately built houses. It seems that even in the case of those houses which were built and actually owned by the state, occupants felt a type of possession of their domestic place, not least because the monthly rent to the state as recorded in the early 1980s was no higher than one or two days' wages for an industrial worker (Schnytzer 1982, 108). At the same time, the 1976 Constitution introduced the concept of "domestic asylum," preventing any enforced house moving. Eventually, in 1992, the occupants of state-owned houses were given the right to purchase them for a nominal sum.

This situation reflected a practical necessity. In other words, although the practical conditions resulting from Albania's economic poverty led the regime to recognize both quasi-private and state-built houses, the government still favored the latter. The quasi-private dwellings were a much more common phenomenon in the rural areas: out of the 266,078 houses built "by people themselves," 251,466 were located in the Albanian countryside. Albanian socialist modernization, in the case of rural areas, concentrated on agricultural reformation, cooperatives, and road-building. Outside of this there was little intervention into the domestic sphere, especially in terms of house reconstruction as there was a lack of resources. On the other hand, city architecture was considered as controlled territory and the majority of the approximately 202,000 state-built houses were located in the cities. The cities were the emblematic spaces of Albanian socialist modernization. It was in the cities where the state built new blocks of flats, boulevards, stadiums, factories, and so on, and where it focused its material modernization project. These state-built houses, mostly blocks of flats, were favored by the regime's imagined classification, the ones which represented and imposed the new ethos. This preference is also reflected in their name, *pallat/pallate*, which means edifice. *Pallate* were the first to be linked to the infrastructure network as they themselves shared the properties of the infrastructure in that they were built voluntarily. Officially, they belonged to the state and were part of the central plan for the production of materials; they were designed, planned, and organized by the same public services and were well integrated into the new state apparatuses. Both the infrastructure and this new housing were incorporated within the concepts of modernization and new socialist ideology. As is claimed elsewhere (Buchli 1999; Humphrey 2003, 91–2), the concept of infrastructure in several socialist countries has to be seen in its Marxist conceptualization, namely as the foundation on which the entire social organization was based. Following this argument, these state-built houses were one more type of infrastructure—a very important one as they clearly defined the preference for modern core family units over the extended family ones dominant in most of Albania. Rural dwellings constructed by people themselves were not perceived by the regime as infrastructures but as individual projects.

In addition to reflecting a necessity, the house allocation process also reflected classification. In Albania, being a member of the party was not obligatory; on the contrary, it was relatively difficult to be included in the "family" of the party. It was a type of award, and various tests in communist ethics were necessary in order to become even a low-ranking member. A similar award system was involved in house allocation; the more communist someone was, the more opportunity they had to get a flat for free, whether in the countryside's few state-built houses or in the city.

The Marxist conceptualization of state-built houses as infrastructure can also be seen in the close material link between state-built houses and actual physical infrastructures (e.g. water supply, electricity). While urban households were linked relatively well with the infrastructure networks, rural households and other quasi-privately built houses in the city had only limited access to infrastructures. An example: on October 25, 1970, the last Albanian village was electrified and renamed "Agim" (Dawn) (Anonymous 1984, 164).

The regime-controlled bibliography states:

> Up to 1945 no village in Albania had electric power. To bring light to all the peasant homes was a difficult and a very costly job. Nevertheless, Albania did it, because it placed the interests, wellbeing, and happiness of the peasant above everything. The electric reticulation of the countryside was done entirely at the expense of the state. The peasants paid nothing, although they assisted in the work to carry out this project. The geographic relief of our country is very mountainous. For historical–social

reasons of the past, the houses of the villagers are built far away from one another. In some cases, the distance between them runs to kilometers. The wire used to take the light to the countryside was enough to go several times around the circumference of the earth. The electric reticulation of our villages paved the way to a profound revolution in the all around development and transformation of the countryside. Together with the electric light, radio, television, and many other household devices entered the peasant homes. (Outline of the People's Socialist Republic of Albania 1978)

This electrification project was very similar to the Soviet electrification campaign of the 1920s. Once again there was a state which was "bringing light to the villagers," which "transformed Albania," and the only request it made for "placing the wellbeing of peasants above all else" was their gratis labor in order to construct such a grand project. This was not the entire truth, however; though the related rhetoric was similar to that of the USSR's 1920s electrification campaign, the latter was mainly concerned with light—the famous "bulb of Illyich" (Buchli 1999, 52). In the 1970s, Albanian electrification "demanded," or allowed for, various other electric devices which were not made available to the owners of private houses, as they were considered less communist than the *pallate* dwellers. In April 1989, according to official statistics, which cannot be verified, for the rural population of more than two million there were 5,601 washing machines, 13,778 refrigerators, and 132,720 television sets (*Vjetari Statistikor* 1991, 35, 367). Other basic household facilities were in short supply. In the mid 1980s, a team of Albanian ethnographers (Gjergji et al. 1985) who conducted surveys in various areas of the country noticed that (although the potential of electrical supply was everywhere) plenty of households depended on an open fire or hearth for cooking and heating. Nevertheless, according to the seventh five-year plan, these open fires should have been replaced by metal, wood-burning stoves; however, in the mid 1980s, in some agricultural cooperatives only 12 percent of houses had and used these stoves; most people still relied on open fires (Gjergji et al. 1985, 11).

By contrast, the cities, where the majority of people lived in state-built houses, enjoyed a relative surplus of electric devices: according to state statistics, for a total of 1,146,500 urban dwellers in 1989 there were more than 192,518 televisions, 80,405 washing machines, and 81,462 fridges (*Vjetari Statistikor* 1990, 35). A further example of this asymmetry is illustrated by access to running water: in April 1989, less than 5 percent of rural Albanian buildings had piped water compared to 63 percent of urban buildings. In total, 53 percent of rural buildings had no water supply at all, while this figure was only 1.3 percent for urban buildings. In 1987, in the regime's English language-press, the deputy minister of the communal economy, Vladimir Meksi, claimed that: "1,100 villages are considered without water" and promised that within the forthcoming period "every village will be supplied with one tap per 60–70 inhabitants or group of 10–12 houses' (*New Albania* 1987, 13). Orjan Sjöberg (1991a, 158) claims that "by the mid-80s, 1,500 out of 2,700 villages were so supplied [with water]." Thus, although infrastructure such as electricity arrived in Albanian villages in 1970, thanks to the labor of villagers themselves, in actual fact people could not really make use of this electricity as they had very few electric devices in comparison to the urban dwellers.

This echoes the aforesaid scheme of road construction, where people were called upon to build the infrastructure of the country for free but their identification with it was deeply fragmented through their inability to make proper use of it. As such, the house emerged as the only material entity they could both build and use, and consequently people could identify themselves with their houses. As the state was not directly involved in the building of rural houses, rural Albanians gradually became completely alienated from the regime and its ideology. This alienation became more obvious during the 1970s when the state nationalized the small domestic production from gardens and the few animals that farmers owned privately. Nationalizing the garden of their own houses had a dramatic impact on people's identifications with the property they had built themselves. People who received next to nothing from the state suddenly saw the only advantage of their difficult rural life—the small production which they sometimes sold at the open-air markets in nearby cities—taken from them. By contrast, urban dwellers of state-built houses lost only a few square meters of common garden, which did not affect them economically. As urban dwellers were living in homes built by the state, they, at least, had the advantage of enjoying the fruits of their free labor as many of them had a fridge or a television in their homes and almost all had running water.

Nonetheless, in both cases, people's homes were the only place they could identify with: the villagers, overseen by the state, formed identities distinct from the state. Urban dwellers developed a relationship of belonging to their state-made houses and hence the state itself. Moreover, it must be noted that this symbolic empowerment of and identification with dwellings was further emphasized in 1997 when the pyramid pseudo-banks collapsed. During this time, the most secure (and, in some cases, only) financial investment was in real estate, and houses were first on the list.

The socialist regime's emphasis on construction was also accompanied by a huge building materials industry. One of the first priorities of industrial production was building materials such as lime, gypsum, and centrifugal poles of ferro-concrete (Papajorgji 1964, 114, 115). By 1965, Albania had over six big cement factories (Papajorgji 1964, 115). Later, a large increase was also noted in the production of bricks. Before the war, bricks had been produced in small furnaces; under socialism, these were incorporated into cooperatives. In addition to these small factories, by 1950 four new brick and tile factories were established in the country and by 1965 this had increased to eleven, in addition to the smaller portable machines (Papajorgji 1964, 115). Given this increase in the number of factories, brick production (nine million pieces in 1948) increased to twenty-three million pieces in 1950 (Skendi et al. 1957, 195–6), representing the boom in construction projects. By the end of the 1970s, Albania was producing almost every type of construction material. In 1978, Albanian economists stated:

> The setting up of new industrial projects, the development of housing, buildings for social and cultural purposes etc. have required the rapid development of the building materials industry. Thus, in 1975 the output of this industry was 185 times greater than in 1938, and had been enriched with new branches that had not existed in the past. The main offshoot of the building materials industry was that of cement and its derivatives, represented by up-to-date factories set up in Vlora, Elbasan, Fushë-Kruja, etc. The production of cement in 1975 was 64 times greater than in 1938. Linked with the production of cement is the production of cement blocks and pipes, asbestos cement sheets and pipes and prefabricated items that were now produced in large quantities. The production of bricks and tiles also increased as a result of the construction of a series of modern factories in the principal cities. Another new offshoot, that of cutting marble slabs based on the many and beautiful marbles of the country, was also added to the building materials industry. (An Outline of PSR of Albania 1978)

At the same time, other kinds of materials such as treated timber, plywood, veneer, parquet blocks and glass, wire, hydro sanitary products, or plastic paint for walls were produced in various industrial units within the country (Papajorgji 1964: 114–16).

Yet, while Albania began producing plenty of new building materials and dramatically increased the production of old ones, these materials were not easily available to the people who built houses by themselves. In the case of the villages, the local cooperative ensured the provision of the necessary building materials (Stoppel 1990, 34, cited in Sjöberg 1991a). Despite this, even in the rural periphery of Tirana, people had to

30 A block of flats in Gjirokastër. In many cases, the socialist government gave material to people who then gathered in groups to build flats. The different materials reveal different periods: white stone in the original part, red brick from Albania on the top floor, industrial brick from Greece on some of the balconies, gray concrete blocks forming extensions on the ground floor.

spend an average of sixty working days to procure the materials needed to build a private house (Sjöberg 1991a, 165). This association between building materials and state-built houses once again produced schemes very similar to those concerning the roads. Just as the political decline of Albanian socialism became evident in the materiality of the road that was washed away due to the rain, the failure of building materials and domestic material culture made the political erosion visible. Gen, who was living in a state-built house, observed:

> You could see that communism was falling, the houses were never very good ... but you could see them slowly losing more and more pieces while the state was falling slowly... . When my mother-in-law sat suddenly on a chair and it crashed, I said it, ask the wife! I said, for sure the state will fall and the next day we heard that people were going out [migrating]. I said it one day before, and we knew nothing about the other communist countries or Tirana, we heard about those later, but the thing shows: every building in Albania was falling-down slowly together with the state.

House poetics: making (incomplete) houses in postsocialism

Today, most houses in Albania have been added to, extended, and refurbished. The World Bank (2006, 47) estimates there were 237,000 urban dwelling units built before 1990 in Albania. Between 1990 and 2004, 45,000 dwellings were built with permission and at least 90,000 without permission. In addition, this figure of 90,000 illegally built dwellings refers only to the cities, not the countryside, nor the coastal zones where the building boom was remarkable. These figures only include newly built houses in urban areas in the postsocialist period. In addition to these, the ongoing renovation and reconstruction of old houses is evident at a first glance at the Albanian landscape. In this sense, Nikolaqi, who lives in Greece with his wife and their children, said to me during a trip from Gjirokastër to his wife's village in Shkodër:

> It is uncounted how many [houses] are being built now in the area. Albania is under construction, and they should put up a board at the borders: "Beware: country under construction," like [the boards] they put up for the road works.

In recent years, not only has the urban topography drastically expanded but rural areas have also changed dramatically, especially those situated near the highways. This indeed gives the impression of a country "under construction." In fact, Nikolaqi identified a very important common property of roads and houses in contemporary Albania: both are constantly under slow construction and thus both have in common what can be considered a fluid, developing and dynamic materiality.

One of the questions raised by this explosion in building concerns how many of these new houses were built by Albanian migrants as opposed to permanent residents. It is difficult to find any social practice which is not connected to migration in contemporary Albania given that, according to rough estimates, almost one-third of the pre-1990 Albanian population, or 800,000 people, have migrated to Greece and Italy alone (Barjaba and King 2005, 12–15). The same goes for house construction, not least because the majority of houses built since 1990 have been built with the assistance of migratory remittances. In 2002, according to a report by the Bank of Albania (2003), international money transfers constituted the main supply of capital to the construction sector of the economy (IMF 2003; de Zwager et al. 2005, 42). In addition, it is important to note that the sums of money sent in these remittances are very large, especially in terms of percentage of GDP. According to a report by the United Nations Development Program (2000, 43, in Mai and Schwandner-Sievers 2002, 941), remittances represent one-fifth of Albanian GDP. According to the Bank of Albania

(2004), remittances in the early 1990s were more than 20 percent of the country's GDP, and were never lower than 10 percent of GDP (de Zwager et al. 2005). As the vast majority of Albanian migrants do not remit via the official banking system, these estimates are almost certainly well below the actual amounts.

In the 1990s, following the mass migration from Albania, for many migrants their first priority, after accumulating some cash from their work abroad, was to build or repair a house in Albania. Statistically, this trend can be seen in various works such as that of the geographers Lois Labrianidis and Antigoni Lyberaki (2001, 223–4) who carried out a questionnaire-based survey among Albanian migrants in Thessaloniki (Northern Greece). Qualitative social research into Albanian migrants demonstrates this practice more vividly. For instance, in a biographical survey of Albanian migrants in Greece (Nitsiakos 2003), the great majority of interviewees refer to their aspirations for building a house in Albania (2003, 131, 169, 195, 219, 255–6, 277). Other qualitative surveys of Albanian migrants such as de Soto et al. (2002) and King and Vullnetari (2003) emphasize this relationship between the house and migration. The latter two authors state that:

> The first priority for remittances is the basic survival needs of the family and an improvement in the quality of accommodation and facilities. This involves various small projects: moving the toilet indoors; repairing windows, doors and roofs; and buying new furniture and key domestic appliances such as television sets, washing machines and, less often, small electricity generators. (King and Vullnetari 2003, 49)

There are two categories of migratory houses: those that remain empty for most of the year and those in which only one or a few members of the original household reside. Generally, many newly built houses in Albania remain uninhabited most of the time as their owners permanently live abroad.

The reader should note the regular use of the verb "make" (*bëj* or *φτιάχνω/ftiahno* or *κάνω/kano*) by the interlocutors when referring to the construction of their houses, rather than the verb "build" (*ndërtoj* or *χτίζω/htizo*). This is a point to which I will return later in this chapter as it explains why Albanian migrants build houses in a country where they do not reside. An example of the use of "make" and of the uninhabited migrants' houses is evident in the statement made by Fatos from Gjirokastër who has a newly built house in the Partizani district of the town:

> Yes, indeed for me I *make* the house. I won't sell my house! But I am not going to return ever to Albania, I was "made" [*ftiahtika*; succeeded

economically] in Greece, I will not go back to Albania to live. Albania needs fifty years to go forward, but it is not nice to have a bad house, is it? [emphasis mine]

Additionally, Nitsiakos remarked:

Of course I am always here [Greece], I do not go up there any more [Albania], if I go it is just for ten or fifteen days, twenty days, but I want to *make* my own house. (2003, 255, translations mine)

A typical example of homes inhabited by only a few members of the original household is the semi-empty block of apartments where I lived in Gjirokastër. It was a stone building from the socialist period, consisting of four apartments. Two of the four households were made up of elderly or middle-aged people whose children had migrated to Greece. My own apartment no longer had anyone from the original household living there, yet all these houses had been renovated and redecorated internally. The walls were painted and the floors retiled, old wooden surfaces were covered with new materials, while new windows and doors had been installed. New furniture was combined with the old socialist period pieces, it was reupholstered and new curtains and pillows had been added. Modern kitchens replaced those from the socialist era and bathrooms were completely refurbished, while balconies and yards were transformed into rooms.

In quantitative terms, the 2001 census (INSTAT 2004, 12) reported a total of 34,268 dwellings in the Gjirokastër prefecture, but 7,528 of them were referred to as "uninhabited" (*banesave të pabanuara*). Moreover, it is possible to claim that the actual number of uninhabited dwellings in 2001 was much higher. This irregularity can be explained by the fact that most of the buildings are under slow construction in Albania. Most of the time, the "making" of houses is perpetual. Even when houses are built relatively quickly, they still have semi-completed sections, or it is possible to attach additional rooms or extra floors. In such circumstances, some of these "houses" have a few rooms built, while the rest of the building is under construction for up to a decade or longer. Often, these two or three so-called closed rooms (*Dhomë te mbylur*; meaning completed rooms with doors and windows) are on the ground floor of a two- or three-story building. Thus, although these *"closed rooms"* form a small apartment within a potentially bigger building, they are not reported as dwellings in the census as, officially, they are still under construction. Furthermore, the census is a quantitative research tool which can miss qualitative aspects: for example, the census reports a house as "dwelled" when only one member of the original household lives there. It is therefore possible to conclude

31 A house built by migrants in Albania which has been under construction for over a decade.

that in a town of approximately 34,000 houses, at least 7,500 of them are uninhabited, with many under perpetual construction. Many commercially built apartments remain empty because there is no analogous demand. This limited demand for flats and apartments built by construction firms is due first to the extended preference of Albanians for building their own house and secondly because some firms, encouraged by the "building fever" for accommodation, mistakenly invested in blocks of flats, as they failed to discern the private nature and the personal-project character of this construction boom. Moreover, in some cases, the building has been used for money laundering, and thus nobody cares for its usage.

The anxieties of postsocialist house building

The evil eye

Building or refurbishing a house in Albania today is not a simple project; on the contrary, it is a risky practice that causes anxiety. One of the most obvious concerns is the consequence of the evil eye (*syri i keq*). Every household I researched had at least one antievil eye apparatus;

moreover, even without doing ethnographic research, antievil eye talismans on dwellings are extremely obvious, as, in order to function, they must be very visible.

The evil eye is frequently mentioned in the ethnographies of the Mediterranean (e.g. in the case of Greece, see Herzfeld 1981; Veikou 1998). One of the most common practices related to the houses under construction in South Albania is the hanging of variously sized anthropomorphic puppets above the thresholds or on the most visible corner of their front walls (these dolls have also been analyzed by Peterson-Bidoshi 2006). Alongside, or as an alternative to these dolls, people also use animal horns—which sometimes belong to animals that are ritually sacrificed in the foundations of the new house—or garlic and other objects like seashells. Furthermore, one of the most interesting antievil eye artifacts in Albania is the use of US flags and even those of the EU or UK. These are placed on the top of houses under construction. In houses owned by members of the Greek minority, these are replaced by Greek flags or flags of the 1914 independent state of Epirus. These talismans are hung on the most prominent corners of the external surface of the house in order to attract the gaze of passersby. This is done so the house itself receives fewer looks and thus has less potential to be influenced by the evil eye.

The evil eye does not merely pose a threat to the house but also to the members of the household. These antievil eye puppets are one of the most important priorities in house construction. Marenglen, who works in Greece as a construction contractor and is constantly expanding and restoring his house in Gjirokastër, explained:

> They say that I became rich and made the house, they envy you a lot if you succeed. I did not steal for this house but I worked hard. Greece is near; whoever is not lazy can go there to work and make one. But people are evil and gossipers. When I started building the house I put it [the doll] there from the foundation brick, yet I almost died twice on my way from Greece in two car crashes and I didn't bother anyone! In Greece they say "look even Albanians can become rich and make houses," here they envy you even more. People are nasty and you do not know how to protect yourself.

Although Marenglen and many others share the fear of the consequences of the evil eye, in the case of house construction the fear is not simply for the evil eye, as such, but also reflects a general situation of risk and insecurity for the conditions of postsocialist everyday life within which this current construction of houses is embedded. Although, according to several people, some antievil eye practices in Gjirokastër were applied during late socialism, their open expression took place only in the postsocialist period. Moreover, migration, remittances, the privatization of immobile property, the market economy, the provision of passports, and cross-border roads are all phenomena which combine to create what is generally called postsocialism or transition. Among other things, they created the conditions which allow people to build these houses today. As the usage of Albanian flags and Greek flags (in Greek minority villages) reminds us, postsocialism also signifies nationalism and conflicts. In addition, as the EU or US and UK flags reveal, it also implies a new type of politics, as Albania is included in a globalized world which did not exist prior to 1990. This fragmented integration of Albania within globalization also implies financial dependency, migration, loss, and, in some cases, undesired gains, as we have already seen. Integrated within this fluid system of risks and the unknown is the construction of the cross-border highways on which people carry the building materials for their houses back home, in some cases befalling accidents or encountering dangers which are in turn often blamed on the evil eye. Thus, these road accidents are inextricably linked with postsocialism. The fear of car accidents while people migrate or return is an expression of the uncertainty involved in postsocialism and migration. More generally, the use of flags to protect against the evil eye and the evil eye's impact on car crashes reminds us that postsocialism and its related phenomena are complex and not always easy to reconcile on an everyday level. Nonetheless, the construction of houses is embedded within them, and thus people cannot avoid the risks when they make their houses.

I suggest that the fears attached to the evil eye, in relation to housebuilding projects in Albania today, are an expression of the anxiety surrounding the complications of the politico-economic transition. I do not doubt the effect of the evil eye, but Albanians today, whether migrants or otherwise, do not have to protect their houses only from the evil eye but also from the many other dangers which are embedded in their daily activities. I will now discuss four further characteristic examples of the anxieties involved in contemporary housebuilding projects: property questions, global market inequalities, unstable political conditions, and corruption.

Property questions

Most of the buildings from the socialist period were built on land that was privately owned before the war. The postsocialist privatization of houses took two opposing directions: the first elections, after the decline of the one-party state (1991), were won by the Socialist Party (Partia Socialiste e Shqipërisë), the political offspring of the Albanian Party of

32 A doll talisman to protect against the evil eye.

Labor (Partia e punës e Shqipërisë). Soon after coming to power, the party issued a law (7652/1992) on the "Privatization of State Housing," which came into force in December 1992. This allowed for the privatization of properties in favor of their then occupants. Then, in 1993, under the government of the anticommunist Democratic Party (Partia Demokratike e Shqipërisë), a new series of laws came into force. Among these was the law concerning the "restitution and compensation of ex-owners" (7698/1993 amended by 8084/1996), issued in April 1993, which dictated that properties and land should be "returned" to the families who had owned them prior to WWII. Not surprisingly, this led to a great deal of confusion and conflict, which created risks and anxiety for those who were building and refurbishing houses. Due to the opposing laws and the complexities of finding rightful heirs, some owners faced the loss of their new or refurbished houses if the history of ownership was unclear.

   The case of Enver, a 76-year-old Gjirokastrit, who was in a state of constant dispute with the descendants of the prewar owner of the plot on which his house stands, is characteristic of the conflicts that may occur:

This land belonged to Geni K., but in 1957 Hoxha built this block of flats here. Geni lives next door, at that time their own house was divided into four apartments, because it was big. Later the other three families left during democracy [postsocialism], he kicked them out, and the state gave us this house here for money. Now Geni, who was not even born in 1957, comes here all the time and parks his car in front of our door, in our own yard, he parks it in someone else's yard! He tells us all of the time that he is going to go to the law-court and take the house. He does not even talk to us, this is the kind of person that he is; he doesn't even say "good morning." Well, all right, we have problems but at least we speak nicely. We have trouble and fuss all the time, as though it is our fault. We got this house with documents; we bought it with money, who will take it now? That was the system at that time, what else could we do? The state had the documents. This is how it was and this is how it is, even the courthouse won't give it to him.

Enver's two children currently live in Greece. One of their first priorities was to refurbish the house where they grew up. The house was spacious, and thus it is the house where they stay when they return to Albania for holidays with their own families. Nonetheless, someone else has claimed the plot on which it stands, creating a deep sense of insecurity for the whole family.

On the other hand, Adil, who owns a shop in the Pazari district of Gjirokastër, recalled how his family lost the house in which they were living during the socialist period and how he reclaimed it in the 1990s, which demonstrates even more vividly the possibility of people losing the houses they reside in today:

We had a three-floor house when we were a big family, then the partisans came. I remember them a little, I was small but I recall some things. They put us down on the ground floor and they brought two other families of communists from other villages. The villagers destroyed it, they did not know how to behave, and they were entering with their boots on the wooden floor. They damaged things; we heard them from downstairs, *bam-bam* with the boots in the house … When there was a democracy [after the collapse of socialism] one of them left, they bought a house somewhere else, but the others stayed. In 1993 I came from Greece [he went with the first current of 1990] and I told them that now we would appeal to the law to get out from here nicely.

Given that the two aforesaid conflicting property-related laws are linked to the two opposing political parties that monopolized the government during the postsocialist period, the political identifications of those involved have come into play. On the one hand, some former political prisoners or others who suffered under socialism due to their anticommunist views formed a powerful lobby, supported by the Democratic

Party and its 1993 law demanding compensation or the return of confiscated real estate. On the other hand, the 1992 law passed by the Socialist
Party favored the socialist period occupants, who in most cases had not
been the owners of the plots during the presocialist phase. In many
Albanian cities, such as Tirana, this situation has led to the building
of high blocks of flats. In these blocks, all of the parties involved—
the offspring of prewar plot owners, socialist period residents, and the
building contractors—have been awarded flats, resulting in a certain
level of social peace and a notable profit for private construction companies. These blocks have also led to a radical transformation of the urban
landscape of Albania since 1993–94.

In the case of Gjirokastër, however, this is a limited practice due to
its urban topographic history. Gjirokastër has three parts: the prewar
section, the socialist period part, and the postsocialist one. In this
third expansion, there are no buildings from before the war, and thus
it is relatively easy for prewar owners and construction companies to
cooperate. The situation is more complex in most of the prewar urban
section. In the 1960s, the old city of Gjirokastër was proclaimed a site of
national and architectural heritage by the socialist government; in July
2005, the prewar part of the city was awarded World Heritage status
from UNESCO. Since the 1960s, strict regulations have banned even
the smallest architectural modifications from being made to this prewar
urban environment. Under these circumstances, the local reaction to
the property question is different from that in most Albanian cities.
The ownership of the old stone buildings acquires further sociocultural
significance: in the case of Gjirokastër's Pazari, for instance, the ownership of the shops emerged as a major symbol of "*puro*" Gjirokastrits
and, for a while, was a subject of dispute between socialist period shop
employees and the heirs of prewar owners. Moreover, there are some
buildings that are claimed by dozens, if not hundreds, of heirs, and cases
such as these keep the local judges extremely busy. The World Bank
(2006) estimates that at least 45,000 urban properties are currently the
subject of legal action, while almost 50 percent of court cases in Albania
have to do with property disputes. As a judge in Gjirokastër told me,
most of the cases in the city's first-degree courthouse until today have
to do with real estate. I replied that at least he did not have to deal with
serious crimes such as murders, to which he replied that these were
easy cases for him—property cases, on the other hand, were incredibly
complex.

Global market inequalities

In addition to the complexities of property ownership, construction materials and domestic decorative items are more expensive in Albania than in migration destinations. Production is at a very low level in today's Albania when compared to the years prior to 1990, and thus most construction materials in Albania are imported and their cost is higher than in Greece or Italy (the phenomenon of importing building materials on an extensive scale is also addressed in UN ECE 2002, 24–6). As such, there is a vast unofficial importation; migrants who temporarily return fill their vehicles with sacks of cement or bricks, pipes, wires, doors, windows, even small cement mixers (to mention but a few of the things I recorded during my fieldwork). This flow of materials is also associated with the inflow of other domestic furniture and decorative items. Many people in Gjirokastër arrange for their furniture to come directly from Greece, as this is less expensive than buying it from Albanian importers in Tirana.

Despite the proximity of Greece and South Albania, importing household items and construction materials still creates a number of practical difficulties. Agim, who is building a new house in Gjirokastër, calculated the expenses:

> Do you know how much this house cost me? So far I would have built ten houses in Greece with this money. First of all count the gasoline I paid for the car during the trips. Put it down and keep notes: gasoline and service to the car, the [car] accident and the damage [he had had a car crash on his way from Greece carrying some construction materials], to pay custom officers over and under the table [both official payments and bribing] to pay the cops who stop you all the time when they see Greek number plates and things on the rack [on the top of the car], to pay double and triple money to the workers because if you are not with them they do nothing ... Plus the wages I am missing back in Greece each time I am coming back to supervise and carry the things, to pay all the agents of the state who come to check for this or that ... Do you want more?

In addition to the high costs, this story also highlights another familiar condition that takes place in the region of Gjirokastër. Agim and the majority of migrants carry the building materials for their new houses directly from Greece; thus, their savings are spent in Greece. In fact, even if they were to buy the same materials in South Albania they would most probably be imported from Greece by the merchants who can easily obtain free visas from the Greek consulate. The way the materials for these houses are carried and thus the way the houses are built represents the aforesaid scheme of dependency where migrants work in Greece, and their life's project, the building of their houses, requires them to

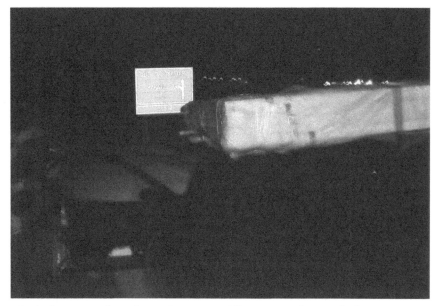

33 A door traveling from Greece to Albania on the roof of a car.

spend the money they earn in Greece. In the case of Gjirokastër, this outflow of people, inflow of materials, and implied outflow of Albanian wealth all takes place on the Kakavijë–Gjirokastër highway.

Political instability

The difficulties and risks involved in housebuilding do not end here. The considerable political instability poses dangers for houses in Albania. For example, Flamur from the Gjirokastër area complained:

> A lot of people had their fingers burnt, they start making houses, they made shops, put money into them and in the war [1997] they lost everything … The thieves stole even the doors and the windows from our house, they broke into everywhere in the village and they emptied the [uninhabited] houses. In Albania nothing had value and nothing was working, we came back and we hardly found the walls, they had stolen even the roof tiles. I remade it, but I am still afraid that something may happen again and this time I won't have the money to redo it.

Despite the fear and risks caused by the political instability in Albania, it should also be noted that this may have a positive effect on housebuilding: one of the reasons real estate's symbolic value in Albania has risen is because property ownership implies a certain degree of personal and financial security. After the 1997 crisis, when many Albanians lost their savings following the collapse of the pyramid pseudo-banks, immobile property gained symbolic and financial value as a type of investment and as a form of security. Cash, at that time, became an unstable resource, one which comes and goes, and sometimes even vanishes completely. Houses, at least, are tangible entities. Nonetheless, these feelings of physical security do not eliminate the risk associated with houses. In the event of a crisis, newly built houses, as the above example indicates, may be damaged, destroyed, or looted. Despite the considerable financial instability in Greece and Italy, Albania is still perceived as more politically unstable by most migrants. This makes the building of a house there a risky practice, one which causes considerable anxiety.

Corruption

Serious risks result from the frequent bypassing of the official state. Rarely are the houses, their extensions, and refurbishments constructed in a manner consistent with formal regulations. On the contrary, the tendency is for people to arrange things informally through personal networks and to avoid the official frameworks. For example, between 1992 and 1996, at least 60 percent of houses were built "informally" (i.e. without the state-required documents and permissions) (UN ECE 2002, 10).

Sali, who lived in Greece for fifteen years and who built a brand new house in North Albania, was one of the many who neglected the state-prescribed method of house construction:

SALI: Everyone knows that this is our building plot; it has always belonged to our grandfathers, so nobody will ask for it. Hoxha took it for forty years, but we have had it for a thousand years!
ME: But without title deeds, how did you get the official permission to build?
SALI: Everyone knows that it is ours, it is not necessary, and nobody says anything.
ME: The architects had no problem?
SALI: I am the architect, Mitso [common abbreviation of Dimitris], everything is mine, and I build 100 percent of it with my own hands.

Most of the time, undermining of the formal state regulation is facilitated by corruption within the public administration. This often simplifies and personalizes the building and refurbishment process. During my brief field trip to a coastal city I met a friend who was working as a building contractor in the area. He invited me for a drink while he was waiting for an appointment:

K: I am waiting for a guy to help him with his house.
ME: Are you building it?
K: No, a friend of mine is building it, I introduced him. I am too busy

with other buildings at the moment. I just know someone from the urban planning office, he is a friend as well and I will help them to find a solution ... because it is not correct.

ME: Solution?

K: The friend does not have permission to build [the house] and they gave him a fine. But he had started the construction [of the house] ten years ago, before the law, so it is not fair, and the other friend can "rub it out" [erase the fine], and because I know him well I ... [can intervene] so that nobody has a problem and my friend can build his house.

While avoiding state regulations drastically simplifies house construction, it can also be expensive. A 1998 World Bank survey found that 72 percent of construction firms admitted paying bribes to public officials (UN ECE 2002, 26); needless to say, this cost is added to the property owner's expenses. As such, those who build a house in Albania today are faced with two options with respect to the state authorities: to simplify the process, or to face a labyrinth of red tape. In another city, in West Albania, Sokol, who was renovating his house there, explained:

In Albania if you build a house you must be prepared to pay a lot of money to the brokers, otherwise they can screw you up as they are with the state and they have all the means. Now that the Democratic Party has come to power everyone in the town planning office is out and new people are in, to get rich, "democracy *a la* Albania." You know N.? He was for five years chief of the town planning office ... He has a new house down in S., a Mercedes Benz, his son studies in Athens and everything! How do you think he gained these things?

In contemporary Albania, there is an ethical hierarchy of the different types of bribery and of the various categories of people involved in this form of corruption. For example, one may notice an obvious division among bribe-receivers, bribe-givers, and mediators who are judged in various ways in each case. In other words, although only a few cases are presented here, the complexity of the situation is analogous to the one Caroline Humphrey (2002, 127–46) describes in the case of post-Soviet Russia. For instance, citizens who bribe a state clerk in Albania today are usually considered innocent, or even victims, while clerks are generally criticized even when they do not ask for money but are offered "gifts" by citizens. Sometimes, what people would call bribery in Northern Europe is a completely legitimate practice integrated into the Balkans' well-established gift-economy relations. In smaller towns like Gjirokastër, for instance, where most of the people know each other, it is common practice to offer an extra gift to other people even if what they do for you is formally included within their official duties. This gift might be cash, another reward, or just a few drinks in the local coffee shop. There are

34 Posters calling owners to register and legalize their buildings.

even semi-standard "tariffs" of gifts for people who want or are forced to pay extra. Ironically, the extended familial and social networks that people in Albanian towns have today have resulted in an unofficial social control of bribery and corruption, as it would be considered unthinkable to accept a financial bribe from a friend or relative.

Given the commonplace nature of bribery and lack of official control over the construction sector, it is a certainty that many of the houses built in recent years will cause complications for their owners in the future. This already became apparent in 2006 when efforts to legalize illegally built houses began.

Migrant remittances and migrant houses

Earlier, I mentioned that as well as the amount of remittances stated in official sources, we must also consider remittances which inflow via informal channels. Albanian migrants, in most cases, prefer to use personalized and informal channels rather than bank and money transfer agencies to remit their money. Quantitative research, such as a survey conducted by the International Organization for Migration (de Zwager et al. 2005, 31), estimates that more than 85 percent of the

Albanians living in Greece transfer money through informal channels (in the case of migrants to Italy, this percentage is slightly lower, but it still amounts to about 75 percent). My research indicated similar findings, as most of my interlocutors preferred to carry cash rather than to use banks, money transfer agencies, or other formal systems. Even those who had bank accounts often kept them for emergencies and not for the regular dispatch of monthly or bimonthly allowances to their families back home.[2] Edi, from Gjirokastër, who was building a house on the periphery of the town despite living in Greece, explained why: "Banks keep the commissions; you give them [the money] and then what? Banks make money out of your money and give you nothing. I prefer to feel it in my pocket, as it is much safer."

The emphasis upon informal channels for remittances also highlights the different intended uses for migratory money. This can be demonstrated through the story of how I met Edi initially. His father was a good friend and helpful interlocutor for me when I was in Gjirokastër. In April 2006, I told him I was going to visit my parents in Athens and he asked me to carry a gift of ten kilos of cheese to his son in Athens, as he would have to go through the long and arduous visa application procedure if he wanted to visit Greece. Edi picked me up from the bus terminal and politely invited me to his house as his wife Mirada had cooked dinner for us. At the end of the night, although we had only met for the first time that evening and despite not even knowing my surname, he gave me a packet of cash to carry back to his father. He explained the money was for the building work that had to be done on his house because he had not visited Albania since the summer. On that occasion, I felt very uncomfortable with such a responsibility. Edi tried to persuade me to help by explaining why he did not use the account his father had with a Greek bank, which had a branch in Gjirokastër:

> It is better if you, as a friend, will carry the money. Oh now, you know elders, I cannot come and it is not nice to put it in the bank, it is a gift. I opened the account for him because he is afraid that he may die and I will need to send money urgently for the funeral, but he is still alive and healthy so I cannot use this account like as if he had died, and, after all, there are works to be done to the house.

Edi was building the house on a plot he bought in the late 1990s, next to his father's house. Before buying the plot, he refurbished his parents' small house, where he and his sister—also a migrant in Greece—grew up. Almost every summer for two or three weeks, Edi and his wife Mirada and their two daughters returned to Albania. They also returned during other holiday periods, but just for a few days. For several years, Edi was a builder and then, in 2004, having worked very hard, he managed to save enough to buy a share of a grocery shop in Athens which he co-runs with a Greek man. When Edi was a builder his wife worked in a restaurant. Today, she works in the grocery shop with him. The couple's joint savings are mainly administered by Edi. Edi explained that one of the reasons they are making this house is because he does not want other people in Gjirokastër to think that he went to Greece and did not succeed economically: "I do not want the others to think that I went to Greece and did nothing," he stated. Similar ideas surrounding prestige are reflected in the words of Fatos, the interlocutor at the beginning of this chapter, who claimed that he was a "made man" in Greece, implying that he became wealthy there and thus he was able to refurbish his house in Albania. Prestige is also linked with fear of the evil eye. The quote from Marenglen in the evil eye section highlights the prejudice that Albanians who succeed in Greece face from some Greeks, and this is most likely due to common anti-Albanian stereotypes.[3] Edi, Fatos, and Marenglen rent their apartments in Greece, where they reside permanently, but they own their houses in Albania, which they visit only temporarily and none of them plan to return.

The expression of prestige in Albania is not only due to discrimination in Greece but also because Albanian migrants want to maintain links with their home country. Edi and Mirada's house is being constructed gradually and slowly; so far, it is only a three-room apartment on the ground floor of the future larger house. This is partly because they do not have the necessary capital to build it all at once but also because this gradual construction provides for their links between Athens and Gjirokastër. Edi, as an experienced builder, occasionally contributes personal labor to the building of his house, but he also appoints other builders to do various projects. When he is not in Albania, his father supervises and administers the construction project, and as such he is in constant contact for various related issues. Moreover, these links are articulated as flows of money and even materials, as Edi has imported the majority of the building materials from Greece. For instance, in the summer of 2006 he came to Gjirokastër with his vehicle filled with materials: "I came to bring the girls to their grandparents and some things for the house," he told me while I was helping him to unload the car. Edi's house is built with the money he has earned and the material he has bought in Greece. Therefore his house, as such, "inflows" gradually, piece by piece, from Greece to Albania. In a discussion we had that summer, in the sitting room of his new house in Albania, Edi and Mirada had the following exchange that highlights the relationship between remittances, their house, and their kinship ties:

EDI: If you won't send [money] back, what is going to happen? We do
          not have anyone else.

MIRADA: Eh! Do not say something like this! We have [friends]! Why,
          don't we have? With who are you hanging around in Greece, are
          you alone? But, your family is different, your mother, your father
          are all here. What are you supposed to do? Abandon them and
          tell them to do everything by themselves? No way! Here they
          have the entire house, and a house has expenses.

EDI: No ... I mean yes, your family is the most important thing. You
          do not vanish, you do not die! It's only that you went a few
          kilometers downward, you get it?

A great proportion of Albanian GDP is made up of migratory remittances, both formally and informally dispatched, and a great portion of
these remittances go toward housebuilding and maintenance. Typically,
the main administrator in the place of origin is a close relative who was
left behind in Albania, such as a father or brother or sometimes even
a spouse. The money that is usually sent or given for various construction tasks is greater than the actual cost of the project. Eventually,
these gradually built houses are a good reason for sending money to
relatives who stay behind in Albania. The widely informal method of
dispatch of cash for the building and care of the house masks the actual
relationship of dependence on the migrant members of the family, and
consequently Albania's financial dependency on the migratory destination countries. Arguably, there is a kind of house fetishism; the asymmet-
rical international relationship is masked via the migrants' houses. The
slow construction of the houses, apart from shaping a certain type of
landscape in contemporary Albania, offers an alternative formation of
the extended money flow and eventually a material link between the
migrants and their people in Albania. This exegesis, together with the
negative sentiments associated with banks in Albania following the
events of 1997, also explains why the mortgage market in the country
is extremely limited. The mortgage issue emerged in a private discussion with a foreign employee of a bank branch in Gjirokastër, as he
could not understand how people managed to build so much without
bank loans. Vullnetari and King (2008) wrote about the "care drain"
in South Albania, and how older people often live in poverty while
their migrant children enjoy relative wealth in Greece. The case study
of Edi shows how the process of "making" the house facilitates caring
for parents who stay behind and the formation of transnational links.

Making houses

The informants' usual phrase referring to the building of their house in Albania is "to make a house" (*Të bëjmë shtëpine ftiahno spiti*). The "making of the house" implies more than simply the technical practice of "building the house" (*ndrëtoj shtëpine/htizo spiti*). Four interlocutors used the phrase "to build a house" only in reference to the technical aspect or construction of house making. "Making" is a much broader and socially significant term than "building." Building consists only of construction from the foundation stone, through the beams to the completion of the whole physical structure. The "making" of a house includes, involves, and enshrines the building of a house. The making of a house is also the making of a home, or a "nest" as some Albanians put it (*bëj çerdhe* or *fole*), from the building phase to the stage of constantly maintaining, repairing, improving, modifying, embellishing, and cherishing both a house and a home.

"Building" a house is a kind of alienating process, like the enforced building of the roads during socialism or the building of houses in Greece for Greek employers, where most Albanian men work as builders. The International Organization for Migration (Chindea et al. 2007, 15; de Zwager et al. 2005, 16) estimated that 49 percent of male Albanian migrants in Greece are active in building and construction. Lambrianidis and Hatziprokopiou (2005, 104) found that the 36 percent of male Albanian migrants who returned permanently to Albania had been working in building and construction while living in Greece.

"Making" a house is the opposite: it is an *inalienating* process. Albanian migrants make their own houses but they also "make" themselves, like the man in the opening of the current section who stated that in Greece he was "made." This is a typical phrase in the region and particularly in the Greek language in which he spoke during the interview; it simultaneously reflects a prevalent way of perceiving the concept of making. Albanian migrants, through their houses in Albania, make their own selves. Let me elaborate: during my pilot survey in Athens, I asked people what they carried with them during their temporary return trips to Albania. Among other things, a typical reply I received was: "things for me" (*gjera per mua, per veten* or *gjera per veten time*, or *pragmata gia mena* or *dika mou pragmata*). It appears that people who live permanently in Greece without any intention of returning "carry things for themselves" to a place where they do not reside. These are personal items (e.g. clothes and cosmetics) that people carry to Albania from their migratory destinations to leave in their empty houses, consciously neglecting the fact that they live somewhere else. Another typical answer I received when I asked what people carry to Albania was "things for the house" (*gjera per shtepine* or *pragmata gia to spiti*), as was the case with Edi, who told me he came to bring the girls to their grandparents and some things for the house. I initially understood these "things for the house," on a basic level, to be household and decorative items or construction materials. During my fieldwork, however, I met migrants who showed me the photo-albums of their house in Albania along with the photo-albums of their children. Someone else, after showing me their landline number in the Albanian telephone directory, called their empty house as though they were ringing a human being. What I suggest is that the phrase "making a house" has a key role not only in the bridging of the migratory destination and the place of origin but that making a house is the making of a self within the very familiar sense of home. This home, as such, carries an almost personified agency, which leads to the formation of self; under circumstances of extreme fluidity, these houses are the making of a self from below. In addition, this making of both houses and selves passes via the cross-border highway in both directions, first flowing out as migration, and later flowing back in the form of building materials, techniques, and remittances. I will illustrate this relationship through the case of one of the "Greek houses" located in Albania.

In addition to the building of a dwelling, the making of these houses by migrants primarily helps the kinship ties to be cultivated from distance. The term *shtëpi* (Albanian) and *spiti/σπίτι* (Greek), used by my interlocutors, stands for house, home, household group, and, occasionally, for the family. This is a celebrated, and even a little clichéd, statement in anthropology, but this articulation of "house" as a "social relationship" has been observed by Claude Levi-Strauss in his analysis of house-based societies (1987, 1982). There are many ethnographic examples (Nuer, Tallensi, Tikopia, Lovedu) in which the term "house" is used to label a social group related by descent or alliance such as the family (Thomas 1996, 283). In this sense, the "making of the house" from distance is the gradual remaking of a new type of relationship, mainly a new version of the existing kinship relationship. The new houses emerge as the catalytic agent, which assists the rearticulation of relationships among the older agents in the transnational era of Albanian society.

The making of these houses emphasizes kinship or other social relationships when some of the members are geographically distanced. Nonetheless, the migrant's absence is directly linked to these houses, because it is they who "supply" the money and even the material for the long building process. The absent migrant is the protagonist in the making of the house, through which he or she is ensuring a degree of presence. In this way, in Albania, the house incorporates a simultaneous absence and presence. This appears to be a paradox of transnationalism: it allows people to live over larger geographic distances while simultaneously creating novel practices to keep their associations across that distance. Despite the major risks and difficulties involved in the building of these houses, as Edi put it, "the family is the most important thing."

Furthermore, the making of these houses, by migrants, incorporates and is incorporated within the Albanian everyday postsocialist cosmology. In this way, the various phenomena of the macroscale politico-economic transition are reduced to the familiarity of the microscale of the individual home-making projects. These are referred to through phenomena such as the property question, political instability, the extensive importation of goods into Albania, corruption, migration, and the Albanian economy's dependency on remittances. It does not matter if these houses are incomplete or if they are under construction for a decade or so. It is not important that people who do not intend to return and live in them make many of these houses. It is the process of making a house per se that matters. Making the house familiarizes and "translates," within the understandable sphere of the home, the fluid and mobile transitional and transnational everyday life in contemporary Albania.

Notes

1 It is important to note, however, that in Gjirokastër most of the houses were private and not state-owned, despite it being a city, due to its historically important architecture.

2 Partly, this distrust of the banking system is due to the 1997 crisis, when the pyramid pseudo-banks collapsed devastating the savings of a great proportion of the population.

3 One of the most notorious examples is the slogan that many fans of the Greek national football team shouted when their team won the European Championship in 2004: "Albanian you will never become a Greek!" (*Den tha gineis Ellinas pote Alvane!*). This slogan became more popular when the Albanian football team beat the European champions just a few months after their triumph, an event which led to nationalist–racist criminality in Greece at that time. Regarding Albanian stereotypes, see Kapllani and Mai (2005).

8

Infrastructures, borders, (im)mobility, or the material and social construction of new Europe

The pathos of all bourgeois monuments is that their material strength and solidity actually count for nothing and carry no weight at all, that they are blown away like frail reeds by the very forces of capitalist development that they celebrate. Even the most beautiful and impressive bourgeois buildings and public works are disposable, capitalized for fast depreciation and planned to be obsolete, closer in their social functions to tents and encampments than to Egyptian pyramids, Roman aqueducts, Gothic cathedrals. (Berman 1982, 99)

After the time of the State's political relativity as nonconducting medium, we are faced with the no time of the politics of relativity. The full discharge feared by Clausewitz has come about with the State of Emergency. The violence of speed has become both the location and the law, the world's destiny and its destination. (Virilio 2006 [1977], 167)

Albania was one of the first European countries with an advanced highway system suitable for automobility, built back in the 1930s before the respective highway construction projects of Italy and Germany had been completed. After WWII, the Albanian socialist regime emphasized highways as well. The only issue was that automobility in Albania was legalized and thus became widespread only in 1991. Similarly, electricity networks were constructed but electricity was not necessarily flowing through them. So, if one takes into account that for almost sixty years Albanians had to build roads and other infrastructures with their own hands without using the infrastructure for the purpose it was meant for, Albania has a very special place in the sociocultural study of infrastructures as infrastructures were very explicitly political and social (engineering) projects. This state-run project paved the way for the future of highways as an international development/corporate project and eventually as another kind of infrastructure.

The most important road for the life of the city of Gjirokastër is the 29-kilometer highway linking it to the Albanian–Greek border. Post-socialist Gjirokastër is a city which has centralized its road networks spatially and socially. Though it is unclear, as the locals believe, if half of the population actually lives in Greece, it is likely that at least one-third of its pre-1990 inhabitants now live there. The road became a highway between 1997 and 2001. The road repair project was undertaken by Greek firms and by the Greek state, using materials purchased and brought from Greece. The blueprints and designs were identical to those used in Greek roads. Materially and visually these 29 kilometers are an inflow of the Greek road network into Albania. The road runs from Greece, alongside Greek minority villages in South Albania, and ends in Gjirokastër, the city which nationalists and Greek expansionists consider to be the capital of this minority area. In fact, the area through which this road runs was a disputed territory between the two countries until 1987.

Although the highway and the various flows along it have a decisive impact on, and central position in, the sociocultural life of the city, the road is perceived via a negative road mythology. In contemporary oral discourse, the road has become the physical location for tales of violence, war, and criminality. The most prominent of these tales are those describing the flow of hazards from Greece into Albania. According to local mythology, the Greek intelligence service has used these 29 kilometers for sinister ends—Greek spies smuggling ancient Greek and Christian artifacts in the coffins of dead Albanian migrants so that future archaeologists would find them and provide Greece with a plausible claim to South Albania or North Epirus (as those on the far-right of Greek politics refer to it). One of the most infamous and important tales is about the 1997 collapse of the pseudo-bank pyramid schemes. It describes how, at various points along these 29 kilometers, people witnessed armored trucks speeding off to Greece, carrying US$2 billion of Albanian savings.

This combination of the migration flows together with global development policies, such as the reconstruction of the Albanian road system, has produced a narrative which corresponds perfectly to contemporary Albanian life. The most productive cohorts of Albanian society migrate to Greece and send their remittances back, providing a welcome income for the Albanians who have come to depend on them. By contrast, Albania itself produces very little in comparison to the past, and thus this inflow of remittances simultaneously implies their outflow, especially to Greece, from where the majority of Albanian products are imported. Hence what travels to Greece is Albanian wealth in the form of productive cohorts and consumption. As such, the inflow of remittances, supplied by the well-meaning migrants who leave to offer their families a better quality of life, has had the unintentional consequence of consigning the Albanian economy to an extended period of stagnation. Albanian society depends on remittances and the Albanian state on international aid. However, as the example of road construction demonstrates, this international aid comes with conditions dictated by the states and transnational organizations that provide it. In the case of the Kakavijë–Gjirokastër highway, Greek expansionist aspirations and the political principles of neoliberalism were incorporated within the project. Hence it is to be expected that the local oral discourse locates these stories of outflow of Albanian wealth and the inflow of dangers along these 29 kilometers that mark the entrance to Greece.

Nevertheless, if we want to examine the narratives of the road and the processes they describe, we must consider an additional dimension. This negatively charged highway mythography, which describes international asymmetries, is merely one aspect of road-related activity. There are additional activities which go beyond the macropolitical and macroeconomic implications of migrating, returning, consuming, and remitting in an unequal world. Paradoxically, these additional road-related activities refer to something which is considered relatively static and very different from the road: the house. In fact, just like the materiality of the road, the houses in Albania are not static but fluid and mobile, so much so that the houses themselves travel along the road.

The ethnographic example of the houses Albanians build in Albania, where they no longer reside, reveals their sociocultural priorities regarding their homeland. It also reveals their houses' direct material and social links with all these aforesaid dependency processes and with the road. In other words, the houses Albanian migrants build exemplify all the contradictions of a transnational existence in a world of international inequalities. On the one hand, through the home, there is a collective effort to dealienate the experience of displacement and the road—the means by which this occurs. On the other hand, the very act of building the home ensures continued dependence on migration, displacement, and alienation.

These houses share the same ontological properties with the cross-border highway. They are being built with Greek materials which come from Greece. They are built with money which comes from Greece and they are constructed on the basis of Greek plans and designs that Albanians (mainly construction workers) learn in Greece. In fact, it is an inflow of a transformed and adopted "Greekness" into Albania, just as the cross-border highway is the material inflow of the Greek network into Albania. Via this Greek road, people migrate abroad; via this Greek road, they return and bring "things for their house." As a consequence, this implies that people spend their earnings from Greece in Greece, further aggravating the dependency of their home country on the neighboring economy. This entire process began with the construction of the Greek highway and is now sustained by this same highway. At the same time, in contrast to the postsocialist roads that are built by Greeks for Greeks in Albania, these houses are built by Albanians. These are the same Albanians who build houses for Greeks, in Greece, a country where the majority of construction workers are Albanian. In this book, roads and migrants' houses built in their home country emerge as different parts of the same process. In fact, there is the paradox of an alienating cross-border highway that is being dealienated within the affective and familiar sphere of the home.

The long post-cold war period

This book starts with the story of a boat full of Albanian migrants that sank after its collision with a vessel of the Italian Navy which was trying to prevent it from crossing EU borders. Almost twenty years later, as the Albanian together with most other European governments were sealing off their borders to Syrian refugees, sinking boats and migrants trying to enter the EU were a common phenomenon in the Mediterranean. Obviously, the Others, of the 1990s who did not have the right to enter into Europe, were of a primarily different ethnic origin than the Others of the 2010s; yet, the persistent refusal of the right to mobility and, more generally, the border securitization regime being witnessed when these lines are drawn, was rehearsed and shaped in the early 1990s. Although the exact location of this border moves, qualitatively the border regime of "Fortress Europe," as we know it today, has remained the same over the last decades, protecting the core of Europe and its strategic peripheries. The issue is that this is the only spatial pillar of post-cold war Europe that remains intact and even enhanced.

Building Europe

Historically, the twentieth century has witnessed two major pan-European construction projects that have taken place over the entire length and width of the continent, renewing its built environment. The first one is the post-WWII reconstruction of the Old Europe powers and the second one is the post-cold war "reconstruction." Besides being a much larger-scale project, the post-WWII project explicitly had a two-fold character. The two sides of the cold war divide were each building their own urban and infrastructural materiality. Via this material reconstruction, they aimed to engineer their respective social and political entities. Moreover, the construction project of the 1940s–50s was to (re)build a devastated continent. The ensuing physical construction project, from the

1990s–2000s, was tied to the metaphysical destruction of the communist regimes' infrastructure and materiality—its very ethos. Thus, the building construction was part of the destruction, both physical and symbolic, of the defeated enemy.

We have detailed ethnographies of the socio-material transformations that occurred in Eastern Europe at that time (Buchli 1999; Dalakoglou 2012; Ssorin-Chaikov 2003; Yurchak 2003), and these have also been recorded and recreated in art. For example, the celebrated film *Good Bye Lenin!* (Becker 2003) describes on a fictional level, this process of deconstruction of the enemy's material culture and its replacement by the capitalist version, which was novel to the former socialist countries. The movie's hero is desperately trying to reconstruct East Germany's material reality for his mother who wakes after a long coma—she must not get shocked to find the world has changed lest she fall ill again. He tries to recreate the GDR's material culture and with every passing moment this becomes more difficult as the material samples of the previous world are systematically erased.

Beyond fiction, the cold war was a war and at the end its outcome was one that most wars share: the winner occupied the territory of the defeated. Because this war was waged between two economic/political systems, this "occupation of territories" meant the instant transformation of the vast majority of immobile resources and real estate of socialist countries from state, public or cooperative hands to private ones. The enormous influx of resources into the West European capitalist economy resulted in its overnight expansion.

Another type of resource that was added to the capitalist European economy was the massively impoverished parts of Eastern European populations who either migrated to the West or worked in their own countries—often for Western European interests and in the interest of the new local capitalist elites who replaced the nomenclature of the socialist period—while drawing on the private property of productive means as yet another source of power. This vast influx of real estate and labor power fueled the European capitalist economy and especially unskilled and low-skilled labor markets all over the continent. Thus, it was only a matter of time until the construction sector evolved into the "steam engine" of economic growth during the 1990s and 2000s, occupying an increasing percentage of GDP all over Europe. Indeed, after 1990 Western Europe witnessed some of the largest construction projects, both in terms of publicly funded works and in terms of private contracts. Within this context the whole phenomenon must also be linked with the emergence of the infrastructural mega-event of which the European continent saw three over the period of twenty years to

2012 (Olympic Games of Barcelona, Athens, London) which fundamentally changed the profile of three of its metropolises in the West.

This particular project of the built environment's reconstruction not only created profit but also engineered the new sociocultural capitalist subjectivities and relationships. For example, in the case of Eastern Europe, these subjects had to get used to the world of private automobility, the private housing market, the cosmology of supermarkets or malls, the new capitalist social hierarchies, etc. Similarly, the West was being reengineered socially, first of all quantitatively, thanks to the intake of human and financial resources and accelerated growth, but also qualitatively. This is evidenced via the influx of a new inferior "social class": "The Eastern Europeans." These were often added to Western Europe's previous "inferiors": the migrants from the Mediterranean countries or those from the former colonies. However, in some cases the influx of Eastern European migrants added an entirely new social class and social category of immigrants that did not exist previously, e.g. in Greece with the influx of Albanian migrants during the 1990s. This transformation caused by East European migration was such that the word "Albanian" became synonymous with the unskilled, underpaid manual worker, with phrases such as "He made me work like an Albanian" appearing in Greek everyday language. Of course, during Greece's enormous economic and construction boom (mid 1990s–mid 2000s) immigrants from Albania dominated the sector's workforce. Thus, Western Europe's periphery acquired its own Others, thereby solidifying its newly found identity of "Westernness."

Borders

Apart from this reconstruction of the built environment, the post-cold war era also had another significant spatial dimension. Following 1990, an ongoing process of internal and external reconfiguration of the European borders ensued. Primarily, the new borders created a new privileged European space and identity, which was promising, or even providing, the dreams of wealth and growth alongside those of a supposed territorial/cultural exclusivity. The sudden collapse of the main division between socialist and capitalist Europe made the previous internal Western division between core Western Europe and peripheral Western Europe much less significant. Just as the Greeks felt more Western, the Old West embraced the periphery in the face of the Otherness of Eastern Europe. Thus, given, the capitalist past that the whole of Western Europe had experienced, the Western periphery and Western core shared commonalities in comparison to the Easterners. Events such as the wars in Yugoslavia or the brief Albanian Civil War (1997) were attributed mostly to the primary "sin" of communism and were used to confirm the former distinction, where the West had to intervene to "civilize" the East of Europe.

Despite the various infrastructural cross-border projects between EU and non-EU member countries on the continent, which attempted to materialize the new links, the new United Europe's identification processes became problematic (see Dalakoglou 2010). The division had strong roots as for over fifty years the archetypal enemy was the "other" Europeans and, as the Otranto tragedy shows, overcoming such old divisions is a long and hard process.

These EU/non-EU borders became the favored arena for testing, developing, and shaping the policies of "Fortress Europe" in the first instance. Indeed, as more and more Eastern European countries enter the EU or gain potential member status, the geopolitical border is constantly redrawn. It is for example worth noting how within just two decades the Western governments' attitude changed toward the Easterners who crossed the borders of the old EU of the 12 member states. When the first Eastern migrants started crossing the (former) iron curtain toward the West, Western governments perceived this as a political success and as a positive development, which indisputably manifested the defeat of the enemy—the socialist regimes. However, only a little later, the Eastern Europeans became an undesired flow for EU member countries. Therefore, the borders were sealed off, and by 1999, with the Amsterdam Treaty, the EU member-state borders were upgraded into common EU borders, secured and sealed by common EU political and policing measures. Despite the gradual inclusion of many Eastern European countries to the EU, the zones of the inexpensive sex or gambling industries along the old East–West European borders are an explicit example of the fact that the whole process is indeed ongoing. The initial example we used, the Otranto tragedy, demonstrates how the Eastern Europeans were the first to suffer from the "Fortress Europe" politics.

Nevertheless, currently we are witnessing the turn of Eastern Europe to claim its right to Europeanness and Westernness over the bodies of the new Others, precisely as the periphery of Western Europe did in the 1990s over the bodies of Eastern European migrants. In February 2016, the Albanian PM announced that he would seal off the borders of his country against Syrian refugees using it as a passage on their way to Northern Europe via Greece. At the same time, several Balkan countries came to an agreement with Austria to seal off their own borders, thus closing down the Balkan corridors to refugees from Syria, other Middle East countries and Afghanistan. Meanwhile, the Hungarian government highlights a growing trend within the Eastern European states of the EU of openly racist and anti-refugee rhetoric and policy. In early 2016 the Dutch presidency of the EU silently accepted all these tactics and decisions. The Western European states thus conveniently export their own racist and anti-refugee politics to the previously excluded Eastern European and new member states.

The confirmation of its Europeanness for Eastern Europe implies better mobility within Europe but also the violent sealing off and guarding of the common European territory. It is not accidental that the most representative event of the communist regimes' collapse is the fall and crossing of the Berlin Wall. At the same period, Albanians overthrew their socialist dictatorship revolting on the street and occupying the embassies in Tirana, demanding the issuing of passports. The core of Eastern Europeans' participation in the new European project consisted in the potential of easier mobility to the West and fewer border controls. This desire has evolved historically as a process synonymous with the reconfiguration of the common European borders into an arena of strict control and violence against non-Westerners echoing the exclusivity of Old Europe. After all, Eastern European "Otherness" may have passed mostly over the bodies of heavily exploited and underpaid employees, but the non-European "Otherness" passes largely over dead bodies of the men, women, and children who wash up on Europe's shores every day.

Crossing borders

After the outbreak of the European Financial Crisis in 2008, one of the main spatial dimensions of the post-cold war Europe—the qualitative transformation of the built environment and real estate—has either been deregulated or has slowed dramatically. In light of such events, the only main spatial axis of reference of post-cold war Europe that remains intact is the border securitization.

Hence, the sudden transformation of the Balkans from Europe's proud border to an express corridor for countless refugees in 2015 was perceived as an expression of a major crisis for the whole of Europe. All the cross-border infrastructures that were built in order to cement (quite literally) the relationships between EU and non-EU member states during the post-cold war period, including port facilities, cross-border highways, border control stations and pan- and trans-European transport corridors suddenly became corridors for refugees. This activity has gravely called into question the planned commercial and touristic purposes of these infrastructures, but most importantly challenged the entire European project.

Thus Frontex, the European Border Police, has for some time now taken the right to operate in the region. This has proved insufficient, however, and as the EU does not have its own navy, in February 2016 a decision was taken to allow NATO to take over the guarding of the sea borders between Greece and Turkey. NATO will officially patrol and control the borders between two NATO member countries, aiming to show explicitly where exactly Europe's borders are located. Indeed, the notion of borders becomes more important than European membership itself, as the Greek government submits the control of the country's borders to NATO in the name of the hypothetical threat coming from the one million refugees from war-torn countries that have crossed the European borders during 2015–16.

In early 2016 the whole humanitarian refugee tragedy that unfolded along the Syrian-Balkan corridor was of little importance—if any at all—compared to the question of the region's border policing. Europe's leaders have spent their time negotiating where exactly the European borders lie, to which countries Europe will externalize the refugees and how it will guard its common borders in order to decrease the flow of refugees. The life of a few million human beings was a secondary question to be debated by the European leadership—acceptable collateral damage for the protection of European spatial exclusivity. On the one hand, this securitization of the common EU border is one of the last things that might hold Europe together; on the other hand, this process exhibits more and more explicitly elements from what Marc Mazower (1999) has called the history of our "Dark Continent." Europe is not only the continent that became, in the post-WWII era, the champion of human rights, refugee rights, bourgeois democracy, etc., but also the continent that produced Nazism and fascism, and previously had produced colonialism, imperialism, and the genocide of various populations characterized as inferior and undesired "Others."

Nevertheless, according to Scott (2014) people who are mobile without permission of sovereign apparatuses are often treated as enemies by them mainly because they challenge the processes of fencing and control. The idea of private property and own-ability of resources are based on these two activities and they are crucial principles for the development of capitalism, and modern state. Infrastructures and their flows are often embedded in the projects of various sovereign mechanisms (e.g. see Graham and Marvin 2001) that aim to create conditions of order and control from above. However, ethnography shows that infrastructures and the mobilities they facilitate in various geographical and historical contexts were traditionally considered, in principle, as peculiar kinds of entities (see Larkin 2013). Roads especially, such as the footpaths and the bridges of the Balkans, were traditionally considered as examples of commons, operating often in a sphere that goes beyond both the control of private interests or the state to become the per se site where such mechanisms were challenged by the everyday practice of the common people (Dalakoglou 2009; Green 2005; Nitsiakos 2010). The road belongs to everyone in US road fiction. Simultaneously the roads are out of control and open to all potentialities in most of the European fiction according to Bakhtin. The road and its speedy flows are the principles of war, violence, and occupation (Virilio 2006 [1977]) but also the principles of freedom and resistance to authoritarianism (Deleuze and Guattari 1986; Scott 2014). Especially the materialities of the roads, the mobilities and flows that cross borders, without the permission of sovereign apparatuses, embed a core problem for such systems of power. As the current ethnography shows, without romanticizing, it is precisely within these sites of cross-border mobilities and materialities that established political and economic (legal or illegal) systems are challenged from below and on the move.

Appendix 1

Notes on language, terminology, and pseudonyms

Pronunciation, transliteration

Isa Zymberi (1991) provides the following table showing the Albanian alphabet and pronunciations:

Letter	A	B	C	Ç	D	Dh	E	Ë	F	G	Gj	H	I	J	K	L	LL	M
	a	b	c	ç	d	dh	e	ë	f	g	gj	h	i	j	K	l	ll	M
Value	a	b	t͡s	t͡ʃ	d	ð	ɛ	ə	f	g	ɟ	h	i	j	K	l	ɫ	m
Letter	N	Nj	O	P	Q	R	RR	S	Sh	T	Th	U	V	X	XH	Y	Z	ZH
	n	nj	o	p	q	r	rr	s	sh	t	th	u	v	x	xh	y	z	zh
Value	n	ɲ	ɔ	p	c	ɾ	r˗	s	ʃ	t	θ	u	v	d͡z	d͡ʒ	y	z	ʒ

The Albanian letters that do not appear in the Latin alphabet or sound different from the same letter/diagraph in English are as follows. For these pronunciations, I follow the *Albanian–English–Albanian Dictionary* (Hysa 2003) and Zymberi's (1991) suggestions. Zymberi (1991) provides the table set out below.

Ç	as check	Q	as cheese
dh	as this	Rr	as in borrow
Ë	as hurt	Y	as the French u in *une*
xh	as gin**ger**	Ll	ll as ball
Gj	as judge	Zh	like vision
X	as jow	Nj	Like **new**

Greek transliterations follow the transliteration tables of other anthropological publications on Greece (e.g. Green 2005, xvii–xviii; Herzfeld 1985, xviii, 275–6).

Letter	Sound	Letter	Sound	Letter	Sound	Letter	Sound
Aα	A	*Hη*	i, e	*Nν*	N	*Tτ*	t
Bβ	V	*Θθ*	th as **thick**	*Ξξ*	X	*Υυ*	i,y
Γγ	g (soft)	*Iι*	I	*Oo*	O	*Φφ*	f
Δδ	th as **the**	*Kκ*	K	*Ππ*	P	*Xχ*	h or ch
Eε	E	*Λλ*	L	*Pρ*	R	*Ψψ*	ps
Zζ	Z	*Mμ*	M	*Σσ(ς)*	s	*Ωω*	O

Diagraphs

Aι	e or ai	*ου*	Ou	*Nτ*	nt or d
Aυ	av or af	*Γκ*	G	*Eυ*	ef or ev
Eι	i or ei	*Mπ*	B	*Oι*	i or oi

Quotations and translations

The interviews for this book were conducted in both Greek and Albanian and all the translations are mine. The same stands for Albanian and Greek literature and press. When the discourse of an interlocutor is provided, my comments and explanations are added between brackets [ ].

Definite/indefinite articles

In the Albanian language, there is an indefinite or definite article in every noun, including proper nouns (e.g. the name of the city in which I worked is *Gjirokastër* [indef.] or *Gjirokastra* [def.]). Albanian nouns are inflected by gender: masculine, feminine, and neuter; and number: singular and plural. There are five declensions with six cases (nominative, accusative, genitive, dative, ablative, and vocative). The definite article is provided by a different suffix at the end of nouns in their various declinations and cases. For example, the singular male in nominative case adds *-i-* or *-u-* and the singular female adds *-a-* or *-ja-*. I use words with both articles.

Pseudonyms—anonymity

To ensure the anonymity of my interlocutors, and following the usual practice in anthropology, pseudonyms are used for all names, and some of the details of their life-stories that I did not consider important in the following discussion were changed. One must note that the same name is used to refer to more than one person, as this is the case in Albania. This is partly due to the limitations set by state authorities. From the late 1960s onwards, the Albanian state issued lists of accepted names for newborn babies, mainly with the aim of eliminating names with religious connotations. The most striking examples of the naming regulations that late socialism promoted are names like *Marenglen* (derived from a combination of Marx, Engels, Lenin).

Appendix 2

Population statistics

Gjirokastër

Ethnic and cultural affiliation	Resident population	Percentage of resident population
Total	72,176	100
Albanian	56,193	77.86
Greek	5,363	7.43
Macedonian	1	0.00
Montenegrin	1	0.00
Aromanian	688	0.95
Roma	91	0.13
Egyptian (Gypsy)	21	0.03
Other	56	0.08
Prefer not to answer	8,729	12.09
Not relevant/not stated	1,033	1.43

Religious affiliation	Resident population	Percentage of resident population
Total	72,176	100
Muslims	27,815	38.54
Bektashi	6,118	8.48
Catholics	1,493	2.07
Orthodox	12,583	17.43
Evangelists	59	0.08
Other Christians	50	0.07
Believers without denomination	6,050	8.38
Atheists	4,550	6.30
Others	52	0.07
Prefer not to answer	10,945	15.16
Not relevant/not stated	2,461	3.41

Bibliography

Abulafia, D. 1976. "Reflections on a Visit to Albania." *Cambridge Review* 26: 46–51.

Adami, J. 1953. "The History of Roads in Albania." *Bulletin of Albanian Sciences* 8 Nentori: Tirana.

ADE-IBM-EPU-NTUA. 2004. "Final Report of the Evaluation of the EC Interventions in the Transport Sector in Third Countries." Brussels. http://ec.europa.eu/europeaid/how/evaluation/evaluation_reports/reports/sector/951655_vol2_en.pdf

Agar, M. H. 1996. *The Professional Stranger: An Informal Introduction to Ethnography*. Bingley: Emerald Group Publishing.

Al-Ali, N., and K. Koser (eds). 2002. *New Approaches to Migration? Transnational Communities and Transformation of Home*. London: Routledge.

Albania. 1978. *An Outline of the PSR of Albania*. Tirana: 8 Nentori.

Albanian Constitution. 1976. Approved by the People's Assembly on December 28, 1976. http://bjoerna.dk/dokumentation/Albanian-Constitution-1976.htm

Alexander, C., V. Buchli, and C. Humphrey (eds). 2007. *Urban Life in Post-Soviet Asia*. London: UCL Press.

Alimehmeti, F. 1986. "Mbi disa veçori të banesës fshatare tëe zonës fushore-kodrinore të Tiranës në vitet e para." *Monumentet*, 31:113-124

Allcock, J.A. 1991. "Constructing the Balkans." In J.A. Allcock and A. Young (eds), *Black Lambs and Grey Falcons: Women Travellers in the Balkans*. Bradford: Bradford University Press, pp. 170–91.

Althusser, L. 1989. "Ideology and Ideological State Apparatuses." In *Lenin and Philosophy and Other Essays*. London: New Left Books, pp. 170–86.

Amery, J. 1948. *The Sons of the Eagle: A Study in Guerrilla War*. London: Macmillan.

Andrea, Z. 1984. "Archaeology in Albania, 1973–83." *Archaeological Reports* 30: 102–19.

Anonymous. 1978. *An Outline of the People's Socialist Republic of Albania*. Tirana: 8 Nentori.

Anonymous. 1984. "Albania: General Information." Tirana: 8 Nentori.

Appadurai, A. (ed.). 1986. *The Social Life of Things*. Cambridge: Cambridge University Press.

—1988. "Putting Hierarchy in Its Place." *Cultural Anthropology* 3(1): 36–49.

—1990. "Disjuncture and Difference in the Global Cultural Economy." *Theory, Culture & Society* 7: 295.

—1996. *Modernity at Large*. Minneapolis: University of Minnesota Press.

—2011. "Disjuncture and Difference in the Global Cultural Economy (1990)." In I. Szeman and T. Kaposy (eds), *Cultural Theory: An Anthology*. Chichester: Wiley-Blackwell, 282–95.

Arendt, H. 1951. *The Origins of Totalitarianism*. New York: Harcourt, Brace & Co.

Ash, W. 1974. *Pickaxe and Rifle: The Story of the Albanian People*. Wimbledon: Howard Baker.

ATA. 1997a. "Italian and Rumanian Soldiers for Reconnaissance in Gjirokastër." www.hri.org/news/balkans/ata/1997/97-04-23.ata.html# 23

—1997b. "Four People Killed in Gjirokaster." www.hri.org/news/balkans/ata/1997/97-7-06-6-11.ata.html#13

—1997c. "Terror Continues in Border Checkpoint of Kakavijë—Two Policemen Injured." www.hri.org/news/balkans/ata/1997/97-05-14.ata.html#11

—1997d. "Situation in Gjirokaster and Nearby Villages is under Control." www.hri.org/news/balkans/ata/1997/97-03-04.ata.html

—1997e. "PHARE Program to Accord 10 Million ECU to Albania." www.hri.org/news/balkans/ata/1997/97-10-25.ata.html

—1999a. "Albania Listed among Countries with Biggest Death Number in Road Accidents." www.hri.org/news/balkans/ata/1999/99-01-12.ata.html#15

—1999b. "Communication Bridge Placed between Lazarati People, Government." www.hri.org/news/balkans/ata/1999/99-01-20.ata.html# 07

Athanassopoulou, A. 2002. "Arvanites and Albanian Migrants." PhD dissertation, University of the Aegean, Department of Anthropology.

Augé, M. 1995. *Non-Places*. London: Verso.

Baba, Rexhepi. 1970. *Misticizma Islame dhe Bektashizma*. New York: Walden Press.

Bace, A. 1984. "The Albanian Roads in the Middle Ages." In *Problems of the Formation of the Albanian People, Their Language and Culture*. Tirana: 8 Nentori.

Backer, B. 2003. *Behind Stone Walls: Changing Household Organization among the Albanians of Kosova*. Pejë: Dukagjini Publishing.

Bakhtin, M.M. 1982. "Forms of Time and of the Chronotope in the Novel." In *The Dialogical Imagination*. Austin: University of Texas Press, pp. 84–258.

—2010. *The Dialogic Imagination: Four Essays*, vol. 1. Austin: University of Texas Press.

Bank of Albania. 2003. "Annual Report 2002." Tirana.

—2004. "Annual Report 2003." Tirana.

Bardhosi, N. 2004. "Veçori të ndarjes së pasurisë sipas së drejtës dokesore" [Particularities of the division of real estate according to customary law]. *Kultura Popullore* 1–2: 99–128.

Barjaba, K. 2004a. "Albania Looking beyond Borders." www.migration information.org

—(ed.). 2004b. *Albania's Democratic Elections, 1991–1997: Analyses, Documents and Data*. Berlin: Edition Sigma.

—2005. "Labour Emigration: From Political Will Towards Collaboration of Migratory Markets." In International Organisation for Migration and Government of the Republic of Albania (eds), *Selected Papers on National Strategy on Migration Workshop*. Tirana: International Organisation for Migration, pp. 31–46.

Barjaba, K., and R. King. 2005. "Introducing and Theorising Albanian Migration." In R. King, N. Mai, and S. Schwandner-Sievers (eds), *The New Albanian Migration*. Brighton: University of Sussex Press, pp. 1–28.

Barth, F. 1964. *Nomads of South Persia*. New York: Humanities Press.

Barthes, R. 2001 [1967]. "The Death of the Author." *Contributions in Philosophy* 83:3–8.

Basch, L., N. Glick-Schiller, and C. Szanton-Blanc. 1994. *Nations Unbound: Transnational Projects, Postcolonial Predicaments and Deterritorialized Nation-States*. Langhorne, PA: Gordon & Breach.

Baudrillard, J. 1988. *America*. London: Verso.

—1994. *Simulacra and Simulation*. Ann Arbor: University of Michigan Press.

Bauman, Z. 2000. *Liquid Modernity*. Cambridge: Polity.

Baum-Snow, N. 2007. "Did Highways Cause Suburbanisation?" *The Quarterly Journal of Economics* 122(2):775–805.

Beaton, R. 1996. "The Greek Ballad: The Bridge of Arta as Myth." In D. Alan (ed.), *The Walled-up Wife: A Casebook*. Madison: University of Wisconsin Press.

Beck, U. 1992. *Risk Society: Towards a New Modernity*, vol. 17. London: Sage.

Becker, W., B. Lichtenberg, Y. Tiersen, and S. Arndt. 2003. *Good Bye Lenin!* Schwarzkopf & Schwarzkopf.

Berger, J., J. Mohr, and S. Blomberg. 2010. *A Seventh Man: A Book of Images and Words about the Experience of Migrant Workers in Europe*. London: Verso.

Berman, M. 1982. *All that Is Solid Melts into Air: The Experience of Modernity*. New York: Simon & Schuster.

Biber, M. 1980. "Albania Alone against the World." *National Geographic Magazine* 158: 530–57.

Biris, K. 1960. *Arvanites, the Dorians of Modern Greece: History of the Greek Arvanites*. Athens.

Birsch, J. 1972. "The Albanian Political Experience." In L. Schapiro (ed.), *Political Opposition in One Party States*. London: Macmillan, pp. 179–200.

Blanc, A. 1961. "Naissance et évolution des paysages agraires en Albanie." *Geogr. Annlr* 43: 8–16.

—1963. "L'évolution contemporaine de la vie pastorale en Albanie méridionale." *Rev. Geogr. Alpine* 51: 429–61.

Blanqui, A. 1972 [1866]. *Instruction pour une prise d'armes L'Éternité per les astres hypthèse astribinuqye et autre textes*. Société encyclopédique français, Editions de la Tête de Feuilles.

Blumi, I. 2008. *Redefining Balkan Nationalism*. London: Tauris.

Boas, F. 1884. "A Journey in Cumberland Sound and on the West Shore of

Davis Strait in 1883 and 1884." *Journal of the American Geographical Society of New York* 16: 242–72.

—1887a. "The Occurrence of Similar Inventions in Areas Widely Apart." *Science* 9(224): 485–6.

—1887b. "Museums of Ethnology and Their Classification." *Science* 9(228): 587–9.

Borchert, J.G. 1975. "Economic Development and Population Distribution in Albania." *Geoforum* 6 (3): 177–86.

Borza, E.N. 1992. *In the Shadow of Olympus: The Emergence of Macedon*, rev. edn. Princeton, NJ: Princeton University Press.

Bottles, S. 1987. *Los Angeles and the Automobile: The Making of the Modern City*. Berkeley, CA: University of California Press.

Bourdieu, P. 1970. "The Kabyle House or the World Reversed." In *The Logic of Practice*. Cambridge: Cambridge University Press, pp. 271–84.

—1977. *Outline of a Theory of Practice*. Cambridge: Cambridge University Press.

—1984 [1979]. *Distinction: A Social Critique of the Judgement of Taste*. Cambridge, MA: Harvard University Press.

Broughton, J.C.H.B. 1813. *A Journey through Albania and Other Provinces of Turkey in Europe and Asia, to Constantinople, during the Years 1809 and 1810*. London: Printed for James Cawthorn.

Brunvand, J.H. 1981. *The Vanishing Hitch-Hiker: American Urban Legends and Their Meanings*. New York: Norton.

—1999. *Too Good to Be True: The Colossal Book of Urban Legends*. New York and London: Norton.

Bryceson, D., and U. Vuorela (eds). 2002. *Transnational Families*. Oxford: Berg.

Buchli, V. 1999. *An Archaeology of Socialism*. Oxford: Berg.

Campbell, J. 1964. *Honour, Family and Patronage: A Study of the Institutions and Moral Values in a Greek Mountain Community*. Oxford: Clarendon Press.

Carter, F.W. 1986. "Tirana." *Cities* 3(4): 270–81.

Castells, M. 2010. *The Rise of the Network Society: The Information Age: Economy, Society, and Culture*, vol 1. Chichester: Wiley & Sons.

Chater, M. 1931. "Albania, Europe's Newest Kingdom." *National Geographic* 59(2) (February): 132–82.

Chindea, A., M. Majkowska-Tomkin, and I. Pastor. 2007. *The Republic of Albania Migration Profile*. Ljubljana: IOM and Republic of Slovenia.

Ciano, Count G. 1953. *Ciano's Hidden Diary, 1937–1938*. New York: Dutton.

Clifford, J., and G. Marcus (eds). 1986. *Writing Culture: The Poetics and Politics of Ethnography*. Los Angeles: University of California Press.

Cole, J. 1998. "The Work of Memory in Madagascar." *American Ethnologist* 25(4): 610–33.

Coles, K. 2002. "Ambivalent Builders: Europeanization, the Production of Difference, and Internationals in Bosnia-Herzegovina." *Political and Legal Anthropology Review* 25(1): 1–18.

Compte, A. 1851–54. *Système de politique positive*. Paris: Le Mathias.

Consociazione Turistica Italiana. 1940. *Albania: Guida d'Italia*. Milan: Unione Tipographica for CTI.

Cresswell, T. 2006. *On the Move*. London: Routledge.

Cresswell, T., and P. Merriman. 2011. *Geographies of Mobilities: Practices, Spaces, Subjects*. Ashgate.

Crew, P.M. 1982. *The Cambridge Ancient History*, vol. 3, pt 3, *The Expansion of the Greek World, Eighth to Sixth Centuries BC*, 2nd edn. Cambridge: Cambridge University Press.

D'Alusio, F., and P. Menzel. 1996. *Women in the Material World*. San Francisco: Sierra Club Books.

Da Matta, R. 1987. *A Casa & a Rua*. Rio de Janeiro: Editora Guanabara.

Dalakoglou, D. 2007. "Kërkimi Etnografik në shtetin fqinj: Vetveja etnografike në Balkan" [Ethnographic research in the neighboring country: ethnographic self in the Balkans]. *Hylli i Dritës* 252 (1): 24–9. Special issue: Social Anthropology in Albania. [in Albanian]

—2009a. "An Anthropology of the Road: Transnationalism, Myths and Migration on the Albanian–Greek cross-border motorway." PhD thesis, University of London (UCL).

—2009b. "Building and Ordering Transnationalism: The 'Greek house' in Albania as a Material Process." In *Anthropology and the Individual: A Material Culture Perspective*. Oxford: Berg, pp. 51–68.

—2010a. "Migrating-Remitting-'Building'-Dwelling: House-making as 'Proxy' Presence in Postsocialist Albania." *Journal of the Royal Anthropological Institute*, 16(4): 761–77.

—2010b. "The Road: An Ethnography of the Albanian–Greek Cross-border Motorway." *American Ethnologist*, 37(1): 132–49.

—2012. "'The Road from Capitalism to Capitalism': Infrastructures of (Post) Socialism in Albania." *Mobilities*, 7(4): 571–86.

—2013a. "Neo-Nazism and Neoliberalism: A Few Comments on Violence in Athens at the Time of Crisis." *WorkingUSA*, 16(2): 283–92.

—2013b. "The Crisis before 'the Crisis': Violence and Urban Neoliberalization in Athens." *Social Justice*, 39(1): 24–42.

Dalakoglou, D., and R. Halili. 2009a. "Albanian Nationalism." In *The International Encyclopedia of Revolution and Protest*. Oxford: Blackwell.

—2009b. "Socialism in Albania." In *The International Encyclopedia of Revolution and Protest*. Oxford: Blackwell.

Dalakoglou, D., and Harvey, P., 2012. "Roads and Anthropology: Ethnographic Perspectives on Space, Time and (Im)mobility." *Mobilities*, 7(4): 459–65.

Dalakoglou, D., and Kallianos, Y. 2014. "Infrastructural Flows, Interruptions and Stasis in Athens of the Crisis." *City* 18(4–5): 526–32.

Dalakoglou, D., and Vradis A., 2011. "Revolt and Crisis in Greece." Oakland: AKPress.

de La Haye, Y. (ed.). 1980. *Marx & Engels on the Means of Communication*. Paris: International general.

De Rapper, G. 1998. "La Frontière albanaise: Famille, société et identité collective en Albanie du sud." Doctoral book. Paris X-Nanterre.

De Soto, H.G., S. Beddies, and I. Gedeshi. 2005. *Roma and Egyptians in Albania: From Social Exclusion to Social Inclusion*. Washington, DC: World Bank.

De Soto, H., P. Gordon, I. Gedhesi, and Z. Sinoimeri. 2002. "Poverty in Albania." Washington, DC: World Bank.

De Waal, C. 2005. *Albania Today*. London: Tauris.

De Zwager, N. et al. 2005. *Competing for Remittances*. Tirana: IOM-Tirana.

Debord, G. 1992 [1967]. *The Society of the Spectacle*. London: Rebel Press.

Dede, M. 1987. *The Greek Arvanites*. Ioannina: Idryma Voreioipirotikon Erevnon. [in Greek]

Degrand, J.A.T. 1901. *Souvenirs de la Haute-Albanie*. Paris: Welter.

Deleuze, G., and F. Guattari. 1972. *Anti-Œdipus*. London and New York: Continuum.

—1986. *Nomadology: The War Machine*. New York: Semiotext(e).

Denzin, N., and Y. Lincoln. 1998. *Strategies of Qualitative Inquiry*. Thousand Oaks: Sage.

Dimitriadis, E., L. Lagopoulos, and G. Tsotsos (eds). 1998. *Roads and Crossroads of the Balkans*. Thessaloniki: Aristotelian University of Thessaloniki Press.

Douglas, M. 2003. *Purity and Danger: An Analysis of Concepts of Pollution and Taboo*. Abingdon: Routledge.

Duijzings, G. 2000. *Religion and the Politics of Identity in Kosovo*. London: Hurst.

Duijzings, G., D. Janjić, and M. Shkëlzen (eds). 1996. *Kosovo–Kosova: Confrontation or Coexistence*. Nijmegen: Peace Research Center, University of Nijmegen.

Durham, M.E. 1904. *Through the Lands of the Serb*. London: Edward Arnold.

—1905. *The Burden of the Balkans*. London: Nelson.

—1920a. *Twenty Years of Balkan Tangle*. London: George Allen & Unwin.

—1920b. "Ritual Nudity in Europe." *MAN* 20: 171–2.

—1923a. "A Bird Tradition in the West Balkan Peninsula." *MAN* (April): 55–61.

—1923b. "Dardania and Some Balkan Place-Names." *MAN* (March): 39–42.

—1923c. "Of Magic, Witches and Vampires in the Balkans." *MAN* (December): 189–92.

—1923d. "Some Balkan Embroidery Patterns." *MAN* (May): 69–72.

—1923e. "Some Balkan Taboos." *MAN* (June): 83–5.

—1923f. "The Seclusion of Maidens from the Light of the Sun and a Further Note on the Bird Tradition in the Balkans." *MAN* (July): 102–3.

—1923g. "Head Hunting in the Balkans." *MAN* 23 (February): 19–21.

—1924. "The Balkans as a Danger Point." *Journal of the British Institute of International Affairs* 3(3) (May): 139–44.

—1935. "Bride Price in Albania." *MAN* (June): 93–4.

—1941. "Albania." *Geography* 26: 18–24.

—1979 [1928]. *Some Tribal Origins, Laws and Customs of the Balkans*. New York: AMS.

—1985 [1909]. *High Albania*. London: Virago.

—2001. *Albania and the Albanians: Selected Articles and Letters 1903–1944*. London: Center for Albanian Studies.

Durham, M.E., and J.G. Frazer. 1912. "Albanian and Montenegrin Folklore." *Folklore* 23(2) (June): 224–9.

Eades, J. (ed.). 1987. *Migrants, Workers and the Social Order*. ASA Monographs 26. London: Tavistock.

EBRD. 2006. "EBRD Strategy for Albania as Approved by the Board of Directors 4 April 2006." www.ebrd.com/about/strategy/country/albania/albania.pdf

Edensor, T. 2004. "Automobility and National Identity Representation, Geography and Driving Practice." *Theory, Culture & Society* 21 (4–5): 101–20.

Elisseeff, V. (ed.). 1998. *The Silk Roads: Highways of Culture and Commerce*. Paris: UNESCO.

Elsie, R. 2001. "The Bektashi Order of Dervishes." In *A Dictionary of Albanian Religion, Mythology and Folk Culture*. London: Hurst, pp. 25–34.

Eriksen, E. (ed.). 2003. *Globalization: Studies in Anthropology*. London: Pluto.

EUC. 2006. "EU Council Decision regarding the Partnership with Albania." 2006/54/EC. Official Journal of the EU 7.2.06–L35. http://eur-lex.europa.eu/LexUriServ/LexUriServ.do?uri=OJ:L:2006:035:0001:0018:EN:PDF

Evans-Pritchard, E.E. 1932. "The Zande Corporation of Witchdoctors." *Journal of the Royal Anthropological Institute of Great Britain and Ireland* 62 (July–December 1932): 291–336.

—1960. "A Contribution to the Study of Zande Culture." *Africa* 30(4): 309–24.

Fakiolas, R. 2003. "Regularizing Undocumented Immigrants in Greece: Procedures and Effects." *Journal of Ethnic and Migration Studies* 29(3): 535–61.

Fanon, F., and J.-P. Sartre. 1963. *The Wretched of the Earth*. London: Penguin.

Farooque, A.K.M. 1977. *Roads and Communications in Mughal India*. Delhi: Idarah-i Adabiyat-i Delli.

Featherstone, M., J. Thrift, and J. Urry. 2005. *Automobilities*. London: Sage.

Ferguson, J. 2006. *Global Shadows: Africa in the Neoliberal World Order*. Durham, NC: Duke University Press.

Fischer, B. 1984. *King Zog and the Struggle for Stability in Albania*. Boulder, CO: East European Monographs.

Fischer, B.J. 1999. *Albania at War*. London: Hurst.

Fitzherbert, M. 1985. *The Man Who Was Greenmantle: A Biography of Aubrey Herbert*. Oxford: Oxford University Press.

Fleming, K.E. 1999. *The Muslim Bonaparte: Diplomacy and Orientalism in Ali Pasha's Greece*. Princeton, NJ: Princeton University Press.

Fortes, M. 1936. "Culture Contact as a Dynamic Process: An Investigation in the Northern Territories of the Gold Coast." *Africa: Journal of the International African Institute* 9(1): 24–55.

Foucault, M. 1975. *Discipline and Punish: The Birth of the Prison*. New York: Random House.

—1980. *Power/Knowledge*. New York: Pantheon.

—2002 [1966]. *The Order of Things: An Archaeology of the Human Sciences*. New York: Psychology Press.

Frazer, J.F. 1906. *Pictures from the Balkans*. London: Cassell.

Friedl, E. 1962. *Vasilika: A Village in Modern Greece*. New York: Holt, Rinehart and Winston.

Frisby, D. 2001. *Cityscapes of Modernity: Critical Explorations*. Cambridge: Polity Press.

Gefou-Madianou, D. 1992. "Exclusion and Unity: Retsina and Sweet Wine." In D. Gefou-Madianou (ed.), *Alcohol, Gender and Culture*. London: Routledge, pp. 108–37.

—1999. "Cultural Polyphony and Identity Formation: Negotiating Tradition in Attica." *American Ethnologist* 26(2): 412–39.

Gell, A. 1998. *Art and Agency: An Anthropological Theory*. Cambridge: Cambridge University Press.

Gellner, E. 1983. *Nations and Nationalism*. Ithaca, NY: Cornell University Press.

Gerarldi, C. 1996. *Lafiglie di Teuta: Donne d'Albania*. Lecce: Besa.

Giles-Vernick, T. 1996. "Ne lege ti guiriri" [On the road to history]. *Ethnohistory* 43(2): 225–75.

Gjergji, A., A. Dojaka, and M. Tirta. 1985. "Ndryrsime në mënyrën e jetesës së fshatarësisë së sotme" [Changes in the manners and lifestyle of the village today]. *Etnografia Shqiptare* 14: 5–33. [in Albanian]

Glick-Schiller, N., L. Basch, and C. Blanc-Szanton (eds). 1992. *Toward a Transnational Perspective on Migration: Race, Class, Ethnicity and Nationalism Reconsidered*. New York: New York Academy of Sciences.

Godart, J. 1922. *L' Albanie en 1922*. Paris: PUF.

Godelier M. 1978. "Infrastructures, Society and History." *Current Anthropology* 14(4): 763–71

Godelier, M., M. Bloch, H.J. Claessen, D.D. Gilmore, O. Pi-Sunyer and Z. Tagányi. 1978. "Infrastructures, Societies, and History [and Comments]." *Current Anthropology* 763–71.

Goffman, E. 1971. *Relations in Public: Microstudies of the Public Order*. New York: Harper & Row.

Goldring, L. 1998. "The Power of Status in Transnational Social Fields." In M.P. Smith and L.E. Guarnizo (eds), *Transnationalism from Below*. New Brunswick, NJ: Transaction, pp. 165–95.

Graham, S. and S. Marvin. 2001. *Splintering Urbanism: Networked Infrastructures, Technological Mobilities and the Urban Condition*. Oxford: Psychology Press.

Gramsci, A. 1995. *Further Selections from the Prison Notebooks*. Ed. and trans. Derek Boothman, Minneapolis: University of Minnesota Press.

Greek Helsinki Monitor. 1994. "Report on Greeks of Albania and Albanians in Greece." www.greekhelsinki.gr/pdf/ghm-greeks-albanians.PDF

Green, S.F. 2005. *Notes from the Balkans: Locating Marginality and Ambiguity on the Greek–Albanian Border*. Princeton, NJ: Princeton University Press.

Gupta, A., and J. Ferguson. 1992. "Beyond 'Culture': Space, Identity, and the Politics of Difference." *Cultural Anthropology* 7(1): 6–23.

—1997. *Culture, Power, Place: Explorations in Critical Anthropology*. Durham, NC: Duke University Press.

Hall, D. 1987. "Albania." In A. Dawson (ed.), *Planning in Eastern Europe*, London: Routledge.

—1990. "Housing Policy in Albania." In J. Sillince (ed.), *Housing Policies in Eastern Europe and the Soviet Union*. London: Routledge.

—1994. *Albania and the Albanians*. London: Pinter Publications.

—1996. "Albania: Rural Development, Migration and Uncertainty." *Geojournal* 38(2): 185–9.

—1999. "Representations of Place: Albania." *Geographical Journal* 165(2): 161–72.

Hall, D., and D. Danta (eds.). 1996. *Reconstructing the Balkans: A Geography of the New Southeast Europe*. Chichester: Wiley.

Hall, D., and A. Howlett. 1976. "Neither East Nor West." *Geographical Magazine* 52: 194–6.

Halpern, J.M. 1958. *A Serbian Village*. New York: Columbia University Press.

Hammond, N.G.L. 1966. "The Opening Campaigns and the Battle of the Aoi Stena in the Second Macedonian War." *Journal of Roman Studies* 56: 39–54.

—1967. *Epirus: The Geography, the Ancient Remains, the History and Topography of Epirus and Adjacent Areas*. Oxford: Clarendon.

—1989. "Review of *L'Illyrie méridionale et l'Epire dans l'antiquité. Actes du colloque international de Clermont-Ferrand (22–25 Octobre 1984)* by Pierre Cabanes; *Les Illyriens de Bardylis à Genthios (IVe–IIe siècles avant J.-C.)* by Pierre Cabanes." *Classical Review, New Series* 39(2): 294–6.

—1994. *Philip of Macedon*. London: Duckworth.

Hann, C. 2003. *The Post-Socialist Agrarian Question: Property Relations and the Rural Condition*. Münster: Lit Verlag.

Hann, C., C. Humphrey, and K. Verdery. 2002. "Introduction: Post-Socialism as a Topic of Anthropological Investigation." In C. Hann (ed.), *Post-Socialism: Ideals, Ideologies and Practices in Eurasia*. London: Routledge, pp. 1–28.

Hannerz, U. 1996. *Transnational Connections: Culture, People, Places*. London: Routledge.

Hansen, T. B., and F. Stepputat. 2001. *States of Imagination: Ethnographic Explorations of the Postcolonial State*. Durham, NC: Duke University Press.

Harrington, R. 1967. "Albania." *Canadian Geographical Journal* 74: 132–43.

Harris, M. 1968 [2001]. *Cultural Materialism: The Struggle for a Science of Culture*. Walnut Creek: AltaMira Press.

Harvey, D. 1989. *The Condition of Postmodernity*. Cambridge, MA: Blackwell.

—1996. *Justice, Nature and the Geography of Difference*. Oxford: Blackwell.

—2010. *Social Justice and the City*, vol. 1. Athens, GA: University of Georgia Press.

—2011. *The Enigma of Capital: And the Crises of Capitalism*. London: Profile.

Harvey, P. 2005. "The Materiality of State Effect: An Ethnography of a Road in the Peruvian Andes." In C. Krohn-Hansen and K. Nustad (eds), *State Formation*. London: Pluto, pp. 216–47.

Harvey, P., and H. Knox. 2015. *Roads: An Anthropology of Infrastructure and Expertise*. Ithaca, NY: Cornell University Press.

Hasluck, F.W. 2007 [1929]. *Christianity and Islam under the Sultans*, vol. 2. Oxford: Clarendon.

Hasluck, M. 1932. "Physiological Paternity and Belated Birth in Albania." *MAN* (February): 53–4.

—1933a. "Bride-Price in Albania." *MAN* 33 (December 1933): 191–5.

—1933b. "Childhood and Totemism." *MAN* 33 (February 1933): 40.

—1938. "The Gypsies of Albania." *Journal of the Gypsy Lore Society, Third Series* 17(2) (April): 49–61; vol. 17, Jubilee Number: 18–31; 17(4) (October): 108–22.

—1939. "Couvade in Albania." *MAN* (February): 18–20.

—1946a. "The Bust of Berat." *MAN* (March–April): 36–8.

—1946b. "The Domestic Cock, Ancient and Modern." *Folklore* 57(4) (December): 184–6.

—1948. "Firman of A.H. 1013–14 (A.D. 1604–5) regarding Gypsies in the Western Balkans." *Journal of the Gypsy Lore Society, Third Series* 27(1–2) (January–April): 1–12.

—1949. "Oedipus Rex in Albania." *Folk-Lore* 60: 340–8.

—1950. "The First Cradle of an Albanian Child." *MAN* 50 (May 1950): 55–7.

—1954. *The Unwritten Law in Albania*. Cambridge: Cambridge University Press.

Hayano, D. 1990. *Road through the Rainforest: Living Anthropology in Papua New Guinea*. Prospect Heights, IL: Waveland Press.

Hecquard, H. 1858. *Histoire et description de la Haute Albame ou Guégarie*. Paris: Bertrand.

Heidegger, M. 1971. *Poetry, Language, Thought*, trans. Albert Hofstadter. New York: Harper Colophon Books.

Herzfeld, M. 1981. "Meaning and Morality: A Semiotic Approach to Evil Eye Accusations in a Greek Village." *American Ethnologist* 8(3): 560–74.

—1982. *Ours Once More: Folklore, Ideology and the Making of Modern Greece*. New York: Pella.

—1985. *The Poetics of Manhood: Contest and Identity in a Cretan Mountain Village*. Princeton, NJ: Princeton University Press.

—1987. *Anthropology through the Looking Glass: Critical Ethnography in the Margins of Europe*. Cambridge: Cambridge University Press.

—1991. *A Place in History: Social and Monumental Time in a Cretan Town*. Princeton, NJ: Princeton University Press.

Holland, H. 1815. *Travels in Ionian Islands, Albania, Thessaly, Macedonia etc.* London: Hurst.

Holley, I.B. 2003. "Blacktop: How Asphalt Paving Came to the Urban United States." *Technology and Culture* 44(4): 703–33.

Hondagneu-Sotelo, P., and E. Avila. 1997 "'I'm Here, But I'm There': The Meanings of Latina Transnational Motherhood." *Gender and Society* 11(5): 548–71.

Horst, H. 2004. "'Back a Yaad': Constructions of Home among Jamaica's Returned Migrant Community." PhD thesis, University of London.

Hughes, T.P. 1996. *A Dictionary of Islam: Being a Cyclopaedia of the Doctrines, Rites, Ceremonies, and Customs, Together with the Technical and Theological Terms, of the Muhammadan Religion*. New Delhi: Asian Educational Services.

Hughes, T.S. 1830. *Travels in Greece and Albania.* London: Colburn & Bentley.

Humphrey, C. 1989. "Perestroika and the Pastoralists: The Example of Mongun-Taiga in Tuva ASSR." *Anthropology Today* 5(3): 6–10.

—1998. *Marx Went Away—But Karl Stayed Behind: Karl Marx Collective, Economy, Society and Religion in a Siberian Collective Farm.* Ann Arbor: University of Michigan Press.

—2002. *The Unmaking of Soviet Life: Everyday Economies after Socialism.* Ithaca, NY: Cornell University Press.

—2003. "Rethinking Infrastructure: Siberian Cities and the Great Freeze of January 2001." In J. Schneider and I. Susser (eds), *Wounded Cities.* Oxford: Berg, pp. 91–107.

—2005. "Ideology in Infrastructure: Architecture and Soviet Imagination." *Journal of the Royal Anthropological Institute* 11(1): 39–58.

Humphrey, C., and R. Mandel. 2002. "The Market in Everyday Life: Ethnographies of Post-Socialism." In R. Mandel and C. Humphrey (eds), *Market and Moralities.* Oxford: Berg, pp. 1–18.

Hymes, D. 1974 [1969]. "The Use of Anthropology." In D. Hymes (eds), *Reinventing Anthropology.* New York: Vintage.

Hysa, R. 2003. *Albanian–English–Albanian Dictionary.* New York: Hippocrene.

Hyslop, J. 1984. *The Inca Road System.* New York: Academic Press.

IMF. 1994. "Second Annual Francisco Fernández Ordóñez Address by Michel Camdessus, Managing Director of the International Monetary Fund." Madrid, December 21.

—2003. "Albania: Selected Issues and Appendix." Country Report no. 03/64. Washington, DC: IMF.

Infrastructure Steering Group. 2003. "Implementing Regional Transport Priorities in the Western Balkans." EC/World Bank Joint Office for Southeastern Europe. http://fs9.rec.org/environment_and_transport/download_page.php?filename=transport%20priorities%20balkans.pdf

Ingold, T. 2004. "Culture on the Ground: Culture Perceived through the Feet." *Journal of Material Culture* 9(3): 315–40.

INSTAT. 2004. *Popullsia e Shqipërisë: Gjirokastër/2001*, vol. 6. Tirana: INSTAT.

Iosifides, T., and R. King. 1998. "Socio-Spatial Dynamics and Exclusion of Three Immigrant Groups in the Athens Conurbation." *South European Society and Politics* 3(3): 205–29.

Ippen, T.A. 1907. *Skutari und die nordalbanische Kustenebene.* Sarajevo: Daniel A Kajon.

Jackson, P., P. Crang, and C. Dwyer. 2004. *Transnational Spaces.* London: Routledge.

Jameson, F. 1984. "Postmodernism, or, the Cultural Logic of Late Capitalism." *New Left Review* 146 (July–August): 52–92.

Johnston, D. 1979. *An Illustrated History of Roman Roads in Britain.* Bourne End: Spurbooks.

Jovanović, M., K. Kaser, and S. Naumović (eds). 2005. *Between the Archives and the Field: A Dialogue on Historical Anthropology of the Balkans.* Münster: Lit Verlag.

Kadare, I. 2007. *Chronicle in the Stone*. New York: Arcade Publishing.

Kaneff, D. 2004. *Who Owns the Past: The Politics of Time in a "Model" Bulgarian Village*. Oxford: Berghahn.

Kaplan, C. 1987. "Deterritorialisations." *Cultural Critique* 6: 187–98.

Kapllani, G., and N. Mai. 2005 "'Greece Belongs to Greeks!' The Case of the Greek Flag in the Hands of an Albanian Student." In R. King, N. Mai, and S. Schwandner-Sievers (eds), *The New Albanian Migration*. Brighton: University of Sussex Press, pp. 153–72.

Kaser, K. 1992. "The Origins of Balkan Patriarchy." *Modern Greek Studies Yearbook* 8: 1–39.

Kaser, K., S. Schwandner-Sievers, and R. Pichler (eds). 2002. *Die weite Welt und das Dorf: Albanische Emigration am Ende des 20. Jahrhunderts* [Wide world and village: Albanian emigrations at the end of the twentieth century]. Vienna: Böhlau.

Kearney, M. 1986. "From the Invisible Hand to the Visible Feet: Anthropological Studies of Migration and Development." *Annual Review of Anthropology* 15: 331–61.

—1995. "The Local and the Global: The Anthropology of Globalisation and Transnationalism." *Annual Review of Anthropology* 24: 547–65.

Kelly, J., and M. Kaplan. 1990. "History, Structure and Ritual." *Annual Review of Anthropology* 19: 119–50.

Kennan, G. 1993. *The Other Balkan Wars: A 1913 Carnegie Endowment Inquiry in Retrospect*. Washington, DC: Carnegie Endowment for International Peace.

Kerenyi, K. 1980 [1951]. *The Gods of the Greeks*. London: Thames & Hudson.

Khun, T.S. 2012. *The Structure of Scientific Revolutions*. Chicago: University of Chicago Press.

King, R. 2000. "Southern Europe in the Changing Global Map of Migration." In R. King, G. Lazaridis, and C. Tsardanidis (eds), *Eldorado or Fortress? Migration in Southern Europe*. London: Macmillan.

—(ed.). 2001. *The Mediterranean Passage: Migration and New Cultural Encounters in Southern Europe*. Liverpool: Liverpool University Press.

—2002. "Towards a New Map of European Migration." *International Journal of Population Geography* 8(2): 89–106.

—2003. "Across the Sea and Over the Mountains: Documenting Albanian Migration." *Scottish Geographical Journal* 119(3): 283–309.

—2004. "Albania: Interrelationships between Population, Poverty, Development, Internal and International Migration." *Méditerranée* 103(3/4): 37–48.

King, R., and J. Andall. 1999. "The Geography and Economic Sociology of Recent Immigration to Italy." *Modern Italy* 4(2): 135–58.

King, R., and R. Black (eds). 1997. *Southern Europe and the New Immigrations*. Brighton: Sussex Academic Press.

King, R., T. Iosifides, and L. Myrivili. 1998. "A Migrant's Story: From Albania to Athens." *Journal of Ethnic and Migration Studies* 24(1): 159–75.

King, R., G. Lazaridis, and C. Tsardanidis (eds). 2000. *Eldorado or Fortress? Migration in Southern Europe*. London: Macmillan.

King, R., and N. Mai. 2002. "Of Myths and Mirrors: Interpretations of Albanian Migration." *Studi Emigrazione* 145: 161–99.

—2004. "Albanian Migrants in Lecce and Modena: Narratives of Rejection, Survival and Integration." *Population, Space and Place* 10(6): 455–78.

King, R., N. Mai, and M. Dalipaj. 2003. *Exploding the Migration Myths.* London: Fabian Society and Oxfam.

King, R., N. Mai, and S. Schwandner-Sievers (eds). 2005. *The New Albanian Migration.* Brighton: Sussex Academic Press.

King, R., and J. Vullnetari. 2003. "Migration and Development in Albania." DRC Working Paper C5, Development Research Centre on Migration, Globalisation and Poverty. Brighton: University of Sussex.

Kipling, R. 1994 [1901]. *Kim.* London: Wordsworth.

Knight, E.F. 1880. *Albania.* London: Sampson Low.

Kola, P. 2003. *The Search for Greater Albania.* London: Hurst.

Kollias, A. 1983. *Arvanites and the Descent of the Greeks.* Athens. [in Greek]

Konidiaris, G. 2005. "Examining Policy Responses to Immigration in the Light of Interstate Relations and Foreign Policy Objectives: Greece and Albania." In R. King, N. Mai, and S. Schwandner-Sievers (eds), *The New Albanian Migration.* Brighton: University of Sussex Press, pp. 64–92.

Kressing, F., and K. Kaser. 2002. *Albania—A Country in Transition: Aspects of Changing Identities in a South-East European Country.* Baden-Baden: Nomos.

Kuper, A. 1986. "An Interview with Edmund Leach." *Current Anthropology* 27(4): 375–82.

Kyriakidou-Nestoros, A. 2001. *The Theory of Greek Folklore.* Athens: Moraitis. [in Greek]

Labrianidis, L., and A. Lyberaki. 2001. *Albanian Migrants in Thessalonica.* Thessalonica: Paratiritis. [in Greek]

Laderman, D. 2002. *Road Films: History and Criticism.* Austin: University of Texas Press.

Lambrianidis, L., and P. Hatziprokopiou. 2005. "The Albanian Migration Cycle." In R. King, N. Mai, and S. Schwandner-Sievers (eds), *The New Albanian Migration.* Brighton: University of Sussex Press.

Lapavitsas, C. 2009. "Financialised capitalism: Crisis and financial expropriation." *Historical Materialism* 17(2): 114–48.

—2014. *Profiting without Producing: How Finance Exploits Us All.* New York: Verso.

Larkin, B. 2008. *Signal and Noise: Media, Infrastructure, and Urban Culture in Nigeria.* Durham, NC: Duke University Press.

—2013. "The Politics and Poetics of Infrastructure." *Annual Review of Anthropology,* 42: 327–43.

Latour, B. 1987. *Science in Action: How to Follow Scientists and Engineers Through Society.* Cambridge, MA: Harvard University Press.

—1993. "We Have Never Been Modern." Trans. C. Porter. Cambridge, MA: Harvard University Press.

—1996. *Aramis, or, the Love of Technology.* Cambridge, MA: Harvard University Press.

—2007. *Reassembling the Social: An Introduction to Actor-Network-Theory.* Oxford: Oxford University Press.

Latour, B., and C. Venn. 2002. "Morality and Technology the End of the Means." *Theory, Culture & Society* 19(5–6): 247–60.

Latour, B., and S. Woolgar. 1979. *Laboratory Life: The Social Construction of Scientific Facts.* Princeton, NJ: Princeton University Press.

Laurence, R. 1999. *The Roads of Roman Italy: Mobility and Cultural Change.* London: Routledge.

Leake, W.M. 1835. *Travels in Northern Greece.* London.

Lear, E. 1851. *Journals of a Landscape Painter in Greece and Albania.* London: Hutchinson.

Lefebvre, H. 1974. "La production de l'espace." *L'Homme et la société* 31(1): 15–32.

—1991 [1974]. *The Production of Space.* Oxford: Blackwell.

—2009 [1940]. *Dialectical Materialism.* Minnesota: University of Minnesota Press.

Leggett, E. 1976. *The Corfu Incident.* London: Seeley.

Levi-Strauss, C. 1966. "Anthropology: Its Achievements and Future." *Current Anthropology* 7(2): 124–7.

—1976. "The Story of the Asdiwal." In *Structural Anthropology*, vol. 2. New York: Basic Books.

—1982. *The Way of the Mask.* Seattle: University of Washington.

—1987. *Anthropology and Myth.* Oxford: Blackwell.

Levi-Strauss, C., and P.B. Kussell. 1971. "Interview: Claude Lévi-Strauss." *Diacritics* 1(1): 44–50.

Lewis, I.M. 1961. *A Pastoral Democracy.* Oxford: Oxford University Press.

Lewis, O. 1964. *The Children of Sanchez.* Harmondsworth: Penguin.

Livy. 1823. *The History of Rome.* Boston: Baker.

Löfgren, O. 2004. "Concrete Transnationalism? Bridge Building in the New Economy." *Focaal—European Journal of Anthropology* 43: 59–75.

Louis-Jaray, G. 1913. *L'Albanie inconnue.* Paris: Librairie Hachette.

Low, S. 2000. *On the Plaza: The Politics of Public Space.* Austin: University of Texas Press.

Luckwald, E. von. 1942. *Albanien: Land zwischen Gestern und Morgen.* Munich: F. Bruckmann.

McHeyman, C. 1994. "The Organizational Logic of Capitalist Consumption on the Mexico–US Border." *Research in Economic Anthropology* 15: 175–238.

MacNichol, D. 2005. *The Roads That Built America: The Incredible Story of the US Interstate System.* New York: Sterling.

Mahler, S. 1998. "Theoretical and Empirical Contributions: Toward a Research Agenda for Transnationalism." In M.P. Smith and L.E. Guarnizo (eds), *Transnationalism from Below.* New Brunswick, NJ: Transaction, pp. 64–100.

Mai, N. 2001a. "'Italy is Beautiful': The Role of Italian Television in the Albanian Migratory Flow to Italy." In R. King and N. Wood (eds), *Media and Migration: Constructions of Mobility and Difference.* London: Routledge, pp. 95–109.

—2001b. "Transforming Traditions: A Critical Analysis of the Trafficking and Exploitation of Albanian Girls in Italy." In R. King (ed.), *The Mediterranean Passage: Migration and New Cultural Encounters in Southern Europe.* Liverpool: Liverpool University Press, pp. 258–78.

—2002a. "Myths and Moral Panics: Italian Identity and the Media Representation of Albanian Immigration." In R.D. Grillo and J. Pratt (eds), *The Politics of Recognising Difference: Multiculturalism Italian Style.* Aldershot: Ashgate, pp. 77–95.

—2002b. "Youth NGOs in Albania: Civil Society Development, Local Cultural Constructions of Democracy and Strategies of Survival at Work." In S. Schwandner-Sievers and B.J. Fischer (eds), *Albanian Identities: Myth, Narratives and Politics.* London: Hurst, pp. 215–25.

—2003. "The Cultural Construction of Italy in Albania and Vice Versa: Migration Dynamics, Strategies of Resistance and Politics of Mutual Self-Definition Across Colonialism and Post-Colonialism." *Modern Italy* 9(1): 77–94.

Mai, N., and S. Schwandner-Sievers (eds). 2003a. *Albanian Migration and New Transnationalism.* Special Issue of *Journal of Ethnic and Migration Studies* 29(6).

—2003b. "Albanian Migration and New Transnationalism." *Journal of Ethnic and Migration Studies* 29(6): 939–48.

Malinowski, B. 1922. *Argonauts of the Western Pacific.* London: Routledge & Kegan Paul.

Mantzios, K. 2007. "Transition Policies: Producing and Reproducing Identities—The Case of Greek Minority in Albania." PhD thesis, University of Ioannina.

Marcus, G. 1989. "Imagining the Whole: Ethnography's Contemporary Efforts to Situate Itself." *Critical Anthropology* 9: 7–30.

—1995. "Ethnography in/of the World System: The Emergence of Multi-Sited Ethnography." *Annual Review of Anthropology* 24: 95–117.

Marcus, G., and M.J. Fischer. 1986. *Anthropology as Cultural Critique: An Experimental Moment in the Human Sciences.* Chicago: University of Chicago Press.

Margary, I.D. 1973. *Roman Roads in Britain.* London: John Baker.

Marmullaku, R. 1975. *Albania and the Albanians.* London: Hurst.

Marx, K. 1993a. *Das Kapital,* vol. 3. London: Penguin.

—1993b. *Grundrisse.* London: Penguin.

Masquelier, A. 1992. "Encounter with a Road Siren: Machines, Bodies and Commodities in the Imagination of a Mawri Healer." *Visual Anthropology Review* 8(1): 56–69.

—2002. "Road Mythographies: Space, Mobility and the Historical Imagination in Postcolonial Niger." *American Ethnologist* 24(4): 829–56.

Mauss, M. 2007 [1935]. "Techniques of the Body." In M. Lock and J. Farquhar (eds), *Beyond the Body Proper: Reading the Anthropology of Material Life.* Durham, NC: Duke University Press, pp. 50–68.

Mazower, M. 2009. *Dark Continent: Europe's Twentieth Century.* New York: Vintage.

Merriman, P. 2007. *Driving Spaces: A Cultural–Historical Geography of England's M1 Motorway*. Oxford: Blackwell.

Meylan, A. 1885. *A travers l'Albanie*. Paris: Libraire Ch. Delagrav.

Merriman, P. 2007. *Driving Spaces: A Cultural–Historical Geography of England's M1 Motorway*. Oxford: Blackwell.

Meylan, A. 1885. *A travers l'Albanie*. Paris: Libraire Ch. Delagrav.

Miller, D. (ed.). 2001. *Car Cultures*. Oxford: Berg.

—2005. "Materiality: An Introduction." *Materiality*. Durham, NC: Duke University Press, pp. 1–50.

—2010. *Stuff*. Cambridge: Polity.

Miller, D., and S. Woodward. 2007. "Manifesto for a Study of Denim." *Social Anthropology* 15(3): 271–411.

Mom, G. 2005. "Roads without Rails: European Highway-Network Building and the Desire for Long-Range Motorized Mobility." *Technology and Culture* 46(4): 745–72.

Mom, G., and D.A. Kirsch. 2001. "Technologies in Tension: Horses, Electric Trucks, and the Motorization of American Cities, 1900–1925." *Technology and Culture* 42(3): 489–518.

Moran, E. 1981. *Developing the Amazon: The Social and Ecological Impact of Settlement along the Transamazon Highway*. Bloomington: Indiana University Press.

Morford, M.P.O., and L.J. Lenardon. 2006. *Classical Mythology*. Oxford: Oxford University Press.

Muka, A. 2003. "Për Fshatin e Malësive të Shkodrës" [On the village of the highlands of Shkodër]. *Kultura Popullore* 1–2: 47–66. [in Albanian]

Natale, M., and S. Strozza. 2003. "Lavoro Reddito e rimesse degli immirati stranieri in Italia." In N. Accocella and E. Sonnino (eds), *Movimenti di Persone e Movimenti di Capitali in Europa*. Milan: Il Mulino, pp. 289–367.

New Encyclopaedia Britannica. 1974. *Micropaedia*, vol. 1. Chicago: Encyclopaedia Britannica.

Newman, B. 1936a. *Albanian Back-Door*. London: De France.

—1936b. "The Law of Lek." *Geographical Magazine* 8: 143–56.

Nicholson, B. 1999. "The Beginning of the End of a Rebellion: Southern Albania, May–June 1997." *East European Politics and Societies* 13(3): 543–65.

—2002. "The Wrong End of the Telescope: Economic Migrants, Immigration Policy, and How It Looks from Albania." *Political Quarterly* 73(4): 436–44.

—2004. "The Tractor, the Shop and the Filling Station: Work Migration as Self-Help Development in Albania." *Europe–Asia Studies* 56(6): 877–90.

—2006a. "Women Who Shared a Husband: Polygymy in Southern Albania in the Early Twentieth Century." *History of the Family* 11(1): 45–57.

—2006b. "L'occupazione austro-ungarica di Mallakastër in Albania e le sue ripercussioni sulla popolazione civile." In Bruna Bianchi (ed.), *La violenza contro i civili durante la Grande guerra: Deportati, profughi, internati*. Milan: Unicopli, pp. 127–46.

Nitsiakos, V. (ed.). 2003. *Testimonies of Albanian Migrants*. Athens: Odysseas [in Greek].

—2010. *On the Border: Transborder Mobility, Ethnic Groups and Boundaries along the Albanian–Greek Frontier*, vol. 1. Münster: Lit Verlag.

Nopcsa, F.B. 1925. *Albanien: Bauten, Trachten und Gerate Nordalbaniens.* Leipzig: Gruyter.

Norris, H.T. 1993. *Islam in the Balkans: Religion and Society between Europe and the Arab World.* Columbia, SC: University of South Carolina Press.

Nowack, E. 1921. "A Contribution to the Geography of Albania." *Geographical Review* 11: 503–40.

O'Donnell, J.S. 1999. *A Coming of Age: Albania under Enver Hoxha.* Boulder and New York: East European Monographs; Columbia University Press.

O'Hanlon, M., and L. Frankland. 2003. "Co-Present Landscapes: Routes and Rootness as Sources of Identity in Highland New Guinea." In P. Stewart and A. Strathern (eds), *Landscape, Memory and History: Anthropological Perspectives.* London: Pluto, pp. 166–88.

Olsen, R. 2004. *Route 66 Lost & Found: Ruins and Relics Revisited.* St Paul, MN: MBI Publishing.

OSCE. 2007. "OSCE Presence Supports Safe Driving Campaign in Albania." www.osce.org/albania/57623

Papajorgji, H. 1964. *The Development of Socialist Industry and Its Prospects in the People's Republic of Albania.* Tirana.

Patton, P. 1986. *Open Road: Celebration of the American Highway.* New York: Simon & Schuster.

Peacock, W. 1914. *Albania.* London: Chapman & Hall.

Pearson, O. 2006. *Albania in the Twentieth Century: A History.* 3 vols. London: Tauris.

Pearson, R. 1983. *National Minorities in Eastern Europe, 1848–1945.* London: Macmillan.

Peterson-Bidoshi, K. 2006. "The Dordolec: Albanian House Dolls and the Evil Eye." *Journal of American Folklore* 119(473): 337–55.

Pettifer, J., and M. Vickers. 2006. *The Albanian Question.* London: Tauris.

PHARE. 1999. "Overall PHARE Assistance in ALBANIA 1991–99 (Mio €)." http://ec.europa.eu/enlargement/archives/seerecon/albania/documents/albania_phare_1991-99.pdf

Pina-Cabral, J. 1987. "Paved Roads and Enchanted Mooresses: The Perception of the Past among the Peasant Population of the Alto-Minho." *Man. New Series* 22: 715–35.

Piperno, F. 2005. "Albanian Migrants' Remittances: A Development Opportunity?" In R. King, N. Mai, and S. Schwandner-Sievers (eds), *The New Albanian Migration.* Brighton: University of Sussex Press, pp. 118–38.

Polster, B., and P. Patton. 1997. *Highway: America's Endless Dream.* New York: Stewart, Tbaori, & Chang.

Postoli, K. 1983. *Bankat dhe veprimtaria e tyre në Shqipërinë Socialiste.* Tirana: 8 Nentori.

Pouqueville, F.C.H.L. 1820. *Travels in Epirus, Albania, Macedonia and Thessaly.* London: Richard Philips.

Prendi, F., and D. Budina. 1970. *"La civilisation illyrienne de la vallee du s"*

Communications de la legation de la R.P. d'Albanie, IIe Congres international des l'Etudes du Sud-est Europeen. Tirana.

Prifti, P.R. 1978. *Socialist Albania since 1944*. Cambridge, MA: MIT Press.

Primeau, R. 1996. *Romance of the Road: The Literature of the American Highway*. Bowling Green, OH: Popular Press.

Pusceddu, A. M. 2013. "Local Brothers, National Enemies: Representations of Religious Otehrness in Post-Ottoman Eprius (Greece)." *Oriente Moderno*, 93(2), 298–622.

Puto, A., and S. Pollo. 1981. *The History of Albania: From Its Origins to the Present Day*. London: Routledge & Kegan Paul.

Rabinow, P. 2007 [1977]. *Reflections on Fieldwork in Morocco*. Berkeley, CA: University of California Press.

Rao, A. (ed.). 1987. *The Other Nomads*. Cologne: Bohlau Verlag.

Rashid, M., V. Dorabawila, and R. Adams. 2001. "Household Welfare, the Labor Market and Social Programs in Albania." Washington, DC: World Bank.

Redfield, R. 1956. *The Little Community*. Chicago: University of Chicago Press.

Riza, E. 1978. *Gjirokastër: Museum City*. Tirana: 8 Nentori.

—1981. *Gjirokastër*. Tirana: 8 Nentori.

Rosaldo, R. 1988. "Ideology, Place, and People without Culture." *Cultural Anthropology* 3(1): 77–87.

Rose, M. 1990. *Interstate: Express Highway Politics, 1939–1989*. Knoxville: University of Tennessee Press.

Roseman, S. 1996. "How We Built the Road: The Politics of Memory in Rural Galicia." *American Ethnologist* 23(3): 836–60.

Rostow, W. W. 1990. *The Stages of Economic Growth: A Non-Communist Manifesto*. Cambridge: Cambridge University Press.

Roussou, E. Forthcoming. "Challenging Perception: The Evil Eye in Greece." PhD thesis, University College London.

Rugg, D.S. 1994. "Communist Legacies in the Albanian Landscape." *Geographical Review* 84: 59–73.

Saltmarshe, D. 2001. *Identity in a Post-Communist Balkan State: An Albanian Village Study*. Aldershot: Ashgate.

Sanjek, R. 1996. "Franz Boas." In *An Encyclopaedia of Social and Cultural Anthropology*. London: Routledge.

Sassen, S. 1990. *The Mobility of Labor and Capital: A Study in International Investment and Labor Flows*. Cambridge: Cambridge University Press.

Schnytzer, A. 1982. *Stalinist Economic Strategy in Practice: The Case of Albania*. Oxford: Oxford University Press.

Schwandner-Sievers, S. 1995. "Freund, Feind, Ehre." In H. Eberhard and K. Kaser (eds), *Albanien: Stammesgesellschaft zwischen Tradition und Moderne*. Vienna, Cologne, and Weimar: Boehlau Verlag, pp. 117–32

—1999. "The Albanian Aromanians' Awakening: Identity Politics and Conflicts in Post-Communist Albania." Working Paper 3. Flensburg: European Center for Minority Issues.

—2001. "The Enactment of 'Tradition': Albanian Constructions of Identity,

Violence and Power in Times of Crisis." In B.E. Schmidt and I.W. Schroeder (eds), *Anthropology of Violence and Conflict*. London: Routledge, pp. 97–120.

—2002. "Introduction: Narratives of Power—Capacities of Myth in Albania." In S. Schwandner-Sievers and B. Fischer (eds), *Albanian Identities: Myth and History*. London: Hurst.

—2003. "Gaps of Concern—An Inconclusive Conclusion." In P. Siani-Davies (ed.), *International Interventions in the Balkans since 1995*. London: Routledge, pp. 194–217.

—2004a. "Albanians, Albanianism and the Strategic Subversion of Stereotypes." In A. Hammond (ed.), *The Balkans and the West: Constructing the European Other, 1945–2003*. Aldershot: Ashgate, pp. 110–26.

—2004b. "Times Past: References for the Construction of Local Order in Present-Day Albania." In M. Todorova (ed.), *Balkan Identities: Nation and Memory*. London: Hurst, pp. 103–28.

—2005. "Culture in Curt: Albanian Migrants and the Anthropologist as Expert Witness." In S. Pink (ed.), *The Applications of Anthropology*. Oxford: Berghahn, pp. 209–28.

Schwandner-Sievers, S., and B.J. Fischer (eds) 2002. *Albanian Identities: Myth, Narratives and Politics*. London: Hurst.

Scott, J. C. 1998. *Seeing Like a State: How Certain Schemes to Improve the Human Condition Have Failed*. New Haven: Yale University Press.

—2014. *The Art of not Being Governed: An Anarchist History of Upland Southeast Asia*. New Haven: Yale University Press.

Scriven, G.P. 1921. "Some Highways of Albania and a Forgotten Riviera." *Geographical Review* 11(2) (April 1921): 198–206

Seely, B. 1987. *Building the American Highway System: Engineers as Policy Makers*. Philadelphia: Temple University Press.

Selwyn, T. 2001. "Landscapes of Separation: Reflections on the Symbolism of By-Pass Roads in Palestine." In B. Bender and W. Winer (eds), *Contested Landscapes*. Oxford: Berg, pp. 225–40.

Seremetakis, N.C. 1991. *The Last Word: Women, Death, and Divination in Inner Mani*. Chicago: University of Chicago Press.

Shai, D. 1976. "A Kurdish Jewish Variant of the Ballad of the 'Bridge of Arta.'" *AJS Review* 1: 303–10.

Sheller, M. 2004. "Automotive Emotions: Feeling the Car." *Theory, Culture & Society* 21(4): 221–42.

Shkodra, G., and Ganiu. 1984. *The Well-Being of the Albanian People and Some Factors and Ways for Its Continuous Improvement*. Tirana: 8 Nentori.

Sivignon, M. 1970. "Quelques donnee demographiques sur la Republique Populaire d'Albanie." *Review de Geographie* 45(2): 73–83.

—1975. "Tirana et l'urbanisation d'Albanie." *Review de Geographie* 50(4): 333–43.

—1983. "Evolution de la population de l'Albanie." *Méditerranee* 50(4): 37–42.

—1987. "Les disparites regionales en Albanie." *Bull. Soc. Languedocienne Geogr.* 21(1–2): 97–103.

Sjöberg, Ö. 1990. *The Albanian Economy in the 1980s: The Nature of a Low-*

Performing System. Stockholm: Stockholm Institute of Soviet and East European Economics, Östekonomiska Institutet.

—1991a. *Rural Change and Development in Albania.* Boulder, CO: Westview Press.

—1991b. *Urban Albania: Developments 1965–1987.* Stockholm: Handelshögskolan i Stockholm, Department of International Economics and Geography.

Sjöberg, Ö., and M.L. Wyzan. 1991. *Economic Change in the Balkan States: Albania, Bulgaria, Romania and Yugoslavia.* London: Macmillan.

Skendi, S. 1954. "Albanian and South Slavic Oral Epic Poetry." *Memoirs of the American Folklore Society* 40.

Skendi, S. et al. 1957. *Albania.* London: Atlantic Press.

Snead, J. , C. Erickson, and A. Darling (eds). 2010. *Landscapes of Movement: Trails, Paths, and Roads in Anthropological Perspective.* Philadelphia: University of Pennsylvania Press.

Soja, E. 1989. *Postmodern Geographies: The Reassertion of Space in Critical Social Theory.* New York: Verso.

Sorenson, R. 1972. "Socio-Ecological Change among the Fore of New Guinea [and Comments and Replies]." *Current Anthropology* 13(3/4): 349–83.

Ssorin-Chaikov, N. 2003. *The Social Life of the State in Subarctic Siberia.* Stanford, CA: Stanford University Press.

Stahl, P. 1986. *Household, Village and Village Confederation in Southeastern Europe.* New York: Columbia University Press.

Stanek, L. 2008. "Space as a Concrete Abstraction: Hegel, Marx, and Modern Urbanism in Henri Lefebvre." In K. Goonewardena, S. Kipfer, R. Milgrom, and C. Schmid (eds), *Space, Difference, Everyday Life: Reading Henri Lefebvre.* Oxford: Routledge.

Stavrianos, L. 1958. *The Balkans since 1453.* London: Holt, Rinehart and Winston.

Stazimiri, G. 1987. *Berati.* Tirana: 8 Nentori.

Stewart, K. 1996. *A Space on the Side of the Road: Cultural Poetics in an "Other" America.* Princeton, NJ: Princeton University Press.

Stewart, P., and A. Strathern. 1999. "Death on the Move: Landscape, Violence on the Highlands Highway, Papua New Guinea." *Anthropology & Humanism* 24(1): 20–31.

Stocking, G.W. 1974. *The Shaping of American Anthropology, 1883–1911: A Franz Boas Reader.* New York: Basic Books.

Swire, J. 1929. *Albania: The Rise of a Kingdom.* London: Williams & Norgate.

—1937. *King Zog's Albania.* London: Robert Hale.

Thomas, H.E. (ed.). 2003. *Globalization.* London: Pluto.

Thomas, P. 1996. "House." In A. Barnard and J. Spencer (eds), *Encyclopaedia of Social and Cultural Anthropology.* London: Routledge.

—2002. "The River, the Road, and the Rural–Urban Divide: A Postcolonial Moral Geography from Southeast Madagascar." *American Ethnologist* 29(2): 366–91.

Thrift, N. 1996. *Spatial Formations.* London: Sage.

Tilburg, C.R. van. 2006. *Traffic and Congestion in the Roman Empire*. London: Routledge.

Tilley, C. 1994. *The Phenomenology of Landscape: Places, Paths and Monuments*. Oxford: Berg.

—2004. *The Materiality of Stone: Explorations in Landscape Phenomenology*. Oxford: Berg.

Tirta, M. 2006. "Marrëdhënie Harmonie në mes Shqiptareve më beshime te ndrysmë" [Harmonic interrelations among the Albanians of various religious beliefs]. *Kultura Popullore* 1–2: 4–16. [in Albanian]

Todorova, M. 1994. "The Balkans: From Discovery to Invention." *Slavic Review* 53(2): 453–82.

—1997. *Imagining the Balkans*. Oxford: Oxford University Press.

Trankell, I.B. 1993. *On the Road in Laos: An Anthropological Study of Road Construction and Rural Communities*. Uppsala: Uppsala Research Reports in Cultural Anthropology.

Trombold, C. (ed.). 1991. *Ancient Road Networks and Settlement Hierarchies in the New World*. Cambridge: Cambridge University Press.

Turner, V. 1995. *The Ritual Process: Structure and Anti-Structure*. New Brunswick: Transaction Publishers.

UN Economic Commission for Europe (ECE). 2002. "Albania: Country Profiles on the Housing Sector." Geneva: United Nations.

Urry, J. 2000. *Sociology Beyond Societies: Mobilities for the Twenty-First Century*. London: Routledge.

—2007. *Mobilities*. Cambridge: Polity.

Vahrenkamp, R. 2002. "Roads without Cars: The HAFRABA Association and the Autobahn Project 1933–1943 in Germany." Working Papers in the History of Mobility No. I/2002.

Vainshtein, S. 1980. *Nomads of South Siberia*. Cambridge: Cambridge University Press.

Vasil, K., and A. Muka. 2003. "Fshati si Vendbanim dhe Tradita Ndërtimore në Luxhëri" [The village as dwelling place and the house tradition in Luxheri]. *Kultura Popullore* 1–2: 101–24. [in Albanian]

Vatavali, F. Forthcoming. "Boundaries, Exchanges and Urban Centers on the Greek–Albanian Border." PhD dissertation, National Technical University of Athens.

Veikou, C. 1998. *Evil Eye: The Social Construction of Visual Communication*. Athens: Hellinika Grammata. [in Greek]

Verdery, K. 1996. *What Was Socialism and What Comes Next?* Princeton, NJ: Princeton University Press.

—1999. *The Political Lives of Dead Bodies: Reburial and Post-Socialist Change*. New York: Columbia University Press.

Vickers, M. 1999. *The Albanians: A Modern History*. London: Tauris.

Vickers, M., and J. Pettifer. 1997. *Albania: From Anarchy to a Balkan Identity*. London: Hurst.

Virilio, P. 2005. *City of Panic*. Oxford: Berg.

—2006 [1977]. *Speed and Politics: An Essay on Dromology*. Cambridge, MA: Semiotext(e).

—2007. *The Original Accident*. Cambridge: Polity.

Vjetari Statistikor i Shqipërisë. 1991. Tirana: Ministria e ekonomisë drejtoria e statistikës.

Voell, S. 2003. "The Kanun in the City." *Anthropos* 98(1): 85–101.

Von Hagen, V.W. 1976. *The Royal Road of the Inca*. London: Gordon & Cremonesi.

Von Hanh, J.G. 1854 [1981]. *Albanesische Studien*. 3 vols. Jena 1854. [repr. Athens: Karavias]

Vullnetari, J. 2013. *Albania on the Move*. Amsterdam: Amsterdam University Press.

Vullnetari, J., and R. King. 2008. "'Does Your Granny Eat Grass?' On Mass Migration, Care Drain and the Fate of Older People in Rural Albania." *Global Networks* 8(2): 139–71.

Wason, D. 1991. *The Albanians of Rrogam*. Manchester: Granada Television.

Watson, J. (ed.). 1977. *Between Two Cultures: Migrants and Minorities in Britain*. Oxford: Blackwell.

Weingroft, R. 2006. The Year of the Interstate." *Public Roads* 69 (4). www.tfhrc.gov/pubrds/06jan/01.htm

Weller, A. 1997. *Days and Nights on the Grand Trunk Road: Calcutta to Khyber*. New York: Marlowe.

White, L. 1993. "Cars Out of Place: Vampires, Technology, and Labor in East and Central Africa." *Representations* 43: 27–50.

Whitfield, S. 2000. *Life along the Silk Road*. Berkeley, CA: University of California Press.

Williams, R. 1960. *Border Country*. London: Chatto & Windus.

Willson, F. 2004. "Towards a Political Economy of Roads: Experiences from Peru." *Development and Change* 35(3): 525–46.

Winner, L. 2010. *The Whale and the Reactor: A Search for Limits in an Age of High Technology*. Chicago: University of Chicago Press

Wollen, P., and J. Kerr. 2002. *Autopia*. London: Reaktion.

Wood, F. 2004. *The Silk Road: Two Thousand Years in the Heart of Asia*. Berkeley, CA: University of California Press.

World Bank 2006. "Status of Land Reform and Real Property Markets in Albania." Tirana: World Bank Tirana Office.

—2007. "Albania: Transport Project." http://go.worldbank.org/5M30PNNR10

—2008. "Secondary and Local Roads Project Will Improve the Quality of Life in Rural Albania." Press release no. 2008/353/ECA http://siteresources.worldbank.org/INTALBANIA/Resources/Status_of_Land_Reform_and_Real_Property_Markets_in_Albania.pdf

Young, A. 1997a. *Albania*. Oxford: Clio.

—1997b. *Religion and Society in Present-Day Albania*. Ithaca, NY: Cornell University Press.

—2000. *Women Who Become Men: Albanian Sworn Virgins*. Oxford: Berg.

Yurchak, A. 2013. *Everything Was Forever until it Was no More: The Last Soviet Generation*. Princeton, NJ: Princeton University Press.

Zavalani, T. 1944. "Resources of Albania." *Geography* 29(3): 80–5.

Zickel, R., and W. Inwaskiw. 1994. "Albania: A Country Study." Washington, DC: Headquarters Department of Army.

Zymberi, I. 1991. *Colloquial Albanian*. London: Routledge.DC: Headquarters Department of Army.

Zymberi, I. 2001. *Albanian*. London: Routledge.

Index

Aani, Maksi 88
Albania 7, 10, 33, 39–40, 43–52
  anthropology of 21–3
  border with Greece 22–3, 36, 53,
    78
  civil war (1997) 85–90, 98–9, 152,
    167–8
  Constitution (1946, 1950 and
    1976) 120, 135–6
  isolationism 22, 124–7
  political instability 152–3
  reliance on remittances 163–4
Albanian migrants 8, 16–19, 22–9,
    104, 112–15, 120–3, 130, 133,
    142–3, 157–9 167
Albanian Telegraphic Agency (ATA)
    83, 86–91, 110
Ali Pasha 24
Amsterdam Treaty (1999) 168
anthropology
  of Albania 21–3
  poetics concept in 131–2
  of the road 1–4, 10–11, 15–16
Antigonea 105–6
Arendt, Hannah 8
Argyrokastron 23
Aronis–Drettas–Karlaftis Consulting
    Engineers S.A. 102–3
asphalt concrete 5–6
asylum seekers 120
Augé, Marc 3
autobahnen 7
automobility 5, 8–12, 52, 74–5, 83,
    94–6, 131, 162

autostrada 7
Azande people 1–2

Bakhtin, Mikhail 82, 95–6, 133,
    171
Bank of Albania 136, 142
Barjaba, Kosta 123
Barthes, Roland 13
Baudrillard, Jean 94
Bauman, Z. 8
Benini, Zenone 35
Berisha, Sali 27, 86, 89–90, 98,
    104–5, 113
Berman, M. 162
Biber, Mehmet 39
Boas, Franz 2–3
border crossings, illegal 115–16
border policing 170
borders, European 167–71
Boulevard 18 (Gjirokastër) 65–9,
    73–5, 78–80, 85
bribery 153–5
bridges 13, 170–1
Budina, D. 106
building materials 140–1, 151, 160

capitalism 8–9, 18, 21, 25, 166, 170
car crashes 83–5, 147
Chater, Melville 33–4
China 26
Ciano, Count 35, 116
cold war 18, 95, 165–6
Cole, J. 94
colonialism 6

Communist Party membership 137
communitas theory 46–7
conscript labor 7, 42
construction work 18–21, 134, 166
   see also road-building in Albania
corruption 153–5
credit, access to 126
criminality 86–93, 116

Debord, Guy 8
Deleuze, Gilles 4
dependency, Albanian 113, 120,
   151–2, 158, 163–5
Dervitsani village 91–2
dialectic materialism 21
dress 124–5
"dromocratic society" 5
Durham, M.E. 44

Eastern European migrants 167–9
electrification 138–9, 162
ELEMKA S.A. (company) 102–3
empty houses 144, 159–61
Epirus 106
ethnocentrism 9
ethnographic surveys 93
ethnography of roads 2–4, 10–13,
   170–1
euro crisis (2010) 19
European Bank for Reconstruction
   and Development (EBRD) 116,
   119
European financial crisis (2008) 169
European Union (EU) 17–20,
   110–18, 168–70
"Europeanness" 118
Evans-Pritchard, E.E. 1–2
"evil eye", protection from 145–7
expressways 8

Fanon, Franz 9
Ferguson, James 3
First World War 6–7
food shortages 124–5
forced labor 39–41, 46–9, 94,
   111–12, 131

Fortress Europe policies 17, 115,
   165, 168
Foucault, Michel (and Foucauldian
   theory) 4, 12–14
free movement of goods, persons
   and capital 114
Frisby, David 7
Frontex 170

gender equality 43
Germany 6
Ghozita, Agim 89
Giles-Vernick, T. 93
Gjergji, A. 138
Gjirokastër 15–16, 23–9, 36–8,
   54–7, 61–9, 71–2, 75–6,
   89–90, 96, 98, 109, 115,
   118–20, 141, 144, 146, 150–4,
   162–3
   geography and population 27–9
   relocation of urban center 62–9,
     72, 75
   social classification in 64
   see also Kakavijë–Gjirokastër
     highway
globalization 132
Godelier, Maurice 11–12
Good Bye Lenin (film) 166
Greece 16–22, 27, 118
   border with Albania 22–3, 36, 53,
     78
   state intelligence service (KIP) 99
Guattari, Felix 4
Gupta, Akhil 3

Hammond, Nicholas 21–2
Hansen, T.B. 14
Harris, Marvin 11–12
Harvey, David 9
Hasluck, M. 44
Hatziprokopiou, P. 159
Hayano, D. 93
Heidegger, Martin 13
Hercules 94
Herzfeld, Michael 3
Holocaust, the 8

house-building in Albania 133–61,
164–5
    anxieties and risks associated with
        145–55
    official regulation of 153–4
    related to migration 143–5
    state-sponsored and *private* 134–9
"house making" as distinct from
        house-building 159–60
household facilities 138–9
Hoxha, Enver 26, 43–4, 53–4,
    59–60, 65, 127
human trafficking 115
Humphrey, Caroline 2, 154
Hungary 168–9

"imagineering" 13, 94
immobility of the Albanian
        population 38–9, 42, 60
infrastructure projects 8, 20, 37–8,
        49–51, 111–12, 117, 137, 162,
        166–7, 170
Ingold, Tim 1
intercity highways 8
International Organization for
        Migration 155–6, 159
Ioannina 115
Italy 16–17, 25, 35–7

Kadare, Ismail 54, 72
Kakavijë checkpoint 83, 87–8, 103
Kakavijë–Gjirokastër highway 42,
        53, 82–9, 96, 98–102, 107–10,
        113–16, 119, 131–2, 152,
        162–5
Kantakouzenos, Ioannes 23
Khrushchev, Nikita 26
King, R. 143, 158
Kokëdhima, Persefoni 58–9
kontribut method of house-building
        135

Labrianidis, Lois 143, 159
Latour, Bruno 13
Lazarat village 86, 90–2
Leach, Edmund 2

Lefebvre, Henri 8–13, 33, 53, 74, 107
Levi-Strauss, Claude 2–4, 98, 160
Libya 7
Livy 106
Löfgren, Orvar 94
Luckwald, Erich von 36
Lyberaki, Antigoni 143

Manaki Brothers 15
Marmullaku, R. 41, 53, 60
Marx, Karl (and Marxist theory)
        9–12
Marxist-Leninist ideology 121, 126
Masquelier, Adeline 93, 131–2
material culture
    and migration 120–3
    of poverty 123–8
Mazower, Marc 170
Meksi, Vladimir 139
migration
    government policies on 17
    and material culture 120–3
    in relation to house-building
        143–5
    see also Albanian migrants;
        Eastern European migrants
militarization of society 41–3
military use of roads 7–8, 33–4
mobility of Albanian society 75
    see also immobility of the
        Albanian population
modernization processes 17, 25,
        43–4, 48, 55, 65, 93, 137
Mom, G. 6
money, perceptions of 70–2
Mullai, Genci 88
Mussolini, Benito 35–6
mythographies of roads 13, 94, 98,
        100, 116–20

Naipi, Bule 58–9
Nano, Fatos 102
national identity, Albanian 45
nationalism 103–10, 119
neoliberalism 18–21, 110, 113–16,
        119, 132, 164

networks 14
Nitsiakos, V. 144
North Atlantic Treaty Organization
　　(NATO) 170

Otherness 17, 165–9

pallate 136–7
Pan-European Corridors 116–17
Papathemelis, Stelios 104
Paris 8–9
Pazari district (Gjirokastër) 55,
　　58–62, 65–9, 72–8, 149–50
Pettifer, James 89, 129
PHARE program 111
Philip the apostle 95
Pina-Cabra, João 94
poetics, anthropological concept of
　　131–2
poststructuralism 12–13
poverty 24, 43, 65, 70, 119–20,
　　123–9
Prendi, F. 106
privatization 116, 147
property rights in Albania 136
pyramid investment schemes 27,
　　69–70, 98–9, 139, 152, 163

Rabinow, Paul 2
refugee flows 165, 168–70
religion 28–9
remittances 70, 113–15, 119–20,
　　129, 142–3, 155–60, 163–4
Riza, Emin 23, 61
road-building in Albania 34–50,
　　110–13, 118–19
　　alienation of Albanians from 118
　　financing of 111–13
　　ideological apparatus of 41–2
　　politics of 118–19
road signs 109–10
roads
　　and dominance over the landscape
　　　107
　　ethnography of 2–4, 10–13, 170–1
　　and the imagination 93

mythography of 13, 94, 98, 100,
　　116–20
old and new networks of 5, 95
and related narratives 94–6
Roseman, Sharon 94, 131–2
Rostow, Walt 6
rural population of Albania,
　　alienation of 139

Scott, James 4
Scriven, George 33
self, making of (through housing) 160
Skendi, Stavro 33–6
Snead, James 5
social duties 126
social formations 74–5
social sciences' interest in roads 10
socialism, building of 42–4
socialist lifestyle 46–7, 96
Sorenson, R. 3
Soviet Union (USSR) 26
Sphinx, the 95
Stepputat, F. 14
Stewart, Kathleen 132
Swire, Joseph 34, 44
Syrian refugees 165, 168

technology studies 6
Theseus 94–5
Thomollari, Vassil 105
time–space compression 9
totalitarian states 5
Trobriand islands 4

Ulysses' Gaze (film) 15
United Nations Educational,
　　Scientific and Cultural
　　Organization (UNESCO)
　　World Heritage Sites 29, 54–9,
　　69, 150
urban sectors, *socialist* and
　　postsocialist 74
urbanization 53

Verdery, Katherine 43, 105
Vickers, Miranda 89, 129

Virilio, Paul 1, 5, 9, 33, 96, 162
Vullnetari, J. 143, 158

"walking" cultures 1
walling-in of women and children
    92
Westernization 17

White, Luise 93
Williams, R. 53
World Bank 111–12, 142, 150, 154

xhiro 67–9, 73

Zog, Ahmet (King Zog) 25, 35, 44